Robert Kanigel is the autho   to
Genius, and *The Man Who Knew*
Kanigel has contributed to   and
other distinguished publicati   ..es in Cambridge,
Massachusetts.

10/2014
21 issues

Also by Robert Kanigel

THE ONE BEST WAY

APPRENTICE TO GENIUS

THE MAN WHO KNEW INFINITY

HIGH SEASON
IN NICE

How One French Riviera Town

Has Seduced Travellers

for Two Thousand Years

ROBERT KANIGEL

An *Abacus* Book

First published in the United States of America in 2002 by Viking
First published in Great Britain in 2002 by Little, Brown
This Abacus edition published in 2003

Copyright © 2002 by Robert Kanigel

The moral right of the author has been asserted.

A CIP catalogue record for this book
is available from the British Library.

ISBN 0 349 11347 5

Printed and bound in Great Britain
by Clays Ltd, St Ives plc

Abacus
An imprint of
Time Warner Books UK
Brettenham House
Lancaster Place
London WC2E 7EN

www.TimeWarnerBooks.co.uk

For Elise Hancock

CONTENTS

PROLOGUE

AGAINST THE BLACKNESS OF THE SEA AT NIGHT, A BRIGHT BLUR OF movement on the beach.

It is near midnight. Late June in Nice, on the French Riviera. Crowds of late-night tourists stroll along the Promenade des Anglais, the broad seaside boulevard, crowned with palms, that follows the great arc of the bay. A fresh breeze wafts in from the sea. Any breezier, any cooler, and it might feel chilly. But it's not chilly. It's perfect; the weather's always perfect here.

You settle back into one of the blue wooden chairs that line the seafront. The ocean air washes over your bare arms and legs. Behind you as you face the sea, a broad walkway divides the car traffic from the beach. Smartly dressed older couples shuffle amiably, arm in arm. Knots of teenagers. A young girl rollerskating alone, blond hair fanning out behind her. And spread out before you, the pebbly beach and softly murmuring sea.

It's from here that you spy the ghostly movement, revealed by lamps that flood the beach in light: Two young men reach down, tug off their shoes, and, almost in tandem, toss them aside. Then their shirts come off. And their pants, which land in a pile at their feet. They stop at their flimsy, colored briefs, and stand up straight. For a moment, they hesitate, then run splashing into the water, limbs flailing, white streaks against the inky sea.

The water's chill shocks them into silence. But soon the two of them, the surf lapping at their waists, are shouting themselves hoarse in

German, frolicking in the water like happy children. Their yells grow rhythmic and they start to sing—smoky Munich beer-hall songs, one imagines, shunted to the coast of France. To the jaunty beat of their tune, they spank the sea in unison, slapping sheets of spray into the air. . . .

Then, abruptly, back on the beach where they'd left their clothes, *another* blur of movement. It was easy to miss him as he stood motionless on the beach, fully dressed, but he'd been there all along—a third young man, friend of the other two. He'd climbed up to the Promenade, carried a chair back down to the beach, and primly stood and watched as his friends cavorted in the surf.

But now he can bear it no longer, and he, too, reaches down to pry off his shoes. Soon all three of them are yelling, splashing, and singing—joyously, exuberantly, happy.

∞

High Season in Nice is a story of pleasure and escape—about what five months or five days in an exotic, strikingly beautiful place, wrested from lives choked by worry, toil, or tedium back home, meant to a few wealthy people 250 years ago, and mean to millions today.

It is about how modern tourism got the way it did.

It is about how Nice and the Riviera became what they are.

It is about the price they paid to do so.

Nice was founded by the Greeks sometime after the sixth century B.C. It has borne the tread of Roman legionnaires, was stopover point for Italy-bound Englishmen on the Grand Tour, port-of-call for Cook's tours, home-away-from-home for Russian expatriates and the Lost Generation. Matisse came here. So did Thomas Jefferson. So did Chekhov and Queen Victoria, F. Scott Fitzgerald and Isadora Duncan. Wounded soldiers back from the Western Front in World War I stayed in its hotels and villas. So did autoworkers from drab Paris suburbs who'd never in their lives seen the sea. So did Jews seeking refuge during World War II, and American GIs after it. And now so do clerks from London and Lyons, software engineers from Silicon Valley, *nouveaux-riches* entrepreneurs from Moscow.

It is a Saturday in late spring at the end of the twentieth century. We are in old Nice, at the Cours Saleya, flanked by elevated terraces where once gentlemen and their ladies promenaded at their ease. The mayor's office has brought a troupe of musicians here to the flower market, a teaser for paid performances elsewhere tonight. It is noon. The Mediterranean sun stands high overhead. Everywhere, flower stalls under striped awnings: seas of bouquets, riots of pink, yellow, and red. Throngs of tourists and local Niçois watch as two women from the company dance to a slow, rhythmic pulse of tambourines, castanets, and drums. A swarthy woman with jet-black hair and tight black pants; another in a long, slinky purple skirt. Their bodies sway to the music. Their faces are lit by rapt smiles. Hundreds, hypnotized, draw near. The dancers smile. The flower vendors smile. The tourists smile.

Dare we judge their smiles shallow for being those of mere tourists? Somehow less authentic for being roused by those whose business is to charm, seduce, and entertain?

Nice has undergone vast change over the centuries. And yet, for all the change, there is this one constant: its beguiling invitation, held out to each new generation of travelers, to come visit, cast troubles aside, enjoy.

❧

They clog the old route nationale and the A8 expressway in miles-long traffic jams, or *bouchons*.

They crane their necks for a view as cloud-covered backcountry gives way to sunny coastal towns that resemble white granite outcroppings as their jet drops low over the blue Mediterranean for the final descent to Nice–Côte d'Azur Airport.

They step from the gloom of the train station into the glare of bright sun and sky, knees buckling under top-heavy backpacks, wrung out from long train rides from Paris or Prague.

By the millions they flock each year to Nice and the rest of the Riviera. Six in ten are French, the rest a mix of nationalities that varies with time of year and exchange rate; Italians, perhaps, are favored one year, Americans the next. The Italians drive over the border in July, head back just before the great French flood in August. British and Germans each account for half a million Riviera trips a year, Americans a bit fewer. Russians flock toward high-end shops with window signs in Cyrillic, buy up champagne, lobster, and caviar. In summer, a Finnish company flies in a weekly charter with 140 Scandinavians; they see Nice, take a day trip to Cannes, visit vineyards. A certain ANDREAS '96, GREEK LOVER, left graffiti by the stairway that climbs the Château Hill. So did ALI ZAIDI. A Canadian woman heralded FREEDOM 1998, SPIRITUAL JOURNEY THRU TRAVEL ART LOVE & POETRY. SYLV expressed eternal love for NICOLAS. *Everybody* comes to Nice.

Visitors check in to luxury hotels along the Promenade des Anglais—palaces left over from the Belle Époque with great spiral staircases, intricate ironwork, vaulted ceilings.

They filter into the streets around the train station, scouting out cheap one-star hotels, climbing stairs up from the street to cramped second-floor reception desks and smoke-filled common rooms crowded with the young from every nation.

They hop the bus up the Moyenne Corniche to the forest road that climbs Mont Alban, hoping for a bed at the youth hostel. "Backpacker Palace," the local paper calls it—bed, ocean view, and breakfast for the price of a *salade niçoise* on the Promenade.

Guidebooks commend them to hotels where Chekhov slept, or Lenin, or Matisse.

Taxis ferry them to name-brand seaside behemoths that look like Miami or L.A., with bars that push cheeseburgers and American pizza.

Friends back home direct them to restored nineteenth-century three-stars with interior courts lush with mimosa and bougainvillea. There they sit at window balconies over cheese and fruit, watch palms sway in the evening breeze, know at last they've discovered paradise.

Maybe a third of Riviera visitors, particularly the French, never get near a hotel. They fill instead the region's thirty thousand camping sites, as well as its *résidences secondaires*—the beachside condo of your cousin's father-in-law's sister.

Some shuttle between their hotels and the convention center, the Acropolis. They listen all day to scientific papers, or wander down windowless aisles lined with manufacturers' representatives peddling lung monitors and miracle drugs.

Mainly, though, Nice's visitors come for a good time, so they do nothing at all—which, for many too-busy people at century's end, is about the same thing. They relax. They explore the town. They shop. They visit museums. They read in bed. They eat. They make love. They sleep.

And, of course, they go to the beach—miles of narrow shoreline blanketed with what the French call *galets*, the British "shingle," and the Americans "pebbles," which is really just a bed of smooth rounded stones. They lie on towels or cane matting on the public beach; or on beach chairs under umbrellas, laid out in neat rows, on the private ones. Once settled there, they do little else. A dip into the mild surf. A lathering of suntan lotion. Take off a top. Put on a top. Read a few pages. Buy a drink. Soak up rays.

You see tourists standing in Place Masséna huddled over a street map, straining to keep it open against the wind. Or wandering down shoulders-wide streets in the old town lined with shops and galleries. Or lumbering wearily down to the basement of the casino to play the slots. Or taking snapshots of ancient ruins, or of themselves. Or standing serenely at the top of the Château Hill, looking down on red roofs and blue sea, as the wind whips their hair and the sun etches memories in their minds.

For many, Nice is base from which to visit the rest of the Riviera, which is known also, more or less synonymously, as the Côte d'Azur. They board the westbound train from the Nice *gare*, and arrive half an hour later in Cannes, home to the film festival each spring. Or the eastbound, for Monte Carlo, to watch rich people drive up to the casino in Rolls-Royces. Maybe they take the bus to Grasse to buy perfume. Or gaze in wonder at Matisse's marvel of soft prayerful color, his Chapel of the Rosary, outside Vence.

Down the coast, off the Corniche d'Or, south of Cannes, a vacationing family stops for lunch at a small hotel perched atop a secluded cove. The three of them, a couple with their teenaged son, settle on the restaurant terrace, beneath a red umbrella. Every so often they glance up from their menus and down to the sea gurgling amongst the rocks below. There, on a wooden dock that spans the few yards to an oxblood-colored rock rising from the sea, a man and woman idle away the hours. She, in a skimpy black swimsuit with a thin strap across the back, sits within his arms and bare, muscled thighs. Mostly, they just look out to sea. But, periodically, she twists toward him and her lips search out his. Up on the terrace, as they wait to be served, husband and wife stare; the teenager tries not to look. Time stretches out. The waves lap the rocks. The couple on the dock draw up closer, their kisses grow more urgent. Then, finally, an intimate whisper; with studied casualness, they rise from the dock and pad up to their room. On the terrace, lunch is served.

What do tourists do on the Riviera? They do what all travelers, and all tourists, always do. They escape their lives back home and search for pleasure.

It is a subtle distortion to say that the Riviera "still" grants pleasure, as if it but feebly managed to do what a century ago it did better. Today, 170 flights a day, four in ten of them international, land at Nice Airport. A thousand hotels shelter Riviera visitors, three thousand restaurants serve them meals, a hundred thousand workers do their bidding. In 1880, with the Belle Époque at its height and Nice as fashionable as it would ever be, thirty-five thousand foreigners came each year for the season; these days, visitors to the Côte d'Azur as a whole number eight million.

This, some say, is just the problem: too *many* millions.

∞

Thirty Americans are on a two-week, university-sponsored tour of the Mediterranean. This morning they left their floating hotel, a three-masted sailing yacht, tied up at the Monte Carlo marina, and boarded a bus that took them along the twisting coast road to Nice. Now, a little after noon, their bus has pulled up to the Chagall Museum, a stark white stone structure that houses the largest public collection of the Russian artist's work. The Americans, all white socks, running shoes, and loose-fitting leisure wear, pile out. They pass through the gate and across an open grassy area to the entrance.

Inside, their guide gathers them up and leads them into the main hall, crowded with other groups of tourists. She wears a dark ankle-length skirt, crisply fitting linen top over a simple white T-shirt, canvas bag thrown stylishly over her shoulder. The Americans crowd round her. Please stay close, she asks them. She doesn't want to raise her voice, lest she interfere with the other groups and guides.

Just beside the main hall is a noisy entrance foyer, the size of an overgrown living room, where tickets are collected, packages checked, souvenirs purchased. Coins clink on wooden counters. Cash registers chatter and whirr. "We've got pink tickets for you to get in," a harried tour guide yells across the room to her flock. Children fuss noisily. People mill about, chatter, compare notes on this poster or print.

Just now, finally, a saleswoman in the gift shop has had enough. She is in her forties or fifties, with a long, regal neck and commanding presence. In the very middle of a transaction, she stops, stands up to her full height, raises her arms in front of her to the level of her shoulders, and claps—three sharp, hard cracks that rise over the tourist din and draw all eyes toward her. Then, in one broad, fluid pantomime, she scrunches up her shoulders, with both hands points toward her ears, and contorts her face in pain.

Briefly, the room quiets.

But it's summer, high season in Nice, and soon the place is jumping and jangling once more.

Return to Nice after years away and chances are you soon lament the price it's paid for popularity. A New York visitor, Jane Huddish, remembers visiting the Riviera in 1967, right after her graduation from college, and loving it. When she returned three decades later, in the mid-1990s, she hated it. The streets were crowded with cars. Parking was impossible. The hotels were overpriced; a hundred bucks got you a cell of a room with tattered rugs, cheap lamps, and chipped furniture. The views from the legendary *corniches*—the roads cut into the sea-facing slopes of the mountains that track the Riviera coast to Italy—were mostly gone, obscured by new construction. A new casino built next to the old one in Monte Carlo was, she recalled, "filled with American tourists in checked Bermuda shorts playing the slots at two in the afternoon."

Of course, visitors returning to the Riviera have felt that way almost from the beginning. "Those blissful days are gone, and the place has been ruined and vulgarized," one writer noted of neighboring Monaco. "The cliffs have been blasted, the copsewood cut away, and the unrivaled scenery defaced by the ravages of speculative cockneydom." Nice, he complained, had been "desecrated by every variety of eccentric architecture." In Cannes, even more than in Nice, an innocent walk in the country assailed you with "peremptory warnings against trespass, and the more serious obstacles of stone walls and barbed wire." The author, Alexander Shand, was writing in 1903. He was lamenting the lost Riviera of the 1860s.

Such nostalgic yearnings for better times now past presuppose a point of origin—a moment when the Riviera really *was* paradise, and from which one might measure how far it's fallen. But Nice's past, like that of the rest of the Riviera, does not reach back only to some imagined time of Edenic bliss. Today, fending off street peddlers or navigating around bodies on the beach, the visitor to Nice may be forgiven his inability to imagine it any other way. Our modest history, however, must take us back to *before* that moment when, through excess, Nice first began to offend some visitors; back to a time when it attracted no visitors at all.

The history of Nice as playground for tourists begins only in the mid-eighteenth century, when Englishmen bound for Italy passed through, stopped, and told their friends back home of their happy find. But by that time, Nice was already a very old place with roots in Greek and Roman antiquity, and hardy *travelers,* a species it is sometimes convenient to distinguish from pleasure-seeking *tourists,* had been coming there for two thousand years.

These travelers waged war, administered provinces, sold olives, carried salt. They came to Nice by mule, along narrow mountain trails that ran along the coast; or by sea, hugging the Mediterranean shore, by sail and by oar. But for the two millennia from the first Greek settlement of Nice through the Middle Ages and beyond, few of those who crossed the broad bed of the Paillon River to Nice could be deemed tourists.

The sweet breath of its soft air was not enough to make Nice anything like the tourist destination it is today. People had first to learn of it. They had to think of it as other than port or fortress. They had to be lured there. And they had to be able to get there—which for a thousand years or more was difficult. The Niçois, meanwhile, had to learn to shelter, distract, coddle, and amuse their visitors. It was never a foregone conclusion that Nice would become a place to which people would come for a good time, and never preordained that it would remain so. The tourist's Nice of today is the work of centuries. Of societal forces, of historical circumstances. Of myriad individual acts, great and small.

Not many years ago on the Promenade des Anglais stood a certain famous and ornate hotel, the Ruhl. It's gone now. The owner decided to tear it down and put up a new hotel in its place.

On the rue de France today, racks of picture postcards crowd the sidewalk outside a gift shop. Most of the cards cost two francs. But some are half an inch longer on each side and cost five francs; a photographer started making them that way a few years ago.

In Biot, half an hour on the bus from Nice, is a glassmaking factory. Today people line up to tour it, then buy the craftware they watch being made. Forty years ago, the factory was there but no one came to visit.

In Nice today, "high season," when the crowds are thickest and prices highest, is July and August. A hundred years ago, the hotels closed for the summer; high season was January and February.

This is a book about the liberation, pleasure, and release one sun-blessed place grants visitors. But it tells also how Nice's touristic landscape evolved. It is the story of what happens when traveler and destination meet, of the forces that bring them together, of what one special place does to travelers, and what travelers and tourists do to it.

One *special* place? Surely, Nice is special to the people who live there—and in the ads, brochures, and Web sites of its tourist-industry boosters. In other ways, though, Nice is profoundly typical, much like Venice or Majorca, Waikiki or Bath: all are well along the great touristic arc that, over the years, leaves fishing villages and market towns clogged with curio shops. In Venice today, your gondolier gets eighty dollars to row you along the canal. At Stonehenge, in England, you're routed through a concrete tunnel beneath the main road, past a crowded gift shop, and assigned an audio headset before you reach the great stones—which you can't touch.

Tourism has become the last, best hope of every stagnant economy, every local booster. Travel and tourism together rank as the world's largest industry. Three or four trillion dollars' worth a year, one in nine jobs around the world; the figures are so gargantuan, of course, they mean almost nothing. But everywhere, it seems, tourism replaces whatever was there before, is the pill popped for whatever ails an economy. In Puerto Rico, the island's tourism agency was elevated to Cabinet rank, a private company was hired to clean the San Juan beaches, and taxi drivers were ordered to learn Puerto Rican history and rudimentary English. In Interlaken, Austria, so many shops sell Swiss-army knives and Heidi knickknacks that some, in disgust, now call it Interschlocken. In Dubrovnik, Croatia, almost as soon as the fighting stopped, the mayor was talking up the city's tourism industry, and soft floodlights were bathing its ancient stone walls.

So it goes. The beaches of the Caribbean given over to tourists, the warehouses of Baltimore, the lamaseries of Tibet. Few, of course, take such proof of tourism triumphant with unmixed pleasure. An undiscovered tropical beach delights; the same beach wall-to-wall with bodies does not. No one wants to be seen as a tourist, or to see herself as one. *Traveler?* Yes. *Tourist?* Never.

Once the two ideas were not so distinct; the word "tourist" first appeared around 1800, as a straightforward synonym for "traveler." But by the mid-nineteenth century—around the time Nice was developing into the first modern resort—"tourist" had already acquired the derogatory tinge it bears today.

The true traveler emulates intrepid figures like Sir Richard Francis Burton, the English adventurer who trekked through Africa and the

Mideast. The tourist moves in "swarms," "hordes," or, better yet, "teeming hordes," and can most reliably be found in air-conditioned buses.

The traveler, historian Daniel Boorstin tells us, explores the un-known and the unfamiliar. The tourist clings to the "antiseptic, pleas-ant, relaxing, [and the] comfortable."

The traveler, says another scholar, James Buzard, "exhibits boldness and gritty endurance under all conditions . . . ; the tourist is the cau-tious, pampered unit of a leisure industry." The traveler boasts of "in-ner personal qualities that amount to a superior emotional-aesthetic sensitivity"; the tourist, sadly, lacks them.

The traveler craves rich, authentic experience. The tourist is never more at home than with the superficial and the secondhand. He lacks taste. He clings to the beaten track. He poisons everything around him with his presence. "The tourist is the other fellow," Evelyn Waugh once wrote.

Others slice up the terminological pie differently; the manufacture of such taxonomies, useful as they may be, ranks as almost a cottage in-dustry among those writing of travel and tourism. Real people, though, never conform so neatly to type. Plainly, traveler and tourist have much in common as well as much that sets them apart. Both leave their daily lives, all that is most familiar to them, at home. Both step into foreign worlds. Bits of both tourist and traveler, in fact, reside in all of us. The fearless traveler sometimes takes refuge in four-star hotels. The timid tourist faces threat, discomfort, challenge, and provocation whether he likes it or not.

Even today.

Land at the airport in Nice, and—traveler or tourist—your senses flood with the colors of foreign uniforms, the sheen of foreign cur-rency. Your mind's thrown into overdrive. Airport signs look like those at Gatwick or Kennedy, yet not quite. Alien French assails eye and ear.

DOUANES.

TAPIS BAGAGES.

GARE ROUTIÈRE.

ENTRÉE INTERDITE.

Wisps of paranoia. Your bags stand briefly apart from the others on the baggage carousel. Two men. Airport security? Thieves? Nice is Mediterranean, maybe like Marseilles, maybe *French Connection*, drugs, criminals.

Outside the terminal, burdened with baggage, alone. The air feels strangely soft. The sun, and the blazing blue of the sky, burn your retinas.

A bus into town? A cab? Find one where? How much? Too much?

The ride into town—the cars too small, the sidewalks too crowded, the beach, just outside the window, too near.

Lunch. *Farcis niçois?* Words on the menu. Try it, taste it. Later, the words mean tastes and textures, tomato and eggplant, tuna. But that's later. Now just squiggles on the page . . .

This is no godforsaken little village in Eastern Protarolia. This is Nice, Tourist Heaven, with 250 years' experience at welcoming guests, a place that knows how to make you feel at home. But you *don't* feel at home, not yet anyway. You're fretful or giddy, but definitely not at home.

The eighteenth-century traveler, arriving in Nice after a month's travel by coach, mule, or boat, had time to acclimate. But today our tourist steps from an airline terminal in London and into a jet—which, like a circus cannon, virtually fires her into the south of France.

It was to cushion the traveler from novelty's jolts that Cook's tours evolved, and Holiday Inns, Visa, American Express: a whiff of the familiar a thousand miles from home. Yet even today international travel is never entirely routine. Even the eight-cities-in-fourteen-days package tourist, ferried around by bus, coddled in American-style hotels, cut off from the locals, faces more of the surprising and the strange than her neighbor back in Topeka on her fourth trip to Disneyland.

Panicky Americans with language problems, reports Janet Ruiz, the American consular agent in Nice, break down into two types. One laments his ignorance of French; the other asks why in the hell the French just won't speak English. But isn't this second type—the Ugly American, Everytourist at his worst—as provoked and challenged, in his own way, as the veteran traveler who sleeps in the tents of the locals?

Every traveler, likewise, is something of a tourist. Consider the medieval mystic on the classic pilgrimage to Saint-Jacques-de-Compostelle, the French writer Simone Mesnil-Grente asks us in her book *Les Vacances*. Even as he sought deliverance at holy places, was he not also satisfying "the Western taste for a break from the gray monotony of daily life," just like every tourist today? She goes on, "Was the open-mouthed wonder of the Crusaders before the Golden Horn so different from that of [to-day's] Cook's tour travelers in the bazaar of Istanbul? The traveler's check has simply replaced the sword as a means of procuring souvenirs."

In *High Season in Nice*, then, I mostly abjure the tired old distinctions between traveler and tourist. I prefer to see the two sitting side by side in each of us, popping up at various times, or in varying proportions, even on the same trip. I have in mind no one favored balance between authenticity and fantasy; adventure and security; challenge and ease. Whether you reach Nice in a month by mule or an hour by plane; whether for a season's leisure or a night's stopover; whether as Victoria, Queen of England, or a faceless package tourist—you still encounter a new, unfamiliar place. You still need a roof over your head, something to eat, and, perhaps, some slight diversion. Nice has been satisfying those needs for 250 years.

ⱄ

This story of tourism as seen through the prism of a single place unfolds mostly in times of peace. War has theatrics to commend it—jet fighters screaming low over the horizon, poignant stories of cruelty and compassion. Peace, by contrast, is humdrum; but it is a precondition for tourism. Its rise-and-fall follows the alternation of peace with war the way a phonograph needle tracks the twisting grooves of an old LP.

When, in 1706, the hilltop fortifications that for five hundred years had made Nice a formidable bastion were razed on the express orders of a victorious enemy's king, the town lost its military value overnight. That, in retrospect, made possible Nice's rise as a tourist destination.

The French Revolution drove aristocrats mindful of their heads to Nice; the flow of ordinary tourists, however, dried up until Waterloo and the end of the Napoleonic Wars opened the floodgates once more.

World War I brought to Nice wounded soldiers from the Western Front. The Armistice brought tourists.

The early days of World War II saw the Riviera crowded with Jews in flight from the Nazis. When the Germans came, they desecrated the Promenade des Anglais with pillboxes and barbed wire. It took Allied victory and the ensuing peace to open Nice to tourists once more, first as a rest-and-recreation center for American GIs.

The sheer tawdriness of souvenir stands, the gridlocked roads out of Saint-Tropez, the American college student on the beach at Nice straining to express in high-school French her deepest thoughts—*Où est McDonald's?*—all these make easy targets. And yet, in their very banality, they testify to prosperity and peace.

In the imposing stone Château Grimaldi in Antibes, just across the Baie des Anges from Nice, hangs a giant painting Pablo Picasso completed in 1946. The war over, the sixty-five-year-old artist had left gray Paris for a vacation on the Riviera. A chance meeting on the beach led to his being offered studio space on the top floor of the old castle, just above the almost shockingly blue waters of the Mediterranean. There, in the first summer of peace after the war, caught up in a torrid affair with beautiful twenty-three-year-old Françoise Gilot, he set to a ferocious cycle of new work. He was in love, supremely happy, inspired by the beauty of his new surroundings.

None of his paintings showed it better than one he called *Antipolis, ou la Joie de Vivre*, the joy of life: against a sunny sky and blue sea, a goat plays the flute and fauns cavort, while a voluptuous nude woman with flowing hair dances on the yellow sand of the beach. Scholars who studied earlier versions of the painting found that, as it evolved, Picasso's figures became rounder and fuller.

Eight years earlier, after the German bombings of civilians during the Spanish Civil War, Picasso had painted his monumental *Guernica*, all tears, death, and devastation. Now, by contrast, the artist's happiness came out in a painting that evokes the peacetime pleasures millions of others have also found on the Riviera.

We see no great historical moment played out against the blue sky and yellow sand of Picasso's canvas, nothing but the simple joy of being alive.

1 THE BILIOUS DR. SMOLLETT

FOR MORE THAN TWO THOUSAND YEARS SINCE ITS FOUNDING BY the Greeks centuries before the birth of Christ, no one seeking health, pleasure, or repose would have looked to Nice or elsewhere on today's Riviera. That began to change in 1763, when Tobias Smollett came to town.

Search the pages of history and literature all you like and you'll find no less plausible candidate than Smollett for the position of Nice's chief publicist, no one less prone to honeyed phrases, or less inclined to flatter. In the very book that helped make Nice a popular travel destination, for example, Smollett wrote that he did not know "a more insignificant set of mortals" than the nobility of Boulogne, the English Channel port where he'd stayed for the summer. They were "useless to the community; without dignity, sense or sentiment; contemptible from pride, and ridiculous from vanity."

He wrote that in French inns you were served "with the appearance of the most mortifying indifference, at the very time they are laying schemes for fleecing you of your money."

Smollett wrote that Frenchwomen's silly, extravagant makeup was doubtless inspired by the Indian tribes of America and the Hottentots of Africa. "When I see one of those fine creatures sailing along, in her tawdry robes of silk and gauze, frilled and flounced, and furbelowed, with her false locks, her false jewels, her paint, her patches, and perfumes; I cannot help looking upon her as the vilest piece of sophistication that art ever produced."

Smollett was pugnacious and gruff. He quarreled with everyone, from innkeepers to physicians. He got into fights. He got sued. He got imprisoned for libel. He inspired another writer, Laurence Sterne, to model on him an unpleasant character named Smelfungus.

On the evidence of his bent for making trouble, then, Smollett was someone any town father or civic booster would want to keep out altogether, yet it was this same Smollett who would, in a series of forty-one letters, published as *Travels Through France and Italy* in 1766, set the admiring eyes of Europe upon Nice.

❧

In the early summer of 1763, when he took the boat across the English Channel for Calais, Smollett was forty-two years old. Trained as a physician, he had traded scalpel for quill, and now was one of that uncommon breed who made their living by their pens. He was the author of one failed novel and two successful ones, the editor of an important English journal, a translator of *Don Quixote*. Well connected, he counted among his friends such literary lights as Samuel Johnson and Oliver Goldsmith.

But just now Smollett was at low ebb. The lung condition he'd acquired some years before—tuberculosis? asthma?—left him weak and painfully thin. His face was shriveled. A high public official had recently betrayed him. Three months earlier, his eldest child, Elizabeth, had died at age fifteen, overwhelming him with grief. "Smollett," as one observer later summed up his state of mind, "needed a change."

With him in France were his wife (the daughter of a Jamaican planter he'd met during navy service), two girls to whom she was governess, and an elderly servant. Though they were bound generally south, it was only after they'd reached Boulogne and met General James Paterson, a fellow Scot, that Smollett fixed on a more specific destination. "The general," he wrote, "talks so favorably of the climate of Nice, with respect to disorders of the breast, that I am now determined to go thither." Armed with directions and a reference letter, he planned to leave in the fall, when the weather would no longer be so hot.

In November, about five months after crossing the Channel, and after stays in Boulogne, Paris, Lyons, and Montpellier, the Smolletts arrived in Nice. There, after a week at an inn, they rented a house with adjoining gardens lush with orange, lemon, peach, and fig trees. The house itself, he reported, had "a ground floor paved with brick, consisting of a kitchen, two large halls, a couple of good rooms with chimneys, [and] three large closets that serve for bed-chambers and dressing-rooms." Upstairs were the butler's quarters and three other rooms.

Over the next year and a half, Smollett explored the city and its surroundings, recording his impressions in letters sent home to England about once a month. (Or at least that's the form in which they were later published; whether they were real letters, to real correspondents, or Smollett's book simply adopted the epistolary style of the day is unclear.)

Like travelers before and since, Smollett noted Nice's charming cultural schizophrenia: "Among the French," he observed, "a Nissard piques [prides] himself on being Provençal; but in Florence, Milan, or Rome, he claims the honor of being born a native of Italy. The people of condition here speak both languages equally well; or rather"—this was, after all, Tobias Smollett—"equally ill; for they use a low, uncouth phraseology."

Smollett wrote of windows fitted mostly with paper instead of glass, bedrooms without chimneys. Both peculiarities grew out of the mild climate; burning a pan of charcoal was usually enough to ward off the winter chill.

He wrote of cats that were "emblems of famine, frightfully thin, and dangerously rapacious"; of fruit "too sweet and luscious." He found the harbor full of small vessels like tartanes and polacres, from Sardinia, Italy, and Spain, loaded with salt and wine.

He learned how, come winter, carnations were harvested, packed in wooden boxes, and sent off to Turin, Paris, and London—where, steeped in vinegar and water, "they recover their full bloom and beauty."

He went up into the hills in and around Nice, from which he could see Antibes and the Esterel mountains, and, on a clear morning, Corsica.

On horseback, Smollett crossed Mont Alban to Villefranche, "a small town, built upon the side of a rock." He reported on the Sardinian galleys there, propelled by legions of rowers—filthy, half-starved slaves and convicts who knitted stockings when they weren't rowing. They seemed "quite insensible of their misery," he marveled, "like so many convicts in Newgate; they laugh and sing, and swear, and get drunk when they can."

He reported how local coffeehouses served sorbet—"iced froth, made with juice of oranges, apricots, or peaches," but so cold he was at first afraid to swallow it.

He saw fishermen hauling their boats onto the open beach. He noted how, in the early summer, fleets of boats, sometimes fifty at a time, put to sea each evening, to return with vast quantities of anchovies.

He told how, at ten o'clock each summer's evening, a curfew bell was rung, "warning the people to put out their lights and go to bed." He described prevalent means of punishment, including the strappado, whereby the criminal is hoisted with his hands tied behind his back to the height of a second-story window, then dropped to within a yard of the ground. That, said the good doctor, "generally dislocates his shoulders, with incredible pain."

This and much else he described with all the lucidity of a man of science, all the vividness of the writer he was by vocation.

But Smollett wouldn't be Smollett if the bile that marked his other accounts simply dried up under the Nice sun. The Niçois, he reported, were "such dirty knaves, that no foreigners will trust them in the way of trade. They have been known to fill their oil-casks half full of water, and their anchovy-barrels with stinking heads of that fish, in order to cheat their correspondents."

The local shopkeepers were "generally poor, greedy, and overreaching." Many had fled from creditors; he pictured Nice as "an asylum to foreign cheats and sharpers of every denomination."

Local artisans were lazy, awkward, and "void of all ingenuity."

In Nice, the arts and sciences amounted to "almost a total blank . . . consecrated to the reign of dullness and superstition." The place was "devoid of taste and literature. Here are no tolerable pictures, busts, statues, nor edifices: the very ornaments of the churches are wretchedly conceived, and worse executed."

And with that typical British contempt for continental Catholicism, he noted that in Nice, overrun by convents and churches, "superstition reigns under the darkest shades of ignorance and prejudice."

Plainly, Smollett did not accord Nice kid-glove treatment; later, when he sought the consulship of Nice, his patrons were told to forget it, that the Niçois would stone him the moment he showed his face in town. But compared with other places he'd poisoned with his pen, Nice got off lightly. And his lapses into praise, touched with that same power of expression that served his darker moods, made Nice fairly glow.

Smollett found it in his heart to describe the locals as respectful, suitably submissive, quiet, orderly, and little inclined to drunkenness. "I have never heard of one riot since I lived among them; and murder and robbery are altogether unknown. A man may walk alone over the county of Nice, at midnight, without danger of insult."

"There is less rain and wind at Nice, than in any other part of the world that I know," he wrote; "and such is the serenity of the air, that you see nothing above your head for several months together, but a charming blue expanse, without cloud or speck."

The climate had done wonders for his health. "I never saw before such sudden and happy effects from the change of air. I must also acknowledge, that ever since my arrival at Nice, I have breathed more freely than I have done for some years, and my spirits have been more alert."

Soon after his arrival, he wrote: "When I stand upon the rampart, I can scarce help thinking myself enchanted. The small extent of country which I see is all cultivated like a garden. Indeed, the plain presents nothing but gardens, full of green trees, loaded with oranges, lemons, citrons, and bergamots, which make a delightful appearance." Around him were "plats of roses, carnations, ranunculas, anemonies, and daffodils, blowing in full glory, with such beauty, vigor, and perfume, as no flower in England ever exhibited."

This was the old sourpuss? This was Tobias Smollett?

His wife had begged him to take her away from England, "where every object served to nourish her grief." He'd hoped "that a succession of new scenes would engage her attention, and gradually call off her mind from a series of painful reflections; and I imagined the change of air, and a journey of near a thousand miles, would have a happy effect upon my own constitution."

The new scenes, change of air, and long journey did just that. Nice exerted its magic.

∞

In July 1765, the Smolletts returned to England. The following year, in May, appeared the *Travels*—or, as its title page had it,

TRAVELS
through
FRANCE and ITALY

containing observations on

CHARACTER,	POLICE,
CUSTOMS,	COMMERCE,
RELIGION,	ARTS, and
GOVERNMENT,	ANTIQUITIES,

with a particular description of the
Town, Territory, and Climate of Nice

Widely and well reviewed, it became an immediate success. Its large first printing sold out. It went back to press in November, twice more in subsequent years. At least half a dozen periodicals carried extracts from its first edition. Two pirated Irish editions came out in 1766, a German translation in 1767, a Swedish abridgment in 1784.

By 1768, the *Travels* had already been widely read, and had planted in drab, dour Britain the seed of a new idea: down by the shores of the Mediterranean lay a lush, beautiful place, with a warm and salubrious climate, whose glorious sun could sweeten even Dr. Smollett's sour moods.

When, in 1775, a traveler bound for Nice reached the summit of the Esterels, from which he could see both sea and snow-capped mountains, he noted, "This is where the English traveler Smollett says he found summer and winter together." The journal of a 1768 visitor casually referred to a customs office Smollett had mentioned. In 1816, a French visitor, the archeologist and historian Aubin Louis Millin, anointed Smollett as "the first to recognize, despite himself, the charms of this country and its people. . . . Since that time," he added, "it's been the fashion in England to pass the winter in Nice."

Smollett, it bears saying, did not "discover" Nice. He wrote that the few friends he'd met were foreigners "who, like myself, only sojourn here for a season." One English visitor in 1764 was the Duke of York, brother of George III. There were enough foreigners, in any case, to constitute their own distinct, and exploitable, market; maids who worked for the locals for three or four livres a month, Smollett wrote, would not lift a finger for an English family for less than eight or ten. (To which he added, with a typical flourish, "They are all slovenly, slothful, and unconscionable cheats.")

Still, it was Smollett's visit, more than any other, that counted. Why?

He was, first of all, not just another journal-scribbling traveler. He was a gifted writer, a literary figure of substantial reputation and large following. And in the *Travels*, with its fetching brew of bile, gleeful asperity, and chiseled pronouncements, he was at the top of his form. One critic would write of a "liveliness and assurance in his style and manner that diverted me even when he was wrong." That vitality bubbled over onto Nice.

Smollett flattered every British prejudice. His downright wicked depictions of the French (with whom a treaty ending the Seven Years' War had been concluded only months before he sailed for France) appealed to British vanity; *The Royal Magazine*, for example, agreed with "the Doctor's severe but just character of the French." Nice was at this time not French but, if anything, Italian. So it basked in that glow that, during the era of the Grand Tour, all things Italian enjoyed in England. Besides, Smollett had paid it the ultimate compliment: he'd dwelt there for two years.

His register of Nice's weather, appended to the text, figured, too.

Modern editions of the book sometimes omit this data-thick, distinctly unliterary appendix, but the original edition noted it on the title page. Here, day by day over a year and a half, Smollett recorded rain, wind, and temperature, the dates on which flowers bloomed or snow appeared on mountaintops visible from town. An Englishman oppressed by low, gray winter skies might be forgiven for thrilling to the vision of a December blessed by mild temperatures and bright-blue sky.

Smollett's readers learned of something deliciously *new* on the Mediterranean. Visit Nice for the first time today (or, for that matter, in 1920, or even 1820) and you'll know a little of what to expect, down to particular hotels, sights, and side trips. Friends tell of their adventures. Guidebooks, brochures, newspaper stories, ads, and Web sites supply information and impressions. But early visitors to Nice had no such guidance; travel literature was in its infancy. Their firsthand accounts are soaked with immediacy, each image, fact, and scene wrested from raw experience. At the time he left England, Smollett didn't even know he was going to Nice, and wouldn't have known how to get there. His *Travels*, as one scholar, Eugene Joliat, a student of Smollett's tortured relationship with France, has aptly written, was, "for England, like an account of new discoveries."

The *Travels* seduced through its sheer bile, its insouciance, its appeal to base British prejudice. But it exerted its more lasting influence through its sunlit vision of a paradise. That vision forever altered the face of Nice. "So ended," wrote Joliat, "the happy, somnolent days of the Niçois—who from then on would be transformed into guides and innkeepers."

A MILE AND A HALF UP THE HILL FROM THE HEART OF TODAY'S NICE stood, for five centuries, an important outpost of the Roman Empire, the administrative seat of the province known as Alpes-Maritimes. The Romans called it Cemenelum. The French call it Cimiez. Tobias Smollett took a mule up to the ruins there in 1764. He found its ancient arena plowed up and planted with crops, its temple a stable for goats and cows.

Archeologists have unearthed from the ruins of Cimiez coins of copper, silver, and gold; ceramic oil lamps, bowls, and vases; earrings and necklaces; perfume jars, ivory knife-handles, amphoras from northern Africa and southern Spain. A few years ago, someone fashioned an architectural model of what Cimiez might have looked like at its height. We see red-tiled roofs, stone walkways, columned porticoes, gardens, public baths, and courtyards; together, they testify to pleasure, luxury, and ease. Historians call the first two hundred years of the modern era Pax Romana, when the Mediterranean from Syria to Spain lay at peace; it was during just this time, and on into the third century A.D., that Cimiez flourished.

It was easier during those centuries to reach Cimiez than it would be, a thousand years later, to reach the medieval town of Nice just down the hill. All roads really did lead to Rome, and Cimiez straddled one of them. The storied Roman roads, fifty thousand miles of them, knitted together the Empire as tightly as railroads would nineteenth-century Europe. The Appian Way came first, beginning in 312 B.C., and for centuries the Empire kept building. Old gravel tracks were rebuilt the Roman way, with deep footings, sloped to the sides for drainage, then topped by great stone slabs, cut and fitted to interlock. Their vestiges today lie all across the Mediterranean Basin—a column-lined main street in Algeria, a roadway rutted by wagon wheels in Spain. Each mile, a great stone monolith, perhaps eight feet high and weighing two tons, engraved with the name of the emperor and the distance to Rome, marked the traveler's progress; several have been found near Cimiez. In 13 B.C., the Emperor Augustus extended toward Marseilles the road running up the west flank of Italy from Rome to Genoa. This new Via Julia Augusta skirted the mountains past Genoa, cut across rivers and steep rocky hills, and climbed up to the plateau of Cimiez, before proceeding west to what is today Antibes.

Today atop this plateau loom the remains of a stone amphitheater built by the Romans in the first century before the birth of Christ and subsequently enlarged. Rising around the elliptical court within, 150 feet across at its longest, stand nine tiers of stone seating, what's left of them, anyway. Before time and marauders reduced most of them to ruins, they could accommodate about five thousand people. That, classical scholars have deduced, meant a city of perhaps fifteen thousand.

Conspicuous among the ruins are three large bath complexes, spread over several acres. No water flows through the town's open drains today. Latrines stand open to the sky. Weeds sprout from white stone walls the color of bones bleached by the sun. But here, seventeen hundred years ago, could be found Roman citizens at their ease, leisurely alternating among cold, warm, and hot baths, and a steam room, the water fed by aqueducts that snaked in and around neighboring hills.

At the baths, a wealthy Roman enjoyed massage, physical exercise, good talk. At the arena, he might witness gladiatorial combat, works of theater and mime. Archeological remains found at Antibes, then Antipolis, the next sizable town from Cimiez, tell of tavern guests invited to select wine and food from a menu engraved on a copper plaque. Plainly, the Romans—at least some favored Romans—knew how to enjoy themselves and indulge their guests. A visitor could find at Cimiez pleasure, entertainment, a good night's rest, and a decent meal.

But, although an important provincial town, Cimiez *was* "the provinces." A few fine works of sculpture have been unearthed from the site, including a dancing faun in bronze and a statue of the Emperor Augustus's niece. But these are conspicuous by their rarity; most relics are more utilitarian. The arena, in contrast to grander ones at Arles and Nîmes to the east, began as little more than a jury-rigged affair for soldiers passing through; scholars have noted its inferior materials, want of decoration, and lack of architectural grace. As for Cimiez's baths, they were *de rigueur* in any substantial Roman settlement, and less imposing than those of such spas as Vichy, Aix, and Bath.

Cimiez, then, might be imagined during much of its five-hundred-year history as a kind of frontier crossroads town—maybe (to offer an American perspective) a little like St. Louis, gateway to the West, in the decades after the Lewis and Clark expedition came through in 1804. A town to which the Empire's business sometimes required a trip; which columns of legionnaires, with their wagons and pack animals, sometimes tramped through; to which couriers, traders, tax collectors, and government officials traveled; but which no one went to any special trouble to visit—certainly not for the sake of a good time.

Long before the Romans came, other peoples inhabited the region. First were the Ligurians, who occupied a large crescent of Mediterranean coastline centered on Genoa. It was at the site of a Ligurian *oppidum*, or fortified hilltop encampment, that the Romans built their town.

Then came the Greeks—Phocaean Greeks, from the west coast of today's Turkey—who established a settlement, Nikaia, at the base of the hill, down by the water's edge, near what is today Nice's old town. They probably settled along the beach near the mouth of the Paillon River, not far from the rocky prominence known today as Les Ponchettes; here, where thousands today bask in the sun, photos from even quite recently show wooden boats beached on the shore much as the Greeks must have done. For centuries, Nikaia was little more than an anchorage with a thin settlement behind it.

Nikaia is Greek for "victory," but scholars don't agree on over whom. Nor do they agree on when the city was founded, some pointing to the sixth century B.C., others to as late as the fourth; nor whether Nikaia was a colony of Marseilles, a hundred miles to the west, which the Phocaean Greeks also founded, or settled independently. The Greeks left behind little that perplexed archeologists have been able to recover.

For centuries after the Romans founded Cimiez, it and Nikaia coexisted, separate and distinct—sometimes in peaceful trade; sometimes uneasily, in conflict. Indeed, Nice can best be imagined as two places, the Roman town and the Greek, stitched together across the centuries—two modest hubs, separated by a mile and a half, three hundred feet of altitude, or an hour's uphill hike. From afar they might blur into one, and today they are bound administratively into one, but for five hundred years or more they were quite distinctly two. Knowledge of these early settlements is fragmentary and uncertain. More certain, however, is that neither of them was in any conceivable sense a tourist destination.

By Roman times, though, places did exist to which wealthy people went expressly for pleasure's sake. Five hundred miles around the Ligurian crescent and down the west coast of the Italian boot could be seen the first glimmers of tourism. In a place called Baiae, two days' travel along the Appian Way from Rome, a resort complex had sprung up during the second century B.C. beside the Bay of Naples. Along the sea, lavish villas were lined up. Cicero had one there. So did Caesar, Pompey, Mark Antony, and Augustus. From some of these sumptuous seaside villas, you could fish by simply dropping a line out a bedroom window. People were borne along the shore in litters, or around the bay or on nearby lakes in oar-powered yachts. Vacationers could buy souvenirs, such as pieces of engraved glass portraying the Baian seafront. Predictably, some complained about excesses of wealth and debauchery. Others worried about the environment; at Baiae, wrote Horace, "lake and sea suffer from the eager owner's fancy."

Some few Romans did travel for the sake of education, self-improvement, and personal enrichment. The wealthy sent their children to study in Athens and Rhodes, or to Egypt (where some left graffiti on the pyramids). But they did not, we may be certain, send them to Cimiez or Nikaia.

∞

Michel de L'Hospital's account of his three-month visit to Nice in early 1560 is almost the first we have that reminds us of the place we know today. "Lit aglow by the setting sun, caressed by soft winds," wrote this fifty-two-year-old French humanist, poet, and statesman, "the city starts at the summit of a mountain and drops gently to the seashore. There, each morning and evening, the local people stroll contentedly up and down the beach."

L'Hospital visited the ruins of Cimiez, including a fourteenth-century convent built near the old baths. He toured neighboring Villefranche and its fort, traveled to the Grotto of Saint-André, savored Nice's gardens and flowers, the sweetness of its evenings, its perfumed breezes. In short, he appreciated the town much as generations of tourists would later.

And this first of the breed was a *foreign* tourist. L'Hospital was French; Nice was not. Nice was part of Savoy, a political entity unto itself. To the Niçois, France was a foreign country.

All across the long centuries since the fall of Rome in the fifth century, Nice fell under the sway of first this, then that fiefdom, duchy, or kingdom. Today, more than many other European cities, it betrays a personality still split by language and culture. Already by 1388, when it passed to Savoy, it and its surrounding backcountry had passed through many hands, including the dynastic houses of Arles and of Anjou. Today these are parts of France. Back then, however, they were all Provençal; today's Provence, out beyond where the Alps sweep down to the coast west of Genoa, was Rome's first province.

When, in 1774, a certain Monsieur de la Lande visited Nice, he noted that in polite society people spoke French; that the laws were published in Italian; but that the common people spoke what he called a "corrupted Provençal." "Today it's raining in Nice" comes out in French as *"Aujourd'hui, il pleut à Nice."* But in Provençal—or, rather, the local version of it, Nissard—it's *"Ancuèi, plòu à Nissa."* Today the street

signs in old Nice bear the ancient Nissard names beneath them. And Niçois cuisine features the likes of anchovy pizza and *socca*, fried chick-pea cracker, which gourmands from the heart of France might scarcely recognize. Nice French? Yes, but Provençal, too.

And, later, Italian.

Today leave the newer part of Nice, cross the barren expanse of park that is the Promenade du Paillon, dart across a noisy, car-clogged thoroughfare lined with shops on one side, and you step abruptly into the past. Here, within the old city, little changed since the seventeenth century, space constricts. Close-packed, stucco-faced four- and five-story buildings rise above crooked, narrow streets; a noisy footfall echoes from the wall of buildings. At every *place*, a convent, church, or chapel. From a little park where three streets meet, you see banks of narrow pastel-colored shutters shut tight against the midday sun.

This could be Italy, whose frontier lies just twenty miles to the east. Indeed, within the 1840s-vintage church that faces Nice's modest harbor, a memorial to the dead of World War I mostly bears French first names and Italian last names: Pierre Chiossa, François Castelli. The fact is, until 1860, when Paris had been French since as long as there'd been a France and when even New World cities like Boston or Philadelphia had been firmly American for almost a century, Nice was still Italian.

Not that it was part of Italy; until 1870, there *was* no Italy, just a jumble of individual states, Savoy being one of them. Savoy itself was actually a French-speaking region that butted up on the north against what is now Switzerland; but since the early fifteenth century it had included Piedmont, part of today's Italy. The result was a kidney-shaped half-breed, about the size of Switzerland itself, *un peu français, un pocco italiano.* Its capital was Turin, or Torino, across the Alpes-Maritimes from the Mediterranean coast. To muddle matters yet more, a 1718 treaty gave to the Duke of Savoy the island of Sardinia, making it, Savoy, and Piedmont all names associated with the same region.

Collapse the centuries a little carelessly, then, and visitors to Nice—or Nizza, or Nissa—might be excused for not knowing just where they were. Liguria? Provence? Savoy? Sardinia? Piedmont? Italy?

France? All political or geographic entities with which Nice has been linked, sometimes at the same time.

Over the years, national identity has hung but loosely upon Nice's shoulders. In 1517, an Italian cleric, Antonio de Beatis, passed through town with his master, a Roman cardinal. De Beatis reported what he called "the common opinion" that Nizza "owes its name to the fact that it is neither [ne] here [za] nor there, that is to say, neither in Italy nor in France." Why, the very emblem of the city, he added, testified to the same thing—"an eagle with one foot raised, and not resting anywhere."

For most of the fifteen hundred years after the fall of Rome, Nice lay under the shadow of larger cities—Marseilles, Turin, and Genoa—roughly a hundred miles to the west, north, and east respectively. During the Middle Ages, it was a modestly scaled town, its few thousand souls clustered within thick walls at the base of the rocky hill near where the Greeks had first settled. The 1500s and 1600s brought a modest growth spurt, but even by the eve of the eighteenth century, Nice did not, as cities go, amount to much.

The occasional arrival of a crowned monarch, like Beatrix of Portugal in 1521, was usually enough to prompt a festival rife with color and pomp. In 1538, Pope Paul III brought the Holy Roman Empire's Charles V and France's François I to Nice, to conclude a peace treaty. Charles entered neighboring Villefranche at the head of twenty-eight galleys and three thousand troops. François, sitting astride a horse adorned with blue velvet embroidered with gold, headed an army of like size. Meeting for two weeks with each of them separately, the Pope finally eked out a short-lived truce. The city fathers put up a marble cross, a *croix-de-marbre*, that is still there, just up from the beach where the Pope disembarked.

But visits like those of Beatrix and Pope Paul were hardly the rule. Nice was a minor town that people had scant reason to visit, and travelers who did stop were usually bound elsewhere. Perhaps north, over the steep white limestone crags of the Alpes-Maritimes, to Turin.

Or east to Genoa, for its churches, palaces, and art.

Or west to Provence, perhaps through southern France, over the Pyrenees, to Santiago de Compostela in northwestern Spain, the great pilgrimage site.

The poet Milton passed through Nice in 1638. But he was on his way to Florence, Rome, and Naples.

In 1644, twenty-three-year-old John Evelyn, a wealthy landowner's son who wished to avoid the civil war then wracking England, left behind his studies at Oxford, crossed the Channel to France, and in October arrived at Cannes. There he got a coast-hugging boat for Genoa. On passing Nice, he noted its "very pleasant aspect towards the sea," but found no cause to stop there.

In 1760, Jean-Jacques Casanova, the infamous libertine, was bound for Genoa by boat with his current lady friend, the fair Rosalie, when rough seas forced them into the port of Villefranche; there they took a carriage to Nice, where they amused themselves for a few days. When the weather improved, they proceeded once more to Genoa.

Always, it seemed, visitors to Nice were passing through it, or by it, or around it, on the way to someplace else.

When they did notice Nice, they gushed not over its civic virtues but its military. Even our Monsieur de L'Hospital couldn't help mentioning its great commanding fortress—which, "protected on one side by the sea and on the other by sheer rocks, may be deemed impregnable." Almost a century later, in 1658, Francis Mortoft set out from England with friends, bound for Italy. In Nice, he noted the town's abundance of oranges and lemons, shipped in chests borne by mules and as common as apples and pears back home. But otherwise he said of it only that it was "a very strong place, having a citadel built upon a rock."

For hundreds of years, this "citadel," perched atop a rocky promontory that climbed straight up from the sea, where scholars suppose the Greeks established their own defensive redoubts, dominated Nice. All through the turbulent Middle Ages and beyond, as the town was threatened, besieged, occupied, and ravaged by a succession of warring parties, this fortified enclave *was* Nice.

Some of the wars, like the Thirty Years' War, made it into the history books. But many others, set against the immutable backdrop of blood and fire that was the Mediterranean Basin during the Middle Ages, never earned names at all. The Goths invaded. So did the Vandals, Burgundians, Lombards, and Saracens. Roman Cimiez, reduced to ruin, gradually slipped under orchards and vineyards. The Roman road from Genoa crumbled. At a high point along the road, about eight miles east of Cimiez, visible from land and sea, the Emperor Augustus had erected, at today's La Turbie, a towering stone monument to his defeat of the local tribes. But during the Middle Ages, marauding Goths and Saracens ripped down the fine white marble, mutilated the inscriptions, and hauled them away.

Today Riviera tourists wander through walled villages topped by battlements, like Èze, ten miles east of Nice, teeming with restaurants and gift shops. *Villages perchés,* the French call these picturesque stone warrens perched atop rocky cliffs. Even today, if you're a little out of shape, they can seem inaccessible; during the violent centuries that spawned them, inaccessibility was just the idea.

Nice's inhabitants, too, dwelt almost entirely within its walls, in the shadow of the fortress that commanded its heights. Beginning in 1270, and for the next hundred years, the walls and battlements began to go up around the town. During the sixteenth and early seventeenth centuries, they were shored up and extended, private houses banished altogether from the top of the hill. What remained was the "very strong place" Francis Mortoft saw in 1658.

A visitor viewing it then from the Cimiez hill, for example, would have seen Nice in all its boisterous tangle of walls and redoubts, spires and pennants, turrets and defenseworks. To the south, the triangularly shaped town was defined by the sea; to the east, by high stone walls and the unclimbably steep slope below the château; and, on the triangle's third side, by the river Paillon, on the far side of which stood open country, speckled with houses and gardens. At least until the early eighteenth century, all Nice was packed into this single square mile, its thick-walled mass punctured at just four places by gates.

And then, abruptly, the great citadel was gone.

The year 1705 saw the end of one of those numerous wars—this one was the War of the Spanish Succession—that left Savoy in constant conflict with its neighbors. Nice had been besieged by eight thousand French troops, who had long been unable to breach the citadel atop the hill. Only after a month and a half of bombardment by cannon and heavy mortars, firing from across the Paillon, did the Savoyard defenders give up, retiring to the north. In revenge for their defiance, King Louis XIV of France ordered his commander, the Duke of Berwick, to expunge, once and for all, the thorn in France's side that was the fortress. From February to July of 1706, great explosions lit up the azure sky of Nice. So industriously did Berwick carry out his orders that promenaders on the Château Hill today find almost no vestige of walls or battlements, no evidence a fort ever existed.

But this one act of destruction had unintended and, for a change, mostly benign consequences. For over the next three-quarters of a century, Nice, for so long hunkered down behind its ramparts, stretched open its arms to the world.

Figuring in this transformation was its geographical position within Savoy, then part of the Kingdom of Sardinia-Piedmont. All that kept the mountainous little duchy from being as landlocked as its Swiss neighbor to the north was the short stretch of seacoast that included Nice and the neighboring anchorages of Villefranche and Saint-Hospice. Back in 1612, Savoy had made Nice a free port, eliminating duties and granting freedom of travel to foreign traders. Then, in 1749, following the eight-year War of the Austrian Succession, King Charles Emmanuel III authorized construction of a new, more substantial anchorage just east of the Château Hill. Nice flowered. Jews and Protestants were given leave to purchase land. A cosmopolitan flavor, an openness to foreigners, percolated through town; one visitor could write, later in the century, "Liberty of conscience and the freedom of the port . . . have attracted a number of strangers." By the mid-eighteenth century, perhaps a thousand of the town's fewer than fifteen thousand inhabitants were foreign, mostly French from Provence. On any day, the port might harbor ships from Sweden, Holland, Denmark, and England.

Especially England, whose policy had long been to ally itself with France's enemies. Savoy and England—which had sided with Savoy in the recent war, and relied on its consul in Nice to keep tabs on the French fleet down the coast in Toulon—grew closer. Commerce between them prospered: English manufactured goods for Savoy's silk, wine, and olive oil. In Nice, Englishmen passing through on the Grand Tour were always welcome.

∞

Others besides the British traveled for pleasure; in 1772, the French envoy in London noted the arrival of many French, "their travels having had no object other than their curiosity." But on the whole, the Grand Tour, whose beginnings scholars sometimes date to the Peace of Utrecht of 1713, was a British affair; by century's end, twenty or thirty thousand wealthy young British men were crowding the Continent each year.

First among the aristocracy and gentry, and later among the professional classes, the idea had taken hold that a gentleman's education was incomplete until he had sampled the Continent—until he had seen the Louvre in Paris, visited the Roman ruins of Arles and Nîmes, strode where Caesar had strode in the Roman Forum, seen the Bay of Naples, climbed Vesuvius. He would tour Europe over a span of two or three years and would come back polished and sophisticated, clutching bronze miniatures of the Trajan Column in Rome, better fit to take his place at England's helm. In his four-volume treatise, *The Grand Tour*, Thomas Nugent conceived travel as a means "to enrich the mind with knowledge, to rectify the judgement, to remove the prejudices of education, to compose the outward manners, and in a word to form the complete gentleman."

Of course, it didn't always work that way. Milord often rushed through museums and ancient sites, clung closely to his British compatriots, picked up just a few pat foreign phrases, and kept a journal full of banal and trifling scribbles. In theory, he enjoyed the benign guidance of a personal tutor, whose watchful eye protected him from debauchery. In fact, tutors were sometimes scarcely more educated than their young masters—who were apt to spend as much time whoring (venereal disease conspicuous among their souvenirs of Paris or Naples) as they ever did learning. One's travels, of course, didn't have to be so wanting. After all, how would you like to have Adam Smith as your tutor? One young English duke did in 1764; Smith worked on *The Wealth of Nations* in his spare time. But idle, empty upper-class life did not, on arrival at Calais, invariably yield to high-minded intellectual zeal. British travelers, it is safe to say, were moved by motives little more elevated than those inspiring most tourists today.

Some of them, during these years before the railroad, brought their private carriages across the Channel and had their drivers shepherd them from place to place. Others bought carriages in Calais, then sold them back before returning to England. Still others hired carriages and drivers as needed. In France, one option was the public *diligence*—an enormous, many-tonned coach holding as many as twenty passengers, with seats inside and outside, leather curtains, baggage tied down by ropes and chains on the top, which plied set routes at set times; you hoped for a lively seatmate, often got a crushing bore.

Nugent's *The Grand Tour* mentions the narrow, dirty streets of Marseilles, the superb port facilities of Toulon, the Roman amphitheater in Arles. It doesn't describe Nice, but does mention it. For Nice lay on the way to Italy, the Grand Tour's culmination. Reaching Italy normally meant crossing the Alps by one of the high mountain passes. But you could avoid the Alps, too. Having reached Lyons from Paris, you could float down the Rhône to Marseilles and from there take a boat that hugged the Ligurian shore directly to Genoa. Or from Marseilles you could go overland to Fréjus, over the wild, red-rocked Esterels to Cannes, across a stretch of flatland to Antibes, then across the frontier to Nice, and on to the rest of Italy.

Not many selected this last option, but a few did, and of those passing through Nice, some stayed for a while. Dr. Thomas Linolett visited in 1714. Lord and Lady Cavendish came in 1731; their son, Henry, the future chemist, was born in Nice that December. Lady Fitzgerald came in 1755. At least one scholar has speculated that the end of the War of the Austrian Succession in 1748 may have helped put Nice on the map. British officers stationed in the vicinity of Nice, scholar Daniel Feliciangeli writes, "had plenty of leisure to appreciate its climate and, once the war was over, to report *viva voce* its advantages to their compatriots."

Still, these visits were but isolated episodes, spelling no change in Nice's fortunes. From a larger perspective, they didn't count.

Then, in 1763, Tobias Smollett came to Nice, and his visit did count.

3 ISLAND NICE

WITHIN TEN YEARS OF THE APPEARANCE OF TOBIAS SMOLLETT'S book, Nice was firmly on the mental map of Europe. The timing couldn't have been better. Europe was, for a change, at peace. Travel was in vogue. "Where one Englishman travelled in the reigns of the first two Georges," wrote one observer in 1772, referring to the period before 1760, "ten now go on a grand tour. . . . There is scarce a citizen of large fortune" not bound for the Continent. Some of them—British royals, sickly lords and ladies, or London social lions who had in the past made predictable choices like France's Hyères or Montpellier—now tried Nice.

One was a brother of King George III, the Duke of Gloucester, and his wife, who stayed at the Hôtel d'Angleterre in the Croix-de-Marbre district. Another was the Duchess of Cumberland, also a sister-in-law of the king. They came for Nice's beauty and winter warmth, but also to duck London scandal-mongering; the king had not sanctioned their marriages. Still, such visitors conferred a royal imprimatur on Nice. Others among England's wealthy and well-born followed.

By 1775, Johann Georg Sulzer, a Swiss German philosopher and mathematician, could write that the English, "accustomed for some years to leave their foggy island in the fall in order to pass the winter in southern Europe, have helped establish Nice's renown for its soothing and restorative powers." A decade later, in 1786, the Frenchman de la Lande noted that Nice served as refuge for foreigners escaping the cold and wet of the north, and that an embryonic "season," spanning the months from October through May, had become established. Another traveler noted "country houses in the vicinity of Nice crowded with English, French, Germans; each forms a colony."

Among the French, a sprinkling of princesses, duchesses, high ecclesiastics, and intellectuals began coming to Nice. One was Antoine-Léonard Thomas, director of the French Academy, whose eloquence on Nice's behalf made him something of a French Smollett. Traveling there in 1782, he found a charming house by the seashore, and soon was writing friends about being lulled to sleep by the muffled, hypnotic rhythm of the waves.

Nowhere is there a more beautiful sky, nor promenades which offer more beautiful views. . . . Here you at once see nature at its wildest and the sheer opulence of fabulous gardens. Higher up, the air seems full of aromas and perfumes. Overhead, a resplendent sky of azure, a sun as brilliant as on the most beautiful days of summer . . .

On and on it went like that—a forerunner in words of the picture postcard, someone would later observe, a century before there *were* picture postcards.

Nice, whose population had by 1787 already swelled 50 percent since Smollett's time, to eighteen thousand, was on the move. "Nice is so astonishingly improved within these eighteen or twenty years," wrote engineer and artist Albanis Beaumont of the period stretching back to about the time the *Travels* first appeared, "that those who frequented it at that time, and have not seen it since, would scarcely know it again."

A building boom was on. Beginning back in the 1740s, a row of low structures serving as shops had been built facing the sea, its flat unbroken roof serving as a terrace, or public walkway, that extended almost a quarter-mile. Handsome stairways brought you up above the grime of the street to where cool winds blew and sea views were unrivaled. All through the remainder of the century and on into the next, these terraces—they are still there—were extended. Six years after publication of the *Travels*, in 1772, the terrace was linked to the new port by a road cut into the Château Hill and jutting out over the sea; winds gathered here, so the locals soon called it Quai Rauba Capeu, from the Nissard for "Hold on to your hat."

By the late 1780s, the terrace was the center of Nice social life. Lodging houses opened directly onto it. It was the place to be seen strolling of a fine winter's evening. In 1789, Englishman Arthur Young remarked on this "noble terrace, opening immediately to the sea, raised above the dirt and annoyance of a street, and equally free from the sand and shingle of a beach. . . . The walk this terrace affords is, in fine weather, delicious."

In 1777, a rich countess founded a theater, for opera, modeled on English theaters of the day and expressly intended to draw English *hivernants*, or winter visitors; it served up fare alternately in Italian and French.

In 1787, local authorities opened a social club where foreigners could gamble and find foreign magazines.

British and other foreigners clustered in the Croix-de-Marbre district, across the Paillon River from the original city. "Their abundance," reported de la Lande, "has stirred the locals to construct and furnish numerous houses aimed especially at the foreigners."

The locals already knew where their bread was buttered. Any handsome villa, with a garden of orange trees laden with fruit, was always in demand. And as demand increased, supply rose to meet it. Little gardeners' houses on the outskirts of town were pressed into service. Sulzer pictured them as "rather picturesque, garlanded with vines, well-constructed, large and clean inside, seducing the English with their charm." You could spend twenty-five livres for a furnished house, with a garden, for the six-month season—or you could spend two hundred. In any case, as an English visitor noted a few years later, some of the locals "accumulated small fortunes." Indeed, it seemed to the British, writes Daniel Feliciangeli, that "the essential character of the Niçois consisted of the nerve and skill with which he fleeced the tourist."

Little Nice, the modest *chef-lieu*, or chief town, of an impoverished rural county, was beginning to do what every tourist mecca in every century would always do—make a living from its wealthy guests. James

Edward Smith, a prominent thirty-seven-year-old botanist who came to
Nice in 1786 as part of a scientific expedition, found himself

> disgusted with the gross flattery paid here to strangers, and the
> English in particular. The whole neighborhood has the air of
> an English watering place. The town is much enlivened and en-
> riched by the concourse of strangers, who resort hither for the
> sake of the climate in winter, and great numbers of people are
> supported by their means.

One local apothecary, a Mr. Faroudi, had gone ahead and learned English, thus capturing most of the visitors' medical business.
　　And so it had begun.

∞

Begun, yes, but on a scale that today seems ludicrously small.
　　In 1789, a traveler stopping in Nice for a few days noted the influx
of English winter visitors, then proceeded to supply their actual number—fifty-seven, a figure probably referring to families; in all, perhaps
three hundred men, women, and children, counting servants and other
household help. However appealing Nice might seem to readers of Tobias Smollett, few of them, in absolute terms, actually got there.
　　To travelers from Northern Europe, Nice was a remote island. Nice,
of course, is *not* an island, and on the map seems near many other cities
and towns. Yet, as exaggerations go, this one isn't outlandish: high mountains, swollen rivers, irresolute winds, and abominable, bandit-stalked
roads made a trip to Nice demanding, expensive, and hazardous. It was
an expedition upon which only a handful could be expected to embark.
　　To later generations of tourists, accounts of such obstacles might
make the heart pulse faster—sheer precipices, the sea washing up on
the rocks below, pirates and storms and moonlit mountain passes.
Eighteenth-century travelers were not blind to romance and stark
beauty, but travel's harsh exigencies compelled their attention more urgently. Consider the English doctor Edward Rigby's account of one hot
August day in 1789. He was near Fréjus, bound for Nice. The road was

rough, he wrote, "and though it led us through uncultivated hills, covered with myrtles, tamarisks, box, cypress, juniper, etc., it was not sufficiently picturesque to make us insensible to the incessant jolts of the
carriage, and to the extreme heat of the atmosphere." In Dr. Rigby's
mental universe, in other words, pretty scenery lost out to the jouncing
and the heat.

And so it was for many an eighteenth-century traveler. The same
wild juxtapositions of jutting rock and blue water that later, defeated
by roads, bridges, tunnels, and airplanes, would leave happy memories
to so many vacationers, then represented danger and discomfort from
which most travelers shrank.

Picture Tobias Smollett approaching Nice for the first time, perched
on the right bank of the river Var, at the frontier between France and
the Kingdom of Sardinia. The Var, which the Romans called the Varus,
discharges its Alpine waters into the sea about four miles west of where
the Greeks founded Nikaia. The river itself is mostly dry, stony
riverbed, cut through by shallow flats and narrow, free-flowing rivulets,
flocks of birds sometimes standing motionless in the shallows. In August, when it's scarcely rained for months, you can sometimes ford its
mile-wide bed.

But Smollett, approaching Nice from Antibes in November 1763,
hesitated at that prospect. The middle of the Var was dry, he wrote, its
water dividing "into two or three narrow streams, which, however, are
both deep and rapid." And the river swelled abruptly after heavy rains,
sometimes rising above its banks in destructive floods, discoloring the
sea for miles around. There was no bridge. In the end, he hired six local
men to help his carriage ford the river. In hindsight, he wasn't sure he
needed them. But, he wrote later, "I did not choose to run any risk, how
small soever it might be, for the sake of saving half a crown."

Twenty-three years later, when the botanist James Edward Smith
approached Nice, he crossed the Var in similar fashion. The local
guides, he wrote, waded "naked . . . to their waists on each side of the
carriage, feeling their way with poles. If any person be lost, the guides
are hanged without mercy." Crossing the Var would not become routine

until 1792. Until then, you forded it the way Smollett and Smith did, or were ferried across by small boat.

Or else you were carried across on the backs of *passeurs*—men from the adjacent riverside town of Saint-Laurent-du-Var, charged with the job by royal decree. "You sit on the shoulders of two men pressed tightly against each other," their arms intertwined, each clutching the top of the other's coat, reported the Abbé Jean-Pierre Papon of his Var crossing in the late 1770s. Whatever you do, he wrote, you don't look down at the water.

∞

All this came only after you'd reached the Var. An Englishman who imagined trailing Smollett to Nice would first face an often stomach-wrenching crossing of a stormy English Channel; then two or three days by carriage to Paris, including perhaps twenty-five "posts"—stopping points arranged every six to ten miles at which to change horses; then five or six days to Lyons. From Lyons, it was two or three days down the Rhône to Avignon on a boat fitted with a dark, dirty cabin crowded with strangers; one English traveler remembered "monks and pilgrims who pray, women who sing, and officers who curse." From Avignon it was across the Durance to Aix-en-Provence, and another three days to the Var. At its best, maybe three weeks of boats, barges, jostling carriages, filthy inns.

Of course, the trip rarely went as planned; certainly it didn't for the Englishman Arthur Young, a quarter-century after Smollett. Young was both an occasional, not entirely successful, farmer and a widely respected student of the art and science of agriculture. At forty-eight, he was a Fellow of the Royal Society, well connected (if miserably married)—and widely traveled, to the tune of some seven thousand miles, in England and Ireland. In 1787, he undertook a series of trips to study French farming. This last one, through the south of France and on into Italy, would bring him to Nice.

On September 11, 1789, in Toulon, just east of Marseilles, Young considered, as he wrote in *Travels in France*, "the method to get to Nice."

The method, as if it were some arcane procedure, worthy of laboratory research or a patent application. Dissuaded from taking into Italy the little one-horse chaise that had already borne him twelve hundred miles, he resolved to rely instead on *vetturini,* hired drivers, and their carriages. He parked mare and chaise in a well-traveled street in Toulon, set out a large sign—*à vendre,* for sale—posted a price of twenty-five louis, and promptly sold both for twenty-two.

Now it was on to Nice. But how? "Will it be believed," he wrote, "that from Marseilles with 100,000 souls, and Toulon with 30,000, lying in the great road to Antibes, Nice, and Italy, there is no diligence or regular voiture?"

One alternative, he was advised at an inn, was to pay three louis for a seat in a carriage as far as Antibes. But he'd have to wait for a second passenger going the same way. No, Young resolved, he'd take a boat instead.

In the morning, his barque pulled out of the great Toulon harbor, studded with many-cannoned men-of-war, the pride of the French fleet. In the evening, it landed at Cavalero, which consisted of precisely three houses. "A more wretched place not to be imagined," wrote Young. "They spread a mattress on a stone floor for me, for bed they had none; after starving all day, they had nothing but stale eggs, bad bread, and worse wine."

And the mules that would take him to Fréjus, next step on the way to Nice and Italy? None on hand. No horses, either. Or asses. "I was thus in a pretty situation."

What to do? Get back on the boat? Despite the unfavorable winds?

Finally, the boat's captain agreed to have three of his men carry Young's bags to a village about six miles away; there, certainly, he'd be able to hire mules. So, the following morning, they set out, through hard, rocky country covered with pines and evergreen shrubs, beside streambeds and over winding mountain paths. Besides Young, the party consisted of a Corsican, a Provençal, and "a mongrel Italian." None spoke English, or even much French. Nobody said much.

At the village with all the mules, there were no mules.

Young negotiated with a man to take his baggage on an ass, a much smaller animal, while he walked another three miles to Saint-Tropez.

From Saint-Tropez, he was ferried by boat across the inlet to Sainte-Maxime.

In Sainte-Maxime, he hired two mules and a guide to take him, over more of "the same mountainous and rocky desert of pines and lentiscus," to Fréjus. Distance traveled for the day, first on foot, then by boat? Thirty miles.

At Fréjus, the ancient Roman town with its remains of aqueduct and amphitheater, he sought a carriage but found none. "I had no recourse but mules" to go over the Esterel hills to Cannes. But "for ten miles on a miserable mule," the man wanted to charge him twice what Young deemed fair.

Taking time to stroll around town and gather plants in bloom, presumably for his studies, the enterprising Young met a woman with an ass piled high with grapes. Would she, and for what price, he asked through an interpreter, be willing to dump her grapes and take his baggage instead? The next day, Young reported, "Myself, my female, and her ass jogged merrily over the mountains." They could scarcely speak a word to one another. Married with three children—that was about all he could get from her. "I tried to know if he was a good husband, and if she loved him very much; but our language failed in such explanations."

Finally, they reached a post house, with horses, and from there it was over the Esterels, with its crumbled red rock and brush underfoot, bushes and small trees fighting up through the dry red soil, blue sea far below, to "prettily situated" Cannes. There he found "no post-house, carriage, nor horses, nor mules to let." And so another woman, another ass, another hike, starting at five in the morning, to Antibes. From there it was a post chaise to Nice, which he reached, after an uneventful crossing of the Var, the next day.

❧

That was what reaching Nice from the Marseilles side of the Mediterranean could be like in 1789. And that was the easy way. From the east, from the Genoa side, the obstacles were not so modest as the Esterels or the Var, but, rather, mile upon mile of rocky precipice that dropped straight down to the sea. Save for occasional inlets, there was no beach, and scarcely a road worthy of the name. All through the Middle Ages, travel had become more difficult, commerce had contracted, roads had withered. The Roman road pushing through the Alpes-Maritimes from the Italian boot, the old Via Aurelia, had long since fallen into disuse.

What now passed for a road twisted up and down rocky paths cut through cliffs. "It would be difficult to imagine," wrote Johann Georg Sulzer, "a road more extraordinary, more terrible, and at the same time," he admitted, "more interesting. . . . Views change with almost every step. So soon as you feel closed in by a wilderness of rocks, where you see no way out, where you feel cut off from all that lives and breathes . . . just then you reach a place where, beyond the rocks, you spy the sea, a strip of coast, bays and tongues of land advancing into the sea."

Oh, it was beautiful, but how were you supposed to cross it? Sulzer climbed atop a mule. So had Smollett before him: "You take a mule," wrote the Scottish doctor, "and clamber along the mountains at the rate of two miles an hour, and at the risk of breaking your neck every minute."

Mules were about as familiar a sight in the Riviera backcountry as sacred cows were in India. They picked their way up narrow, treacherous paths along the coast route from Genoa. Their backs heaped high with sacks and crates tied down with rope, laden with salt, oil, and wine, they climbed up from Nice along switchbacks to L'Escarène and Sospel, along the Sorgio gorge, and over the Col de Tende toward Turin; that's how Thomas Jefferson, in the middle of a five-year European sojourn, made the trip in 1787. They were almost preternaturally surefooted. "They always march upon the brink of the precipice," wrote Smollett, but "you must let them take their own way." They could carry six hundred pounds. They were tireless. "When we arrive at the post," one traveler wrote of a trip through northern Italy in 1787, "the driver takes them into an open place, spreads a little straw; the mules then lay down, and begin to tumble over their backs, in a diverting manner, for

several minutes. They then get up, shake themselves, and after a small
feed, are as fresh as the hour they set out."

And if you *didn't* want to travel on the back of a mule? In many
stretches of rocky coast and mountainous backcountry, the only alternative to walking was to be borne across the mountains by six or eight
strong men, in a straw chair, a wooden plank for your feet, a piece of
oilcloth to protect you from the elements. "Our porters," wrote one
such traveler, the spirited Madame de Genlis, countess, author, and governess to a future king, of a trip in the late 1770s, "were the lowest
people in the world." They understood neither French nor Italian. They
drank. They swore. They argued without letup. "It is hard to feign indifference to their arguments when, carried by them, you see them at
the edge of the cliff, staggering, shaking with rage, and holding your lit-
ter with only one hand, so they can make menacing gestures with the
other."

The sea, of course, was the other road to Nice, but that did not
necessarily mean *sailing* upon it. Since time immemorial, the chief means
of travel in the Mediterranean was the *felouque*—which was a kind of
Roman galley, only smaller. It had sails, typically two masts, but
couldn't sail against the wind, relying instead on a dozen or so oarsmen;
one was as apt to be rowed to Nice, then, as to be borne there by the
wind. Smollett saw *felouques* in Nice all the time, in the harbor waiting
for passengers, or else passing offshore, bound for Marseilles, Antibes,
or Genoa, loaded with goods and passengers. Aboard a *felouque* passing
within sight of shore, Nice was a tight cluster of church steeples, ships'
masts, and red-tiled roofs at the base of the Château Hill.

The *felouque*—*feluca* in Italian—might be large enough to bear a
name; the *Sainte-Thérèse* and *Les Âmes du Purgatoire*, the souls of purgatory,
were two plying the Mediterranean in the late eighteenth century. But,
typically, it was smaller than the ninety feet or so of a Roman galley.
Oarsmen sweated and strained in an open forward section. Aft, a sheltered area, under a canvas awning, was fitted for passengers and their
baggage. Accommodations were spartan; you carried your own pillows
and bedclothes, improvising a bed as best you could. From Antibes, on
the French side of Nice, to Genoa might take two or three days under

oar, one with favorable winds. Bad weather, when the captain typically clung close to shore, charting a course in and out of little bays along the sinuous coast, might extend the ninety-mile trip to 120.

Weather, of course, was the great unknown. In 1760, an Italian writer returning from Barcelona, Giuseppe Baretti, "impatient to go to Nice and have Italian soil under my feet," got stuck in Antibes during a storm. Floods had washed away a bridge then spanning the Var; land passage was out. At last he prevailed on the captain of a *felouque* to take him the sixteen miles to Nice. A mistake, he realized later. "I have run the risk once or twice in my various voyages of losing my life," Baretti wrote his brothers two days later from Nice, "but I have never seen death so near as yesterday afternoon." A terrible wind from the south produced enormous waves. Everyone on board was seasick. Two of his traveling companions vomited up blood. As the storm pushed them toward the rocks, Baretti was struck by how the rowers, pulling at their oars "in the most doleful silence," seemed oddly pensive, as if confronting their fate.

Another danger to sea travel was not nature's but man's. Pirates marauded the Mediterranean; travelers' accounts routinely mentioned either being held up by pirates or the fear of it. Incidents of piracy, one scholar has estimated, were as frequent as dangerous storms.

Likewise on land. An early-seventeenth-century traveler bound for Fréjus after passing through Nice and Cannes told how "three French murderers set upon me in a thievish wood twelve miles long, one of which had dogged me hither from Nice." Smollett reported that the Esterels, very likely the thievish wood in question, though long "frequented by a gang of desperate banditti," were just then safe. But a few years later, in 1787, the Swiss geologist Horace-Bénédict de Saussure described how the main road through the Esterels was a trap for the unwary. Robbers, often escapees from the galleys of Toulon, would calmly wait for travelers to pass a fixed point, "then rush out upon them from the wood in which they were hidden, and rob them of everything," while sentinels, commanding a view of the road, stood watch for mounted police.

To a modern tourist, such tales may evoke the romantic "highwayman" of the Alfred Noyes poem, a dashing figure who woos the land-lord's black-eyed daughter and gallops through the night pursued by the king's soldiers. But Noyes's poem dates to 1907; it was only much later, the real danger past, that poets and publicists could afford to romanti-cize such criminals. In the eighteenth century, they remained a menace, like brutal muggers in dangerous neighborhoods today—and repre-sented an obstacle to travel quite as great.

For a venturesome few, of course, danger added a tang to travel. In 1780, Madame de Genlis and her party in Antibes were forced to wait ten days for favorable winds; the indomitable countess played her harp to while away the time. When they finally set sail for Nice, a *felouque* full of soldiers escorted them "to assure our safety from pirates. This pre-caution," she wrote, "thrilled my romantic imagination," inspiring in her reveries of danger, kidnapping, and battle with which she enter-tained her traveling companions for the rest of the trip.

A few years later, a priest named Eyrard set off from Nice at dusk, in a *felouque* bound for Italy and the start of a two-and-a-half-month trip. The moon lit up the distant shore. The songs of the oarsmen carried across the water. He was aware of being in a tiny boat in the middle of a great sea, far from shore, among strangers who spoke a language he didn't understand. Yet he felt happy and alive. "Winds, reefs, pirates—I feared nothing."

Then, too, peril, or just the prospect of it, was always good for a story; the tortuous topography around Nice inspired deliciously danger-fraught accounts. Albanis Beaumont wrote how the road east of Nice crossed "a wooden bridge, which is literally nothing more than three beams covered with planks, badly put together, without either railing or support"; travelers were left to fairly dangle 250 feet above a tongue of the sea. And down the road, he went on, came "another frightful pass. . . ."

Danger dressed up, or defeated, or confronted at a safe remove spiced up the trip for a few travelers. But they were the exceptions. The risks were real. Getting to Nice meant reckoning with substantial dis-comfort, inconvenience, danger, trouble, and cost. It was never routine.

Consider the trip from Genoa to Nice, roughly a hundred miles.

One eighteenth-century traveler decided that taking the treacherous road that linked them was better than going by sea. A second concluded otherwise: "Having been dissuaded from going by land along that for-midable road, the *corniche* to Genoa, on account of the badness of the roads and the danger of the *banditti,* we hired a *felucca.*" A third traveler, Thomas Jefferson, set out for Nice by boat. But when strong winds rocked his little craft, he became hopelessly seasick. So the captain put into a little fishing port forty miles up the coast, and Jefferson pro-ceeded to Nice by land—"clambering up the cliffs of the Apennines, sometimes on foot, sometimes on a mule, according as the path was more or less difficult."

The problem of those hundred miles, in other words, inspired three different solutions, none of them good; a trip to Nice could never be contemplated lightly. And that fact was enough to dissuade the frail, the timid, and the irresolute. Smollett may have put Nice on the map, but as long as simply getting there was so difficult, a winter holiday in Nice could never, even by eighteenth-century standards, be a mass phe-nomenon.

Still, as we've seen, *it had begun.* As he looked back to the 1780s from across a divide of fifteen tumultuous years, it seemed to John Bunnell Davis, an English physician, that Nice had already become a magnet to visitors from across Europe. For six months of the year, they enjoyed "a place where the pleasures of an agreeable society, joined to the mildness of climate, restored the valetudinarian to health, and afforded a source of amusement to him whose pursuit was pleasure."

Those pleasant circumstances, however, were shattered in 1789, with the coming of the French Revolution, the Terror, and years of almost uninterrupted strife. Nice, one French scholar has written, "lost its tranquility, its well-being, and its guests."

4 RECOLLECTIONS OF DANGERS PAST

AT ABOUT NOON ON A BREEZY AUGUST DAY IN 1789, DR. EDWARD Rigby, traveling with three friends, arrived in Antibes, on the French frontier, just across the Var from Nice. Asked for his passport, issued to him in Paris, Rigby sent his servant with it to the local commandant. The servant returned, Rigby wrote to his wife and daughters later, "in a fright." The commandant had never seen such a passport, and ordered Dr. Rigby and his party to present themselves to him in person. Two weeks before, a mob had stormed the Bastille prison in Paris, precipitating revolution. Europe shook. The French monarchy was crumbling; Rigby's passport bore the imprimatur of the new revolutionary authorities.

In Antibes, everybody from the owner of the little shop where they bought a watermelon to the commandant himself (who let them leave France without a fuss) begged them for information. *Tell us of Paris. Tell us of the Revolution!* In Nice, it was the same. The British consul visited them. "He said he came to pay his respects to us," wrote Rigby, "but the true reason was to hear news from Paris."

Rigby, who at forty-two had never before stepped off English soil, had news aplenty. In Paris, on July 7, he and his friends had taken rooms in a hotel near the Palais-Royal, from which they'd seen the Revolution develop. The streets surged with protest. Banned newspapers circulated freely. In Versailles, seat of the Court, Rigby witnessed a meeting of the National Assembly, heard a speech by Lafayette, the American Revolutionary War hero. Later, he glimpsed the hapless king, Louis XVI, and his queen, Marie-Antoinette, on their way to Mass.

In Paris again, he saw crowds armed with guns, swords, and pikes looted from shops and homes. On July 14, he joined throngs just back from the Bastille, all "shouts and shrieks, leaping and embracing, laughter and tears." As an Englishman, a species then still esteemed by the revolutionaries, he was welcomed. Swept up in the fever of the streets, he joined in the shouting, clasped hands with people around him. But he saw, too, another face of the mob's zeal—two bloody heads perched atop pointed pikes.

Nice, in those days before the telegraph, was cut off from the furor in Paris by six hundred miles and a national boundary; on arriving there, Rigby and his friends sat down to a familiar English dinner of roast beef, boiled potatoes, and beer, then went out for a quiet evening's stroll. He enjoyed the play of moonlight upon the calm sea, the easy ambience of people walking about. A month later, Arthur Young (whose troubles in getting to Nice we traced earlier) likewise savored his tranquil time on the Italian side of the Var.

> The first approach to that country so long and justly celebrated . . . fills the bosom with too many throbbing feelings to permit [even] a bush, a stone, a clod to be uninteresting. . . . Here I am, then, in the midst of another people, language, sovereignty, and country—one of the moments of a man's life that will always be interesting, because all the springs of curiosity and attention are on the stretch.

At dinner that evening, at the Hôtel de Quatre Nations, Young, like Rigby, found "the French revolution only talked of," nothing more, remote.

But what was in 1789 only a distant storm would thunder through Nice, too. Young saw around him fine lodging houses, handsome squares, new streets and houses; all testified to the prosperity the winter visitors brought. But now, he reported, the Niçois worried that revolution would keep the fat-walleted English away, even as it brought "a great resort of French." They were right on both counts.

Even by the time of Young's visit, in the late summer of 1789,

French nobles and clergy from those highborn classes soon to face the guillotine had reached Nice. Most were from Provence. The Duke and Duchess of Rohan were among them. So was the Duchess of La Trémoille, and the Marquise of Cabris. Priests and monks by the hundreds came, including the bishops of Toulon and of Grasse. For three years, Nice, just across the border from France, was haven for two thousand émigrés; *un petit Coblentz*, it was called, in reference to an émigré refuge in Germany. For three years, they were safe.

But from almost the beginning, revolutionary France warred with its neighbors, including the Kingdom of Sardinia, and by September 1792, a French republican army stood poised to cross the Var; seven thousand Sardinian troops faced them on the opposite shore. When Mariana Starke, whose *Letters from Italy* recounted her seven years there, arrived in Nice on September 22, she found lodging houses filled with Sardinian soldiers and a "smothered apprehension" settled across the city.

Should she and her party hire a *felouque* for Genoa and get out? No, they were assured, Nice was safe.

But two days later, Starke saw French émigrés packing up to leave.

On September 27, the Sardinian government ordered anyone with horses or mules to place them in the service of the king.

The next day, sixteen French warships hove into view offshore. The king ordered his troops to abandon Nice for the mountains; that threw the city into panic. "For three or four hours," wrote Starke, "Nice waited in silent expectation of her fate."

The French émigrés began to flee over the Alps. So did many among the Piedmontese and Nissard nobility. So, finally, did the whole Sardinian army, including its commandant.

With the Sardinians gone and French forces still outside the city gates, order broke down. Escaped galley slaves plundered abandoned houses. Starke and her family huddled together through the night. The next morning, anyone with strength enough to walk fled for the hills. "Truly melancholy it was," she wrote, "to see decrepit Age and helpless Infancy toiling, for the first time in their lives, up stony mountains, exposed to the baleful rays of a scorching sun." A priest, part of this exodus, probably a French émigré, wrote how the Turin road was crowded with people of every age, sex, and status, including bishops from Provence who, "canes in hand, overwhelmed with fatigue and covered with dust," trekked up into the mountains toward Sospel.

The Revolution reached Nice. French troops, ten thousand of them, crossed into Sardinia atop a bridge of boats thrown across the Var. Starke pictured them as "raw, turbulent and rapacious" men whose looting their officers did little to curb. Anyone seen as noble or high-born risked the wrath of the Revolution. In heading for the docks, where a ship was to take them to Genoa, Starke and her party were advised to be inconspicuous; she herself dressed as a servant. It was only after one final scare, when soldiers boarded the ship "swearing we were aristocrats and threatening to rob and murder us," that she and her family at last sailed to safety.

A few months after Starke left, a rubber-stamp plebiscite legitimized the triumph of French arms, and Nice was absorbed into France; on February 4, 1793, the county of Nice became the *département* of Alpes-Maritimes. "Thus began," one historian has written, "the deculturation of Nice," its passage from distinctively Niçois to French. In a frenzy of anticlerical zeal, the old Sainte-Réparate Cathedral was renamed Temple of the Supreme Being; its pews were requisitioned for use by local hospitals. Filthy streets in the old town left in perpetual gloom by close-packed houses that crowded out the sun got names like "rue de Lumière," Street of Light. One, harboring the city's most desperately poor, was renamed Happiness Street.

About a month after France's absorption of Nice, two representatives of the National Convention arrived to organize the new *département*. One was Henri Grégoire, a Jesuit-educated *abbé* who had taken a leading role in early revolutionary activity. In a report summarizing his two and a half months in the region, Grégoire advised the taxing authorities in Paris to go easy on Alpes-Maritimes. A meager olive harvest, a bad freeze the previous year, high prices, the lack of work, and, as he acknowledged, the ruin wrought in revolution's name had left the new *département* prostrate.

It was not a good time to visit Nice. In years past, noted the *abbé*,

"The beautiful climate of Nice each year attracted many foreign families, English especially, who went to pass the winter there," contributing much to the economy. But since the Revolution, "no one has come."

And no one came, by and large, for the next twenty-five years. The period from the fall of the Bastille in 1789 to the fall of Napoleon in 1815 were years of turmoil, marked by the cries of angry mobs, the tramp of marching troops, and the icy, thudding fall of the guillotine; in Nice, they set it up in the old Place Saint-Dominique, which was renamed Place de l'Égalité. Many people, of course, traveled to Nice during these years. But except insofar as they were fleeing for their lives, they were hardly traveling for their health, or their pleasure. During these years, indeed, our story grinds almost to a halt.

∞

It would have done so entirely were it not for a year-and-a-half-long hiatus that history records as the Peace of Amiens, which ended the fighting between Napoleon's France and several of its neighbors, including England. On October 3, 1801, word of a preliminary truce was greeted by the pealing of church bells in London, by torchlit processions, tambourines, and trumpets in Paris. The following March, the powers of Europe met at Amiens, north of Paris, and signed a formal treaty. Who could know that peace would be so short-lived?

After thirteen years during which pleasure travel on the Continent had been virtually a contradiction in terms, Europe opened up once more to English visitors. "All the idle captives of the land of fogs," wrote one French historian, "shook their damp wings and prepared to take their flight toward the regions of pleasure and brightness." Most British had looked with scant favor on the Revolution, yet were enthralled by its sheer drama. During that summer of peace, two thousand of them arrived in Paris to see what revolution had wrought. Some went to recover property, others for business, a few for study. Most went for pleasure. In Nice, fifteen British families arrived in November, more the following month.

Nice's newest visitors did not, it seems, bring out the best in local residents. From merchants to carriage drivers, income-starved locals doubled or tripled their prices at the expense of sun-starved visitors. "The stranger generally drinks adulterated wine," wrote one Englishman, "and pays dearer for an inferior quality." Renting a house, especially in the Croix-de-Marbre district, was famously expensive.

One visitor during these months was John Bunnell Davis, who, like Smollett and Edward Rigby, was a physician. Davis saw that many who stepped through the newly open portals of Nice did so feebly; they were ill, often consumptive, seeking in the gentle climate a balm to their health. Davis, writing to those back in England tempted to follow them south, injected a note of realism. The sickest among them, he observed, arrived in Nice sicker than when they left England, "their coughs more violent and accesses of fever more frequent." Too often they never reached Nice at all, or died soon after.

Davis's book, which appeared in 1807, on every page attested to the Revolution's toll on Nice. The public library had "escaped the pillaging hands of the revolutionists," he wrote, but little else had. Their rage, "carried to an almost inconceivable excess, has scarcely left any hotel or mansion of grandeur without marks of degradation." The richest families were ruined, their property consigned to the flames. Many homes in the Croix-de-Marbre district had been destroyed. So had many villas in the surrounding hills. So had even the vines and olive trees adorning them. The quartering of thousands of ill and hungry troops had nourished an epidemic fatal to a sixth of the population. Meanwhile, the disappearance of winter visitors, in and of itself, had warped the pre-revolutionary economy. For example, oranges and grapes were still plentiful, Davis noted, but cauliflowers and other vegetables were scarce. Why? Because the visitors who'd formed the primary market for them, and so made them profitable to farm, were gone.

In June 1803, the Peace of Amiens crumbled. Napoleon arrested all British subjects in France; Dr. Davis, then in Verdun, bound for England, was one of them. But the memory of Nice, which left him with a vision of "tranquil retirement from the tumultuous turmoil of civilized life," lingered with him, nurturing his hope for peace: "May the period soon return when the inhabitant and stranger shall again partake of ancient gratifications, endeared by the recollection of dangers past!"

The Napoleonic Wars would grind on for twelve more years. Lives were lost, homes destroyed, economic life was disrupted. But any final reckoning of war's toll must figure in a further loss—one perversely illustrated by the great good fortune of a certain Michael Faraday. Faraday, it seems, enjoyed a trip to the Continent—including passage through the south of France and several days in Nice—in the very midst of war, while armies bled, and with the personal approval of England's sworn enemy, the Emperor Napoleon.

Born in a village now part of South London in 1791, Faraday was the son of a fitfully employed blacksmith who could scarcely feed his wife and four sons. At age fourteen, he apprenticed to a bookbinder, took to reading books in the shop, grew interested in electricity, made batteries and electrostatic generators, and began doing experiments. Then, beguiled by a lecture given by Humphrey Davy, England's most illustrious chemist, he wrote Davy and, in 1812, became his laboratory assistant. He was twenty-one years old.

The following year, Davy, thirty-four, just knighted and just married, sought leave to enter France, with which England was still at war, as part of a scientific tour of the Continent; Napoleon, patron of science, consented. Though reproached in the English press for doing so, Davy crossed the Channel in October 1813. With him were Lady Davy, her maid, and Michael Faraday. Faraday had never strayed more than three miles from London. He had never seen the sea.

They landed at Morlaix, spent two months in Paris, traveled south to Montpellier, Nîmes, and Avignon. In Aix they stopped at an inn where the Pope was supposed to have stayed six days before, even got the Pope's bed, or so they were told. In Fréjus they saw the Roman amphitheater and were warned of highwaymen in the Esterels, but they got through unscathed and crossed the wooden bridge Napoleon's men had built across the Var. On the Nice side, Faraday wrote, "the houses are painted and ornamented externally, the dress of the people has changed, the gardens glow with oranges and lemons which stand in forests and the vines creep to the top of the highest trees."

In Nice, Faraday strolled along the town's famed terrace, the elevated walkway beside the sea. He saw a ropemaker twisting strands of fiber along the beach. He saw a laundress bleaching linen. He looked hard at the orange and lemon trees, whose peculiarities of cultivation he described in detail, and which, it seemed to him, gave "a striking and forcible idea of a happy climate." He wrote how, in February, he and his party enjoyed themselves at meals "without a fire and with all the doors and windows open, so genial and mild is the winter here."

Their two days in Nice were followed by a harrowing, if memorable, trip across the snow-capped Col de Tende to Turin; by inspection of Galileo's first telescope at the Natural History Museum in Florence; by Rome, where "every day presents sufficient to fill a book"; by a climb of Vesuvius, where they cooked their evening meal by the heat of volcanic steam.

Faraday, who became one of his era's great scientific luminaries, wrote much in his journal of rocks, chemicals, and barometer readings, little of what his travels meant to him personally. But in a letter to his brother from Geneva a few months after leaving Nice, in July 1814, he was more revealing. "As all parts of my travels have pleased me," he wrote, "it will be useless to say I liked Aix, or I like Nice, etc." And then he added this:

It is now nine months since I left London, but I have not forgot and never shall forget the ideas that were forced on my mind in the first days, to me who have lived all my days of remembrance in London, in a city surrounded by a flat green country [where] a hill was a mountain and a stone a rock.

To most Englishmen other than soldiers, war and revolution had meant Europe unvisited, sights unseen, experiences unsavored. From these constraints young Mr. Faraday had enjoyed the happiest of exemptions.

5 RETURN TO LIFE

TWO MONTHS AFTER FARADAY'S RETURN TO ENGLAND IN APRIL 1815, Napoleon's armies suffered their final defeat at Waterloo. The Treaty of Paris restored Nice to the Kingdom of Sardinia, and Italian became once more the language in schools and government offices. European and British visitors began to return to Nice.

It started slowly. In the first year after Waterloo, some ten thousand British tourists visited the Continent; only a handful of them made it to Nice—perhaps a hundred families. But by the time Marguerite Gardiner, Countess of Blessington, stopped there for a few weeks in March 1823, Nice had more than recovered its standing among the British. Conspicuous among these British visitors were consumptives, victims of tuberculosis. The countess pronounced herself sick with pity to meet

some fair English girl with the bright hectic tinge on her delicate cheek, and the lustrous eyes, which betoken the presence of that most perfidious and fatal of all diseases, consumption, mounted on a pony, led by a father, a brother, or one who hoped to stand in a more tender relation to her. I tremble when I see the warm cloak in which she is enveloped, swept by the rude wind from her shrinking shoulders, and hear that fearful cough which shakes her tortured chest. A few weeks, and such invalids (and alas! they are many) are seen no more.

In his 1807 book, Dr. John Bunnell Davis had advised only the very sickest to stay in England rather than risk travel to Nice; he'd encouraged the milder cases to come—and, more, to "look with confidence" toward recovery. One French historian would see Davis as a prime spur to Nice's popularity after Waterloo. "This physician," writes Paul Gonnet, "sent to our shores a colony of pale, blond Englishwomen and listless sons of the nobility near death."

The defeat of tuberculosis, many appreciated, needed more than the soft breezes of Nice (or, for that matter, the pure country air of a Black Forest sanatorium). But the discovery of *Mycobacterium tuberculosis*, the bacterial agent responsible for the dread disease, and of streptomycin and other antibiotic drugs to treat it, lay far in the future. Well into the twentieth century, a change of climate was, with bed rest, still the treatment of choice for tuberculosis, as for many other maladies. It was an age before air-conditioning and central heating; you couldn't make it cooler, or warmer, or drier at the flick of a switch. You had to *go* somewhere, where nature itself might be more benign.

All during the nineteenth century, this idea was enshrined in the collective mind of Europe and America. And the embryonic Nice tourist industry benefited from it enormously. Climate could be an agency of cure? Well, Nice had the best climate of all.

∞

In the Matisse museum in Nice today hangs a canvas entitled *Tempête de Nice*, Nice storm. From a perch in his room in the Hôtel de la Méditerranée in 1919, Henri Matisse painted a lone walker with an umbrella on a storm-swept seaside boulevard under low, seething skies. It *does* rain in Nice, though a summer visitor might be loath to believe it. During his second winter there, Smollett encountered a stretch of bad weather so prolonged the locals could not remember its like. Why, it even snows; in February 1956, the streets were covered with a foot of the stuff. In Nice—which is north of North Korea, and at about the same latitude as Toronto—sometimes it's as nasty, raw, and gray as anyplace you wouldn't want to be.

But that's weather, with its maddening day-to-day surprises; climate is different. If weather is the fickle here-and-now, climate is the aggregate of here-and-nows across years and decades, the piling up of sensory-data points over time and their smoothing over into mathematical averages, likelihoods, tendencies. If you live someplace any length of time, climate, more than aberrations of weather, is what impresses you about it: *snowy Quebec, sultry New Orleans.*

In London it rains 150 days a year, in Nice 60.

On only five days a year in Nice, on average, does the thermometer dip below freezing.

London gets 1,500 hours of sunlight per year, Nice 2,700.

It would be impossible to overstate how forcibly early visitors to Nice were struck by its climate. Everyone spoke of it—especially its winter, which was no winter at all but, as the Swiss scientist Sulzer wrote, "a perpetual spring." Yes, wind and rain visited the city while he was there, Sulzer wrote, but even then, in January and February, they had enjoyed delightful days.

As soon as the rain stopped, the season became lovely once more, like the sweetest springtime in Germany. The air here seems clearer and purer than anywhere else. You can tell by the bright sparkling of the stars and by how many small stars you discover here, visible in Germany only on the best winter nights.

Another visitor, Jean-Pierre Papon, wrote how during the winter of 1803 he'd found the road down the hill from Cimiez

lined with daisies on which you see butterflies fluttering. The presence of these insects, together with the temperature of the air, the beauty of the sky, the green of the fields, the orange and olive trees, let you enjoy in midwinter all the pleasures of spring. . . . Strolling there last Christmas, I recall, the sun was so warm that I lay back at the foot of a lemon tree, on grass sprinkled with flowers the color of violets.

Readers accustomed to shuffling through Chicago slush or shivering in London flats need suffer no more of this; the early accounts all read about the same. First-time visitors enjoyed even the very act of describing Nice's climate, as if indulging in an illicit pleasure. And when facts bound them to report a spell of bad weather, they were apt to dismiss it as an aberration, a petty annoyance soon to burn away in the sun. When the Abbé Dupaty visited Nice in 1780, he noted that, although its winter was never harsh, he had actually encountered snow; his Niçois host, he wrote, apologized.

Nice's climate drew praise not only compared with England and the rest of Northern Europe—which, after all, offered little competition—but even to elsewhere in southern France and Italy. It wasn't that Nice and the Riviera were simply the South, therefore warmer, therefore pleasant; rather, Nice was seen as the best among appealing alternatives. Smollett himself said as much. He'd met some English who'd spent the winter in Aix, just ninety miles east, "on the supposition that there was little or no difference between that air and the climate of Nice; but this is a very great mistake." In 1789, Dr. Rigby traveled by carriage from Marseilles to Toulon, then over the Esterels; but it was only the shoreline road out of Antibes, just across the bay from Nice, that inspired this paroxysm: "Such beautiful water! Such a blue unclouded sky! Such a landscape of hills, woods, and rocks! And such a clear atmosphere!"

When, years later, a Nice newspaper solicited slogans for the city, one reader proposed "Nice, City Without Winter." It was to escape winter, of course, that well-off Northern Europeans came to Nice—hivernants, winter visitors, the French called them. They stayed from November to April. Then, with the first hot breath of summer, they headed home (the Mediterranean sun deemed too harsh for delicate English constitutions and pink English skin). For most of two hundred years, from Smollett's time to well into the twentieth century, "the Season" in Nice meant winter.

The hope that Nice's benign climate might restore health went back at least to Smollett, whose physical and mental afflictions had prompted his trip. Herr Sulzer likewise wanted to believe "that travel to southern Europe would contribute to my recovery"; Nice's climate, he'd been told, was "particularly suitable to my condition." Voltaire wrote of an actor friend who, coming down sick in Lyons, despaired of his life, went to Nice, and promptly recovered. Another visitor, the Abbé Dupaty, told of Englishwomen who arrived in Nice half dead yet soon "recovered their bloom." Both before the Revolution and all through the early nineteenth century, it was this habit of mind—good climate restores health—that made Nice a destination. Unlike eighteenth-century Grand Tourists apt to pass through Nice, stopping there but briefly, many now set their sights on it.

Sick people came to Nice, and many died there; the town had its first English cemetery in 1780. Many of the health benefits imputed to the climate were, of course, illusory. Smollett's year and a half in Nice did him little good in the end; soon after his return to England he was as sick as ever, and five years later he was dead, at the age of fifty. "The public promenade inspires a kind of sadness," a French visitor wrote in 1826, soon after construction of the Promenade des Anglais. "There you see young English women—charming, blond, pale, and near death." Indeed, Niçois physicians ministering to tubercular patients often sent them *away* from Nice.

In anything like the simpleminded, cause-and-effect way implied by testimonials to its healthful climate, then, Nice fell short. Today it's easy to snicker at our credulous forebears for their readiness to imagine serious medical problems melting away in the Mediterranean sun. Still, maybe they were on to something? If visiting a place like Nice did not necessarily restore health, maybe it could, at least, nurture happiness and well-being?

Sometimes after a gentle rain in Nice, wrote Dr. Davis in 1807,

the softness of the climate, the serenity of the sky, the brilliancy of the sun, and the numerous beauties of nature that on every side surround you, may be better conceived than described. The breathing is free, the body light, and the same harmony seems equally to prevail in the human frame as in the circumjacent scenery. The valetudinarian has a respite from his sufferings, and the voluptuous man finds new pleasures occupy his mind.

The Nice air, the good doctor was saying, served both health *and* pleasure. To put scientific niceties aside, Nice simply made you feel better. "Who can for a moment doubt," asked Davis,

> but that health is more likely to return when the path to the acquirement of it is strewn with flowers; when the painful burden that overwhelms the soul is alleviated by agreeable occupations, and when anxiety is exchanged for patience and resignation? [In my book], it has been my endeavor to combine remedy with amusement, in the full persuasion that a change of scene never fails of brightening the couch of sickness.

To combine remedy with amusement—health and pleasure somehow made one. Could easy days, spent in a beautiful place, help drive you back to life with new resolve?

It was 1831, and Berlioz was in Italy.

Hector Berlioz, the brilliant twenty-eight-year-old French composer, already acclaimed for his recently premiered *Symphonie fantastique,* had come to Rome as a winner of the prestigious Prix de Rome. Left behind in Paris was his precious Camille, a bewitching eighteen-year-old pianist he'd met the year before. She had "a figure slim and graceful," he'd written his sister, "with magnificent black hair and large blue eyes which shine like stars." She was, as well, a consummate musician, whom some compared to Liszt. Berlioz was smitten—and, he thought on leaving Paris, betrothed; had they not, after all, exchanged rings? Of course, he'd detected no great enthusiasm for the match on the part of Camille's mother. And in Rome, where he'd expected his beloved's letters waiting for him, they were not. For three weeks he waited, riven by fears. Finally, he decided to return to Paris.

He had gotten as far as Florence when, on April 14, a letter from

Paris finally caught up with him: Camille had married a Monsieur Pleyel, the wealthy forty-two-year-old head of a Paris firm of piano manufacturers.

Berlioz was enraged, inconsolable—and resolute: he would return to Paris, kill Camille, kill her mother, kill Pleyel, then turn the gun on himself. (What else to do for a man whose genius and gift for self-dramatization would make him one of the most romantic figures of his age?) He boarded a carriage for the French capital, intending to go via Turin, but got only so far as Genoa; there the Sardinian police decided he was a troublemaker—these were politically volatile times—and re-fused to let him continue to Turin. He was ordered instead to Nice.

On the way, Berlioz rehearsed in his mind "every point of the little *comedy* I intended to play in Paris"; that was the word he used later in his memoirs. He would go to Camille's house around nine one evening dis-guised as a countess's maid—he actually had the costume made up—and declare he had an urgent message in hand. Then, duly ushered in, and with his intended victims crowded round, he'd produce his pistols and start shooting.

But during the night, as his carriage proceeded toward Nice, less apocalyptic thoughts undermined his resolve. Murder? Suicide? Why, a great future awaited him! What of his unfinished symphonies? When the carriage stopped at a little cafe near Ventimiglia, he dashed off a note to the director of the academy in Rome, which he'd impetuously quit. Might he yet come back? Could his name be restored to the rolls? He would await the director's reply in Nice.

In early May 1831, the letter came, assuring Berlioz that, yes, he'd be welcomed back. Berlioz slid back to life. He'd rented a tiny room in a house virtually in the shadow of the Château Hill. "I drink deep draughts of the sunny, balmy air of Nice, and life and joy return to me," he recalled of his weeks there. He wandered through groves of or-ange trees. He bathed in the sea. He dozed on the heather on the hills between Nice and Villefranche. He looked out over the silent traffic of ships coming and going from around the world. Pencil and notebook in hand, he strolled silently beside the sea, composing, creating—indeed, sketching out the overture of his opera *King Lear*.

The young man's movements once more roused the suspicions of the police. "Musician," was he? What sort of musician spends his days lolling upon the Villefranche rocks and is never seen attending the theater? A spy more likely, waiting for a signal from some passing ship of revolutionaries, hmm? He was hauled in for questioning. Just what was Monsieur Berlioz up to?

"Recovering from a painful illness," he replied. "I compose, I dream, I thank God for the glorious sun, the blue sea, and the great green hills."

The police ordered him out of town.

Berlioz returned to Rome, on the way sketching out the scenario of a piece entitled *Le Retour à la vie,* return to life. "These were," he wrote later, "the three happiest weeks in my life. Oh, Nizza!"

∞

A footnote to the Berlioz story, slight yet telling: His trip from Genoa to Nice was uneventful. No mules. No treacherous mountain trails. Most of the way, he went by carriage. "The horses trotted on, bearing me nearer and nearer to France," he wrote. "It was night, and we were traveling along the Corniche road. . . ."

Corniche. The word simply means "cornice," or "ledge," in this case a ledge of rock carved into the side of the mountain. Along the Riviera today, the word refers to the three fine mountain roads—high, middle, and low *corniches*—that cut through the Maritime Alps from Nice east toward Genoa at varying heights above the sea, and which grant tourists astonishing Mediterranean vistas. Once, the word applied as well even to primitive hill-clinging mule paths so narrow a single person could scarcely pass. In the worst sections, wrote Madame de Genlis of a 1780 trip, they could not even trust the mules, and she and her party had to walk, arm in arm, holding on to one another for dear life; this, too, she termed a *corniche.*

Then Napoleon built the Grande Corniche. In his first Italian campaign, in 1796, his army had faced the same travel obstacles as had everyone else, and in 1803 his troops began building a road that would surmount them; at times, two thousand laborers worked on it. The *cor-*

niche reached San Remo in 1814. But Waterloo, and Nice's return to Sardinia, slowed progress. Crews were still working on a final link in 1826, when at least one traveler reported that twelve hours of the trip still had to be done by mule.

When the Countess of Blessington traveled it in 1823, she remarked that the *corniche* as far as Menton "bears the indelible mark of *him* who planned it; boldly designed, and solidly executed, with a disregard of difficulties." An American, Nathaniel Carter, leaving Nice in 1826 had looked with dread to the notoriously difficult hundred miles to Genoa. But thanks to Napoleon's road, "the craggy and precipitous acclivities of Montalbano," the first stretch, proved easy going. Carter marveled at the "long terraces, often hewn from the solid rock, and hanging upon the crags thousands of feet above the sea." Its vistas made the *corniche* a Riviera must-see; by 1848, Edwin Lee, author of *Continental Travel*, could refrain from describing them because, as he wrote, "the scenic beauties of this route have been dwelt upon by abler pens."

From the east, then, this first *corniche* made Nice less of an island. But from the north, from Turin, Nice had also become less of an island. The year 1792 marked completion of a project to replace the old *chemin muletier*, or mule path, by a *chemin carrossable*, or carriage road. The new road, cut from bare rock, followed the Paillon out of Nice, climbed up to L'Escarène, to Sospel, over the Col de Braus, up to Breil in the Roya Valley, and, finally, zigzagged over the mist-enshrouded, eight-thousand-foot-high Col de Tende into the broad plateau of the Italian Piedmont.

And from the west? In the early days of the Revolution, French republican troops had hastily constructed a wooden bridge over the Var. Fifteen feet wide, flanked by wooden railings, and resting on wood piers set into the riverbed, it was a long, low, rickety structure, not entirely confidence-inspiring; the swollen river sometimes washed away sections of its two-thousand-foot span. And yet, periodically renewed, it would endure for seventy-seven years, well into the railroad age.

For much of that time, two sentry boxes stood side by side in the middle, one painted blue, white, and red, the other red, white, and green; from midspan to their respective shores, French and Sardinian sentries would march back and forth. "Short, puny, pale-faced troops, in blue uniform and tight black cloth gaiters," one traveler described the Sardinians; but getting past them held him up only twenty minutes. After crossing the bridge in 1830, a twenty-three-year-old American student from Virginia, Louis Cazenove, spied the Sardinian king and queen; the king's nod to his doffed hat earned a place in Cazenove's journal. Later, at the customs house outside Nice, "a few francs slyly slipped into the hands of the officer insured our entrance into town free from molestation or vexatious examination." For Cazenove, reaching Nice meant a royal acknowledgment and a modest bribe; the Var passed unnoticed beneath him.

The Var had ceased to be an obstacle, then, just as seaside crags across the Maritime Alps had ceased to be an obstacle. Indeed, all over Europe getting around was easier. Roads were better; from Paris, Nice was now reckoned as just an eleven-day trip. And easier land travel weakened the sea alternative, reducing the role of the *felouques*.

It was turning out much as Tobias Smollett had predicted. "If," he'd written in 1765, "there was a bridge over the Var, and a post-road made from Nice to Genoa, I am very confident that all those strangers who now pass the Alps on their way to and from Italy, would choose this road as infinitely more safe, commodious, and agreeable."

Smollett was not the only seer. "A superb road might be made along the margin of the sea" from La Spezia to Nice. "All the little insulated villages . . . would communicate together, and in time form one continued village along that road." The year was 1787, and the writer was Thomas Jefferson. By 1830, much of his and Smollett's vision had been realized. Now it was almost easy to get to Nice. And it would get only easier.

"In port today is an American ship which travels without sail and by means of fire," a visitor to Nice recorded in April 1832. "It is called a steam ship. It goes in any wind and even against the wind, and at great speed." Soon Nice was fourteen hours from Marseilles or Genoa, versus two and a half days on the muscled backs of rowers. The disparity was not always so great; in favorable winds, a *felouque* under sail could do it in almost the same time. But steam—Fulton's first commercial steamboat by now went back twenty-five years, the original Watt steam engine more than fifty—offered predictability and security. Travelers liked that.

By 1840, steam was a fact of life on the Riviera. The *felouques* were mostly gone, the Var was bridged, the Grande Corniche was completed. Nice was no longer an island. In 1820, one scholar has estimated, Nice had a thousand *hivernants*. By 1860, that figure had doubled, doubled once more, and doubled yet again. Waterloo opened up the Continent to travel. But it took prodigious feats of engineering, and the back-breaking toil of thousands, to open up Nice.

By the time William Farr's *A Medical Guide to Nice* was published in 1841, fewer among Nice's visitors were coming for their health. "Nice once had a reputation for the cure of consumption," wrote Farr, but "this reputation . . . was not founded in fact." Each year Nice drew fewer consumptive invalids, yet more visitors overall; they were not coming only to convalesce. "Persons coming from abroad have commonly two motives, an avowed and a concealed one," wrote Farr; "the avowed motive is health—the concealed one, pleasure."

6 SAUCY LITTLE THING

AT NINE O'CLOCK ONE APRIL MORNING IN 1830, AFTER A STARLIT
trip along the *corniche* from Menton and her arrival at the Hôtel des
Étrangers in Nice, a married Englishwoman rose from bed to begin her
day. She had a light breakfast, wrote letters, paid social calls, and then,
along with a friend, set out to explore the town. "We found," she wrote
in her journal, "that there was really nothing to see in Nice."

It was a pretty town ("or rather a village," she corrected herself), at
least in the wide-streeted part near the hotel. She ventured into shops
that sold boxes crafted of olive wood. She marveled at the wide straw
hats of the local women, which looked to her like inverted scallop
shells. She strolled around town till about five, then returned to the hotel for dinner; the meal itself was fine, but she had to endure an Englishman whose French was both execrable and loud. After dinner, she
spent several hours with some of the same friends she'd seen that morning. Then she returned to her room and went to bed.

And that was about it for her day in Nice on April 13, 1830. Next
day, she and friends visited a convent, then went by horseback to see a
waterfall. Two days later, she and her party were crossing the Var into
France.

Especially in the early years of the Sardinian restoration, Nice was
still a down-at-the-heels sort of place whose want of physical amenities
and cultural attractions belied its growing popularity. In 1816, French
archeologist Aubin-Louis Millin lamented that Nice's bookstores sold
only prayer books and schoolbooks, that there were few private li-

braries, that in the whole town not a painting or statue was worth mention. As for music, you'd scarcely believe you were in Italy. In 1823, the Countess of Blessington described Nice as "more deficient, in not only the elegancies but the comforts of life, than a place could be imagined to be where so great an influx of wealth is poured in from England."

Nice was still in its touristic adolescence, which it would not outgrow until much later in the century. In 1901, with Nice the preferred destination of the crowned heads of Europe, a London magazine would look back wistfully to how Tobias Smollett forsook Montpellier for "quiet" and "inexpensive" Nice. Yet, right up to the 1850s, both words applied.

"The rents of houses and apartments," wrote William Farr in 1841, "are lower at Nice than at any other place of general resort on the continent." You could get the first floor of a fine south-facing house for 850 francs a year. You could hire a cook for thirty francs a month, rent a horse for a morning's ride into the country for five, get your laundry done for half what it cost in England. Much like Third World destinations today only just beginning to catch on with tourists, the future queen city of the Riviera was still seen as exotic, unspoiled, and cheap.

Cheap, of course, because it was desperately poor.

When he visited back in 1775, Johann Georg Sulzer saw little of Nice's old town—he spent most of his time in the country—but what he saw of it was bad enough. Step into one of its tall, dark buildings and you faced dirt, stink, decay. "No one," he wrote, "thinks even to wash the windows," which in some homes were opaque with dust and insect remains.

Most of Nice's clergy, Sulzer reported, were poor; even the bishop customarily went about on foot, dressed in the habit of a common friar. The nobility mostly lived in poverty, "often in indigence and misery." Gentlemen who would never think to be seen in public without the épées that marked their class were often so poor, their swords so rusted and worn, that they were loath to draw them from their scabbards.

And these were Nice's upper crust.

Two decades later, charged with reporting back to the National Convention on what he'd seen of the territory just absorbed by revolutionary France, the Abbé Grégoire sketched a bleaker picture yet. "The traveler in pursuit of pleasure praises the beautiful sky and charming countryside of Nice and Menton"—but head into the backcountry and you'd see the underlying economic rot, the "hovel hidden behind a superb façade." There were a few economic bright spots, like olive oil, oranges, lemons, and silk. But, generally, the new Alpes-Maritimes department could scarcely feed itself. The land, so appealing to the eye, couldn't fill the belly. The terrain was rocky and mountainous, with few meadows for grazing; the want of grazing animals meant you had to import beef, husband scarce fertilizer. Wine production was enough to quench maybe a month's thirst out of a year's. And industry? Manufacturing? Commerce? In the new *département*, he despaired, these were largely nonexistent. Perfume. A few soapmakers and tanneries. That was about it. The region was hopelessly in debt. Beggars swarmed the countryside; Nice's mayor had practically to bat them out of town with a stick.

Nice and its environs were poor during Smollett's time, and Sulzer's, and Grégoire's; in the decades after Waterloo, they were poor still. When the Kingdom of Sardinia got Nice back in 1815, it also annexed the Republic of Genoa, whose great port it then granted economic privileges Nice alone had enjoyed since 1612. In 1853, the king withdrew them entirely from Nice, and the town suffered one more blow.

❧

From all this misery and want the British *hivernants* were comfortably remote. When Richard Blair, a forty-seven-year-old Englishman just back from a long stay in Nova Scotia, visited a relative in Nice for a few months in 1829, he found the old town "narrow, dirty, and stinking," whereas "the part where the English are is open and clean." Dividing the two was the Paillon River, which, until it was channeled into aqueducts, paved over, and erased from awareness toward the end of the nineteenth century, marked off old Nice from new, host from guest, poor from rich, servant from master.

For centuries, visitors unmindful of the Paillon's vagaries would smirk at what was normally just a dried-up riverbed—dusty, rocky, overgrown with vegetation, with a few sad rivulets running down its length. Women washed clothes in what water there was, then laid them out to dry on the rocks. The locals scooted across crudely laid planks to avoid a detour to the stone bridge. "No one," Irish physician Percy Fitzpatrick wrote reasonably enough in 1858, "could imagine that this broad line of dry stones and gravel could ever be metamorphosed into a mighty torrent . . . carrying all before it like a Balaclava cavalry charge."

But that's just what sometimes happened. Eighteenth-century maps called the Paillon not *fleuve* or *rivière*, the more familiar terms, but *torrent*—a river with origins high in the mountains that floods with the melting of the snow. Fed by mountain streams, the Paillon, nearly as wide as the Seine at Paris, would roar down from the Alps, uprooting trees, sweeping away homes, hurling into the sea a roiling brown muddiness of debris. A 1744 flood drowned hundreds of French and Spanish soldiers as they tried to cross during a battle with the Sardinians. In times past, the story goes, a man stationed upstream would, at the first sign of a flood washing down toward town, blare out the warning with a trumpet call.

It was the potential for these sudden floods, together with the breadth of its rocky bed, that helped make the Paillon, otherwise so pathetic, an important dividing line. On its left bank stood a shabby Italian town; on its right, a little bit of England—the Croix-de-Marbre district, its prerevolutionary luster restored, flourishing once more with the peace that followed Waterloo.

There, along the road set back from the sea that bore carriages from the French frontier, stood the great villas, their lush gardens leading down to the shores of the sea; "long ranges of neat white houses, with Venetian blinds and uniformly surrounded by gardens, line the sides of the street," the American Nathaniel Carter noted in 1826. The English had their own cemetery and, after 1821, their own Anglican church; the King of Roman Catholic Sardinia sanctioned its construction as long as it did not actually look like a church. In a book appearing in 1841, a few years before he finished *The Three Musketeers*, Alexandre Dumas dis-

tinguished "*l'antica Nizza*," the old Italian Nice, from "*Nice new*" (he used the English word), with its "perfectly straight streets, whitewashed houses, its doors and windows lined up neatly, its residents—under umbrellas, in veils, and in green laced boots—who say, *Yes*."

Others besides the British came to Nice during the decades before 1860. A few Americans, as we've seen, were showing up. And toward 1850, numerous French, especially from Provence, Languedoc, and, of course, Paris. And some Russians and Germans. But to the Niçois, *any* foreigner was English.

Once, while he was staying at Nice's Hôtel d'York, wrote Dumas, a carriage pulled up bearing guests.

"Who are your newcomers?" he inquired.

"They are English, certainly," replied the innkeeper in Italian, "but I cannot say whether they are French or German."

The English kept largely to themselves in the Croix-de-Marbre, which some of them insisted on calling Newborough. One early guide-book pictures them as having their own doctors and pharmacists, specialty-food stores, jewelers, dressmakers, perfumers, and teachers of French, Italian, music, painting, fencing, and dance. The English lived under the same big beautiful sky as the Niçois, but scarcely touched them.

Of course, this was an old story with the English, in Nice as elsewhere; the British consul told him once, wrote Tobias Smollett, that "he had lived four and thirty years in the country without having once eaten or drunk in any of their houses," meaning those of the Niçois. Seventy years later, little had changed. One Italian observed of the British in 1834 that they lived in the Croix-de-Marbre "just as if they were in Brighton," the English seaside resort south of London made fashionable by King George IV. "During the day, they go out for walks, and horseback and carriage rides. In the evenings, they see one another, read Galignani, speak of politics, take tea or canapés, always in their own way, and nearly always without mixing with foreigners."

As for the Niçois, writes historian Robert Latouche, "they accepted with indifference the homage of foreign visitors, seeking neither to seduce nor hold them"; to pamper or entertain their guests seems scarcely to have occurred to them. It was the sun and the air, the blooming countryside, the amiable intercourse among themselves, and the opportunity to do nothing at all that charmed visitors. The town itself, by contrast, offered little.

It was that early visitor Johann Georg Sulzer who best took the pulse of the place. Don't look for fine goods in Nice, he wrote; the local artisans were so inept that if you wanted even ordinary hats and shoes you'd best order them from Genoa, or perhaps France or England. Don't look, either, for stimulating conversation: "The least little story or uninspiring morsel of gossip passed around at a ball becomes in the next few days the sole subject of conversation." Nice was a provincial backwater, redeemed only by its natural surroundings. The town's prettier precincts boasted walled gardens, crisscrossed with little paths, that had "no other beauty" than their lemon trees and vegetable patches. These were not sculpted, sophisticated affairs worthy of an English squire's country house, or the gentrified gardens of Versailles. They were artless, unspoiled.

Some visitors, no doubt, sorely felt Nice's lacks; but its simplicity, its freedom from cosmopolitan swagger, appealed to many. Consider, for example, Alexander Herzen, the aristocratic Russian intellectual and political thinker who, on first seeing Nice in 1847 with his family, found it barren. "I could find there neither the *Journal des débats*, forbidden by the Jesuits, nor a single Tuscan paper, forbidden by the king. After [the cultural riches of] Paris, I was as surprised by this in Nice as by its river without water," by which surely he meant the Paillon.

Yet Herzen returned to Nice a few years later, following the calamitous, mostly fruitless revolutions that had shaken Europe in 1848. Herzen had lost faith in ideas he'd once cherished, felt defeated and exhausted. "At last," he wrote in June 1850, "I am in Nice once again—in warm, sweet-scented Nice, quiet and now completely empty." He was mindful of the changes three years had wrought on him. Before, he'd sought bustle and activity. But now, in Nice, he asked only "to rest in its serene emptiness." Actually, he didn't rest long; drawing to his side Russian, Italian, and French exiles, he was soon writing as much as ever. But just then, at that crucial moment in his life, Nice had granted relief; indeed, he'd selected it "not only for its gentle air and its sea, but also because it has no significance—neither political nor scholarly nor even artistic."

George Bemis's stay in Nice during the first winter of America's Civil War was less eventful even than Herzen's. It was the time of the Trent Affair, an international incident provoked by American seizure of two Confederate agents on a British ship, the *Trent*. And what did Bemis do in Nice? He talked, and walked, and, the truth is, didn't do much of anything—which, to men and women ground down by illness, fatigue, and worry, can seem the most precious luxury of all. A distinguished Boston lawyer who'd helped prosecute a Harvard chemistry professor for murder ten years before, Bemis suffered from a hacking tubercular cough, and had been ordered to Nice by his doctor.

Soon he was savoring the happy, impossible facts of Nice's climate in his journal. "I have now been here ten days and I have never once had on my thick coat," he wrote a few days before Christmas. On one walk, he got so overheated he had to remove his hat, wipe away perspiration. Another time, still in December, late at night, he wrote "with two windows wide open."

During his stay at the Hôtel de l'Univers, Bemis met with Boston friends. He became the much-sought-after dinner companion of a certain Mrs. Wurts, from whom he gleaned details of an engagement gone sour and "the whys and wherefores of its dissolution." With his new friends, Dr. Sargent and his wife, he went on long walks. "Last evening, the two joined me on the Promenade des Anglais at sunset."

Bewitched by the sun, his cough better, Bemis put off his departure, ultimately staying in Nice four weeks longer than planned. Each day, he'd study French for an hour in bed. Then he'd breakfast, maybe read the *Messager de Nice*, and amble over to the hotel reading room, where he'd tear through the English and French papers. After that, a walk, another hour's reading, a predinner stroll . . .

On the whole, he conceded, his six-week stay was "rather unenterprising and unimproving." Yet by this he seemed not in the least troubled. Always he'd remember Sargent, and their "hilarious evenings, laughing over stories that we told each other." And their walks in town, and out in the country—to Villefranche, to the top of Mont Vinaigrier, to Beaulieu with its thick-trunked olive trees—stopping to rest whenever they wished. A glass of good wine. An hour of good talk.

For visitors like Herzen or Bemis, there might not be much to Nice, but what little there was resided in its climate, its beauty, its native peasantry not yet grown too knowing or too sophisticated. As it became more popular through the first half of the nineteenth century, Nice changed. But slowly. Not enough, even by 1858, to leave Percy Fitzpatrick, for example, with a much different sense of the place from Smollett's in 1764, Sulzer's in 1775, or Davis's in 1802: "In describing Nice as a town," he wrote, "there is not much to be said. It has neither pictures, nor statues, like Florence, nor palaces, like Genoa, nor ruins like Rome. It can be celebrated for its natural beauties alone."

Later in the century, the philosopher Friedrich Nietzsche would write his sister from Nice that he'd never seen a winter so perfect. "The days succeed one another here," he declared, "with a beauty that I would describe as brazen." Nice was like a beautiful fourteen-year-old girl, a saucy little thing who, without sophistication, education, or fancy clothes, gets by on the strength of fresh looks and charm alone. Nice before the railroad didn't need finery and fashion; it had nature on its side.

But nature would not always be enough.

BACK DURING THE WINTER OF 1821, THE ALREADY DESPERATE circumstances of the local peasantry worsened. A freeze killed the oranges. People went hungry. Begging grew rampant. The local English prelate, a persuasive and persistent gentleman known as the Reverend Lewis Way, resolved to help. He collected money from the wealthy British colony and hired local people to lay out a walkway beside the seashore. Everyone benefited. Hundreds of hungry Niçois got work and wages. The *hivernants* got a pleasant seaside thoroughfare that extended from the mouth of the Paillon westward along the shore.

The authorities gave it the Italian name Strada del Littorale, but the Niçois never called it that. They called it the Camin dei Anges; it looked out on the Baie des Anges, the Bay of Angels. Or else the Camin dei Angles, the English road. In 1844, it was extended west and took its current name, the Promenade des Anglais. Later it was widened and prettied up, provision made for carriages, and a walkway of white and gray stone fashioned into a mosaic of squares and diamonds. In 1854, it was extended another half a mile west.

By 1858, Percy Fitzpatrick could say of the Promenade des Anglais that it was "not surpassed by any other in Europe." Flanked by fine villas with gardens, it was already frequented by dukes, princes, the Dey of Algiers, the composer Meyerbeer. At one end stood the public garden, where the French and Prussian consulates stood; from there, along the Paillon's right bank to the Pont-Neuf, were arrayed lodging houses and hotels.

Soon the Promenade wasn't just another pretty place to walk but, in the proverbial formula, the place to see and be seen. Visitors during these years didn't lie out on the rocky beach, soak up rays, and cavort in the surf. They extracted pleasure from the sheer social spectacle of it. The Promenade in late afternoon and evening was crowded with carriages and walkers, men and women at their ease. Little knots of finely dressed people, some stopping to look out to sea, others clustered together in conversation. Men with walking sticks. Women under parasols, saving their creamy complexions from the sun. La Voie Royale of Nice, somebody called it, the Royal Way. It reminded somebody else of Longchamps in the avenue de Neuilly in Paris.

Word of Nice's charms spread through the capitals of Europe. More hotels sprang up. Villas climbed the *collines.* Nice was growing more sophisticated and fashionable—less saucy little thing, more debutante in diamond necklace. With the flowering of the great Promenade, Nice lost some of its sweet simplicity.

And the Niçois, for their part, lost some of theirs.

❧

"Quiet people content with little, and consequently devoid of enterprise." That's how Fitzpatrick depicted the "Nizzards"—which explained, it seemed to him, why much of the town's business was run by foreigners. "I often ask myself," noted another observer, "what would become of Nice in the hands of a more energetic population"; he had in mind the Germans, English, Belgians, or northern French. Although the Niçois in many respects made for an admirable specimen, an early guidebook noted, "his fickle temperament ill-suits him to keep on task for long."

Of course, the Niçois had all along rented the English their villas, served them their meals, chauffeured them around town. But to many of their guests they were also, like the sea and the cloudless sky, part of the landscape, a source of curiosity and amusement. In their costumes, their artless simplicity, their earthy, warm-blooded mix of French and Italian, they were "local color," their chief virtue being to entertain and divert.

"We have the drollest *fille de chambre* that you can imagine," Margaret Maria Brewster, daughter of a Scottish scientist, wrote of her servant at the Cimiez villa where she stayed during the winter of 1857—"good, merry, laughing, stumpy Marie, with a fine *old* brown face, though she is almost young, and a pair of glorious southern eyes." Marie spoke no Italian, only a smattering of English. She'd start out in French, slip into a mongrel of French and the local dialect, and then wind up "in *patois* pure and undefiled"; at one point, Brewster became certain that Marie's husband had two wives—a linguistic imbroglio soon cleared up.

"Perfect strangers to vices engendered by luxury, and to the violent passions which agitate the great," was how John Bunnell Davis described the Niçois following his stay in 1802. They clung to the dress and manners of their forefathers. Fashion exercised no sway over them—or wasn't supposed to: When Miss Brewster asked to sketch her, Marie showed up the next day with her best, her "smartest," clothes. These, however, displeased her employer, who deemed them too modern. So she dressed up Marie in an old black velvet jacket, pink apron, and coarse blue petticoat that she decided were more authentic.

To some visitors, the locals could seem the next-best thing to noble savages, guileless and simple yet possessing preternatural abilities. Davis reported that the backcountry people had no clocks, no sundials, no barometers. Yet, with only the crowing of the cock to go by, and the position of the sun and stars, they could tell the time as accurately as a clock. They could predict the weather as well as any meteorologist—by the hue of the clouds and the chirping of birds, and by "a kind of confused foresight that resembles . . . that instinctive presage of approaching changes of weather which we observe in animals."

Davis wrote of Nice's version of Carnaval, the Lenten festival celebrated in many Roman Catholic countries; the gaiety of the peasants at wakes; their music, dance, and song; their masquerades; their burlesquing buffoons and gaping spectators. "How frequently . . . have I seen with secret pleasure and delight the rural amusements of the peasants," he confided, how captivated he'd been by "scenes of mirth and innocence."

Maybe they weren't Bushmen or Hottentots, but to many visitors the Niçois seemed quite exotic enough. An American visiting Nice in 1837, a Mrs. Evan Philip Thomas from Baltimore, wrote how goats were driven in herds of two dozen at a time to the houses of customers, then milked on the spot. Women toiled in the fields, while men cleaned and made the beds back at the hotel—"a very disagreeable state of things," to her way of thinking. During Carnaval, Mrs. Thomas waded out into the crowd, apparently enjoying the music and the masks, the sight of grotesquely dressed locals doing quadrilles, peasants and fashionable ladies bombarding one another with candies.

Another American, Benjamin Silliman, recorded in an 1851 journal written for his children how the narrow lanes of Nice's old town swarmed with picturesquely costumed natives, how children were stowed among baggage in the panniers of heavily laden donkeys. Twenty miles up the *corniche* from Nice, in Menton, he saw women launder clothes in small streams that washed across the road, then spread them out to dry, stones weighting them down so they wouldn't fly away. Children followed Silliman's carriage for miles to collect horses' excrement, which they loaded into baskets they carried atop their heads.

Riviera commerce was borne on the heads of women and girls, from beds and cradles to washtubs and copper vessels full of water. "They appear unconcerned, holding their arms pendant or akimbo, and looking carelessly around," wrote Silliman. "But we have never seen them drop anything, or observed the head to vibrate, or the foot to stumble."

Just as Haiti and Bhutan today inspire fashion trends in Paris or New York, so did the ways of the Riviera among visitors to it. Local women wore a traditional hat consisting of a shallow cone of straw secured by a broad velvet band threaded through it and slung winsomely around the chin. It had been "adopted by some of our most fashionable ladies," noted Percy Fitzpatrick in 1858. The *cappellino*, he declared, was "the prettiest covering that ever was invented for a pretty face."

But not every visitor saw the Niçois as good only for their rustic ways and oddities of dress. For example, Johann Georg Sulzer was struck by Nice's garden terraces, chiseled into the hills one atop another, buttressed by stone walls, and maintained only by prodigious effort: "Suppress from your mind's eye these terraces, so that the mountains are reduced to their original form, with their arid and un-productive soil, and you could scarcely predict that one day they would house and nourish so many people." How *did* the Niçois manage? Even their wood was scarce; they built from stone, didn't heat their homes, and restricted bread-baking to public ovens, all to husband this scarce resource. Sulzer was likewise impressed by how the Niçois conserved water. And with how, faced with the lack of grazing land—hence of grazing animals, hence of fertilizer—they'd devised an elaborate system for collecting what manure there was, including human waste.

Simple peasants? Well, men and women so industrious and re-sourceful just might be able to deduce that their wealthy guests were a resource, too. Indeed, as the flow of visitors to Nice grew, not all the locals, as one twentieth-century French historian wryly pictured visi-tors' attitudes toward them, sat around playing darts.

In April 1826, a few years after the Promenade des Anglais made its debut as a modest path beside the sea, a Nice *abbé* noted that foreigners had occupied 116 houses that past winter. They'd spent six hundred thousand lires, or 5,172 per household. From that figure he deducted the amount of a typical house rental, divided the remainder by the length of an average stay, and came up with twenty-six lires per day; this, he figures, was how much the average visitor spent on "items of fashion," on music and language teachers, and in otherwise sustaining the local economy. It was a calculation of which any modern tourist-board offi-cial might be proud.

The flow of visitors to Nice had become regular enough, their numbers and the amount they spent important enough, that they were being *tracked*, their ups and downs duly noted. The year 1825 was a bad one, seventeen houses in the Croix-de-Marbre being vacant. The year 1827 was a good one; receipts were double those of the year before—or, as the *abbé* noted, using a yardstick familiar to any Niçois, the equivalent of a good year of olive-oil sales.

There was money to be made, and some Niçois were learning how to make it. Certainly the peasants around Cimiez were; they sold off so many antiquities to tourists, a tour guide lamented in 1861, that the most precious of these were already lost. By the 1850s, Nice guidebooks once given over to history and climate now fixed on Nice's flowering *industrie d'accueil*—its welcome industry of hotels, furnished rooms, cafés, and restaurants, and the instructors, physicians, shopowners, and others who served foreign guests.

Sink money into a house, spruce it up, then rent it to foreigners; that still counted as "an unusual type of industry," according to an 1844 Nice guidebook, as if describing a new phenomenon. Seven years later, a visitor wrote how, come winter, "the Niçois retreats with his family to the darkest corner of his house and rents out all the apartments to foreigners." Always it was the locals who surrendered their comfort, the foreigners—notably the English—who got the kid-glove treatment. "If, as I got off the diligence at the Hôtel des Étrangers, I had been able to ask for a room in perfect English," he went on, "I would not be lodged right now in the dark, cramped attic room from which I write."

Of course, English milords had stirred resentment in Nice for as long as they'd been coming there. One early visitor seeking peaceful retirement in Nice, a Provençal, finally gave up and left for Genoa rather than suffer the English any longer, with "their pride, their arrogance, their haughtiness, their presumption." Most of a century later, many Niçois felt similarly. "Their bearing toward the strangers," Fitzpatrick wrote in 1858, "is polite but cold."

But host and guest were by now bound in a marriage of convenience. The Niçois had to learn to rein in their avarice, keep their opinions to themselves, please and pamper their worthy guests. And by and large they did. When, in leaving Nice in 1851, Benjamin Silliman boarded a carriage to take him over the *corniche* to Genoa, he and his party all got a cheerful *bon voyage* from the hotel staff gathered at the door to see them off. "Their deportment was more like that of friends taking leave," Silliman wrote, "than that of mercenary people who, having received our money, were willing to see us depart."

At least one Nice *hôtelier*, it seems, had raised deference to a high art.

Back then the hotel, and all it implies today of comfort, service, and luxury, was still almost a new idea. Records from the fifteenth century do cite hotels in Nice, including the Épée and the Angel. And a certain Auberge de la Lune was of sufficiently high repute that a Neapolitan duke stayed there in 1676. But most visitors to Nice, like most visitors everywhere, counted on the hospitality of local residents. Even by the early nineteenth century, hotels as we know them were scarce. The conditions at inns and *auberges* were often primitive at best. Typical was the nameless inn on the Nice-Turin road that Mariana Starke described as "a crazy hovel, containing scarcely one whole window, and no sitting room, except that which serves in common for postillions, porters, gentlemen, poultry, and hogs." In town, the situation was little better; Smollett could declare that, "in the town of Nice, you will find no ready-furnished lodgings for a whole family."

By 1830, however, Nice had perhaps a dozen hotels, and twice that many *auberges*. By the late 1850s, a little after Benjamin Silliman got his cheerful *bon voyage* from the hotel staff, it had many more—fifty, by one count. Names evoking England figured large among them, including the Victoria, the Hôtel de la Pension Anglaise, and the Hôtel de Londres. One of the largest of the new hotels was the six-hundred-room Chauvain, which stood on Quai Saint-Jean-Baptiste, on the right bank of the Paillon, set back from the river by a retaining wall and a row of trees.

Among its British guests in February 1857 was Margaret Maria Brewster. Ill at the time, she'd been stuck for a few days in a bleak, north-facing room, nothing else being available. But, finally, she'd landed one much better, a room with a southern exposure on a mezzanine so close to the busy quai below she could practically reach out to pedestrians and touch them. From her high, sun-flooded window she'd look out and see priests scurrying by in their three-cornered hats; "motley groups of passers-by" on the Pont-Neuf. One time she was treated to a concert by three Italian singers—a man with castanets, his pale wife in black dress and gold earrings, and a woman who played guitar. "How beautifully their voices harmonize in that wild half-plaintive, half-cheerful melody," she wrote in her journal. They sang for Nice's visitors—but few, by Brewster's account, stopped to listen.

Her room was still far from the hotel's best, but if she squeezed herself over to one corner of it, she could glimpse the sea, "sparkling and quivering to the rays of that golden, wonderful sun." She could look out, too, on the mostly dry bed of the Paillon, where washerwomen, hundreds of them, knelt wherever they could find a little pond or rivulet, "washing and wringing, scrubbing and spreading," laying clothes out to dry along the shore. The Niçoises wore bright skirts, with red or yellow kerchiefs; they weren't scrubbing their *own* clothes, it struck Brewster, but much drabber *English* garments, those of their guests and patrons.

❧

When Nathaniel Carter passed through Fréjus on his way to Nice in March 1826, he stayed at the hotel where Napoleon was supposed to have slept on the eve of his first exile a decade earlier; or so his attentive landlord informed him. The place was falling apart, its floorboards so swaybacked they reminded him of the aftermath of an earthquake, its walls hung with tattered silken tapestry. But the bed! Why, it was *the very one*, he was assured, in which Napoleon had slept; to judge by their condition, its pillows and bedclothes had gone unchanged since the emperor's visit. As Carter lay upon that pillow, in that canopied bed, in the darkness of the night, his imagination ran riot with "the pageantry of other times; and the spectres of war and conquest, fields of carnage and conflagrated cities."

Cimiez, on the hill above Nice, inspired kindred musings; its Roman ruins, one visitor wrote, "must necessarily awaken melancholy reflections on the fragility of human labors." Here was Nice's own Coliseum, with its ghosts of gladiators, now "heaps of ruin where once majestically arose the noblest ornaments of human industry. . . ."

Cimiez, Croix-de-Marbre . . . or wherever Napoleon stayed for the night: such places became hallowed, and lucrative, ground. In a scenario played out again and again on the Riviera, as elsewhere, events lend luster to a site. People come to look, muse, reflect. Innkeepers and tour guides spring up to serve them. So, finally, do restaurants, museums, souvenir stands, and gift shops.

In Nice itself, the locals would be justly able to say, *Napoleon slept here;* for several months in 1794, the future emperor stayed in a house on the road to Villefranche; in fact, he fell in love with his landlord's daughter. The address today is No. 6 rue Bonaparte; a plaque marks the spot.

∞

Capturing the francs and pounds of *hivernants* by offering them the emperor's bed for the night, building them villas, putting them up in hotels, washing their clothes, and otherwise catering to their needs was, during these years, largely the work of private initiative. So was the Librairie Visconti, a lending library and cultural center in Nice's old town catering mostly to foreigners, established in 1839. So was the Théâtre Français, a right-bank alternative to the Italian theater on the other side of the Paillon. So, for that matter, was the Promenade des Anglais itself. So were the growing number of restaurants and cafés.

But Nice's Sardinian rulers and its own officials began paying heed to the winter visitors, too. A new Consiglio d'Ornato, a kind of Make Nice Beautiful architectural-review board, proved duly solicitous of visitors' needs. The Consiglio drew up a master plan for the Paillon's tourist-frequented right bank; laid out a gridwork of streets and boulevards where once there'd been orange groves; regulated the size and appearance of new buildings; developed a large central square, Place Masséna, on the other side of the Pont-Neuf from the old city, which would become the city's fashionable new hub. Near the mouth of the Paillon, a public garden, intended expressly for foreign visitors and their children, was created from a jungle of unruly vegetation. "Every effort Nice makes to clean itself up and become more attractive," wrote Auguste Burnel, author of an 1856 study, would draw more of "the elite population that each year brings it the wealth it so needs."

Nice was altering its face to suit its foreign guests. In those days, the Paillon River separated the Promenade des Anglais on the town's right bank from the Quai du Midi on its left. But after a bridge was built across it, the city fathers began to think in more grandiose terms—of an unbroken seaside promenade from Nice to Villefranche, maybe even around Cap Ferrat all the way to Beaulieu. "Astute Niçois, looking beyond the horizons of their city," writes one historian, "were envisioning the climatic exploitation of the whole Riviera."

∞

Meanwhile, a new fraternity of literary publicists and propagandists were picking up where Smollett had left off a century before. One was Alphonse Karr, journalist, satirist, and founder of a journal named *Les Guêpes*, the wasps, for the sting of its prose; to Karr is owed the epigram, *"Plus ça change, plus c'est la même chose."*

After the 1851 coup that made Louis-Napoleon emperor, the forty-four-year-old Karr, in trouble for his republican ideas, sold his house and fled to Genoa, where he asked leave to travel to Venice and Rome. The Austrians, who occupied much of northern Italy, turned him down flat; who needed this troublemaker? Meanwhile, satirical articles Karr had sent off to Paris led to his being charged with an outrage against public morals. He was acquitted, but came away bitter and hurt.

It was at just this susceptible moment that he remembered a conversation he'd had with a Russian princess in Paris. "If one day your cares assail you," she'd advised him, "leave for a place that is nothing less than heaven on earth . . . the magnificent city all Europe calls *Nizza la Bella.*"

Karr wrote to a friend, Léon Pillet, the former French consul in Nice, who only confirmed the princess's high opinion of the town. "If you don't find all you want there," Pillet replied, "the beauty you do find will temper your regret for whatever you miss." Nice's climate, of course, figured large in his tribute. Why, once he'd given a picnic for visiting royalty where the women didn't bother with hats! In February! Out in the sun, on the grass, in the middle of winter!

Did Karr wish to mix in society? Well, from November to March, Nice was filled with French, English, and Russians bent on having a good time and spending money. If he wanted none of that, he could head off for the countryside; no one would care. Books, newspapers, French intellectual life? These poured into town with each new surge of visitors. "You have in Nice," wrote Pillet, "the rare advantage of being able to live precisely as you wish."

Here, thought Karr, was precisely the haven he needed. He gathered up what money he had, bought a carriage and horses, made for Nice, and installed himself in a two-story house on a *colline* just outside town encompassed by gardens and lush vegetation. It wasn't long before he'd taken up a new calling, that of gardener, and had made a name for himself for the cut flowers he dispatched all over Europe, and for a clientele that ran to princes and kings.

But the *écrivain-jardinier*, as he became known, didn't entirely forsake writing. His book *Promenades Outside My Garden*, appearing in 1856, introduced its readers to the Nice countryside; to the flower market, with its jasmine, roses, jonquils, and violets; to the market's dark-haired girls, baskets atop their pretty heads filled with fruit and flowers. Nice, to Karr, was a "blessed country where, under the ardent embrace of the sun, the earth begets generations of flowers without end." Such language only tightened Nice's hold on the imagination of Europe.

So did that of Théodore de Banville, a poet and dramatist in his thirties, who arrived in Nice a few years later. With his actress companion, he moved into a cozy *bastide*, or country house, flanked by two stone Madonnas, and fell under Nice's spell; *La Mer de Nice*, published in 1861 and cast in the form of letters to a friend, was his declaration of love. In Nice, he wrote, town and country had made a secret pact. "Gardens full of palm and orange trees, all scents and smells, drowning in flowers, unfold in all their glory in the midst of residential neighborhoods. . . ."

Neither Banville nor Karr was a literary figure of the first rank; neither is much read today. To us, their lyricism may seem gaudy and overblown. But during that era of romanticism triumphant, both men were major literary figures. Both dressed Nice in a silken web of heightened feeling, made it a destination all the more exotic and irresistible.

∞

One day in March 1857, a Scotswoman staying at a villa near Cimiez took a day trip with friends to Villefranche, which had the best natural harbor east of Toulon. A century later, American Sixth Fleet ships would call there, but just now it was empty, save for a few sailboats and, as this visitor noted, "the Russian vessels which brought the Empress." The empress was Alexandra Fyodorovna, widow of the Emperor Nicholas I, dowager empress of Russia, and sister of the King of Prussia.

The 1856 peace treaty sealing its defeat in the Crimean War forbade tsarist Russia to reconstitute its Black Sea fleet. But why not a naval base, or at least a coaling station, in the Mediterranean? Soon Russia was making overtures to its former enemies, France and Sardinia. A little later, in October 1856, the dowager empress arrived for a Riviera holiday shot through with political significance. From Villefranche, she was driven in an open carriage to a villa just outside Nice; her retinue of more than a hundred people got a hotel to themselves.

Nothing was too good for the empress. They lit up the town for her. A succession of villas was placed at her disposal. Midway through her stay, Victor Emmanuel, King of Sardinia, came to pay his respects. The next few days were crowded with Sardo-Russian dinners, balls, receptions, concerts, and expressions of undying good will between the two countries. A Russian naval squadron soon lay at anchor in the Villefranche harbor, and for months the streets of Nice were crowded with Russian uniforms. The British were not amused. Some London newspapers urged tourists to spurn Sardinian Nice for Cannes or other French resorts, but no one much listened.

When Alexandra finally left Nice in April 1857, her health was said to be much improved; by one account, she could now "get down from her carriage and climb back up without the least assistance." Her visit did not inaugurate a Russian presence in Nice; her compatriots had been coming in modest numbers for years. But it forever etched Nice into the mind of Russia, and Russia into the civic mind of Nice. In coming years, the Riviera would see Russian-language newspapers, a Russian church on Nice's rue Longchamps, and a flow of Russian luminaries that ranged from the playwright Chekhov to the revolutionary Lenin.

Alexandra herself was back in Nice two years later. But this time she returned prematurely to Russia, and died in November, at the age of sixty-two, in St. Petersburg. A Nice newspaper devoted precisely three lines to her death. "Perhaps," one historian wondered with the benefit of more than a century's hindsight into the workings of a tourist town, "no one wished to draw attention to the fact that the benefits of her stay had been neither . . . durable nor deep."

Of course, by then it hardly mattered; the connection had been forged. Of five thousand *hivernants* visiting Nice in 1861, Russians numbered one in six of them, the largest national group besides the English and the French.

∽

Every year for five years running, and then at least one time more, a certain Monsieur Paccard came to Nice for the winter. We know little of this gentleman, not even his first name. We do know that each fall he traveled down from Chalon-sur-Saône, a river port in Burgundy, just south of Dijon, with his wife and one or two servants. And that he came for his health; he suffered from gout, a heart problem, and a cold that never seemed to go away. Later, when French scholars got hold of his notebooks, they pronounced him a *"Français moyen,"* an average Frenchman, not terribly well read, not particularly insightful, a good provincial *petit bourgeois*.

His first time in Nice was 1851, when, one November evening, after a twenty-seven-hour coach trip from Marseilles, he and his wife arrived at the Hôtel d'York, got a room with two beds on the second floor, had a little soup, and went to bed. The next morning, they went out looking for a place for the winter and suffered a nineteenth-century version of sticker shock: *eighteen hundred francs* for the six-month season. The place was beautiful, overlooked the quai, had a great southern exposure, but cost way too much.

Monsieur and Madame settled for smaller, much cheaper digs—five hundred francs—on the route de France. The furniture was old, but the place was comfortable, and its seven windows looked south, to the sun and sea.

Over the next few days, Paccard and his wife exchanged money, and signed up for a commercial reading library near the Pont-Neuf that carried English, French, and Sardinian newspapers. That winter, they watched Russian New Year fireworks on the Quai du Midi. They sampled

Mardi Gras. Like so many other travelers, Paccard kept a journal; his was flat, factual, littered with prices and travel times, little struck by wonder, content simply to record the raw data of his stay.

So it went, year after year—the trip down, checking into the hotel, finding and renting a house, signing up for the reading room, excursions and amusements, the occasional excitement of a storm (or, in 1854, of a modest earthquake that shook windows and sent inhabitants of the old city, half dressed, crying, and in shock, fleeing to Place Victor).

But in February 1860, Paccard's journal took a new turn. "Demonstrations for and against the annexation of Nice by France have taken place in the Theater. They've had no great impact in the city, which is perfectly calm. But on Sunday, the 12th, they barred music in the Public Garden for political reasons."

Paccard was living through a seismic shift in the political life of Nice. In 1858, France's Louis-Napoleon had met secretly with Camillo di Cavour, the Sardinian prime minister, the two contriving a Machiavellian gambit to remake the map of Europe. Cavour was a prime architect of the Risorgimento, the movement to unite the Italian-speaking peninsula, then a restless crazy-quilt of duchies and kingdoms, many under the dominion of foreign powers. In the North, neighboring Austria, with whom Sardinia had warred in 1849, occupied Lombardy and Venetia; Cavour wanted Austria out. He prevailed on France to intervene should Austria invade Sardinia-Piedmont (an event he was scheming to provoke). Louis-Napoleon agreed, but at a price—that Nice and Savoy be restored to France; the final step, for form's sake, was to be a plebiscite.

Paccard knew nothing of these intrigues—only that a vote was to determine whether Nice would remain part of Sardinia-Piedmont or become French. At a demonstration on Sunday, March 4, 1860, he heard cries of "*Nice italienne*," and at another, "*Vive la France, Vive l'Empereur.*"

The following Sunday, more demonstrations, which this time threatened to spin out of control. Knives were drawn. Soldiers arrived. Order was established.

Tuesday. The city was calm, except for unrest among the lower classes. The English and the Russians, noted Paccard, opposed annexation.

On March 23, a local newspaper declared that France's annexation of Nice and the rest of Savoy was a *fait accompli*. French troops were said to be arriving on Monday. They didn't, but after more weeks of rumor and uncertainty, the plebiscite took place. The vote was peaceful.

April 15, a beautiful Sunday. From that morning on, Paccard reported, groups marched through town to the sound of tambourines under the French *tricolore* surmounted by the imperial eagle. "Cries of *Vive la France, Vive l'Empereur* were continual and energetic. . . . There is no trace of opposition. All is free and spontaneous."

And then Paccard gave himself over to an unwonted bout of eloquence: "Truly, it is a beautiful spectacle to see a people willingly change their nationality without intrigue, without intimidation, by its own wish and following the movements of its heart. One can scarcely avoid the thought," said this elderly Frenchman, "that for forty-five years they have remained French to the depths of their souls."

The next day, the vote was tallied—eleven against and some seven thousand for—for what the history books would call the *rattachement*, Nice's unification with France. Two days later, French troops entered the city.

Paccard, meanwhile, had grown sicker, lost weight, and probably had only a short time to live. But the union with France, whose endorsement by the Niçois he'd witnessed, would launch a new era on the Riviera. Soon it would be harder to enjoy the sort of quiet times that he, and Alexander Herzen, and George Bemis had been able to take for granted.

In 1862, a woman we'll call Madame Brunet—her account was published anonymously the following year—was staying in Nice with her husband, a French government official. "We live in the aristocratic quarter," she recorded in her journal, "in the middle of everything, ten minutes from the sea." Socially, it was the best year anyone could remember. The King of Bavaria was there. So were dukes, counts, and millionaires—Beautiful People, circa 1862.

On the evidence Madame Brunet's journal offers of a sharp and sardonic eye, one might have hoped not to appear within its pages. At a lavish charity concert that left the performers awash in huge floral displays supplied by Alphonse Karr, the English, she recorded, fairly "sparkled by their absence; it's said they keep away any time they must part with their money." Another time, at the prefect's costume ball, a woman arrived brightly anticipating the stir her costume would cause. But after half an hour, she slipped away, mortified by the reactions of the other guests—who, smirked Madame Brunet, were "less indulgent than her mirror."

Late in her stay, a soft, steady rain discouraged jaunts into the country. So she found herself back on the Promenade des Anglais, seeing as if for the first time its "long sandy walk running along the blue sea," its lush gardens and charming villas, its foreign visitors turned out in all their finery. Nice, she exclaimed, "has never had such a brilliant season."

Yet, a few years later, Belle Époque in full flood, Nice's seasons would prove more brilliant yet; its rich would be richer, its hotels larger, grander, and more numerous, its charity balls finer, its amusements more various. In comparison, the winter of 1862 could seem like its last quiet time.

8 O NIZZA!

IT WAS 1885, AND ANNA DE L'ÉPINOIS WAS BACK ON THE RIVIERA.
Thirty-two years before, in 1853, she and her two grown children
had spent the spring there, touring and sketching Nice and its surrounding countryside. They'd hiked into the country, visited local ruins. From nearby Mont Boron, they'd looked out across a bowl of arid
hills that dropped down to the deep, sail-speckled harbor of Villefranche. In sepia-toned watercolors, they'd pictured trails snaking under
rocky ledges; a hunter with felled game draped across his shoulder.
Then the three had set off for Genoa, managing long stretches of the
trip on foot, periodically stopping by the side of a road or the base of
a waterfall to sketch.

Anna, born in 1804, came from a family of landed gentry that had
lost one of its own to the guillotine during the Revolution. At twenty-
one, she married into a family, the de l'Épinois, which enjoyed a long,
lively interest in art and history (and which had also suffered a loss to
the guillotine). In her mid-twenties, she'd had her children. In 1853, in
her late forties, she took them to the Riviera.

Now, in 1885, she and her daughter, Aurélie, were back once more.
And it was while stopping off at one of the little seaside towns they'd
visited before—Noli, three-quarters of the way to Genoa from Nice—
that memories of the earlier trip swept over her with sudden, sharp in-
tensity. Was it the sight, again, of the great rocks poking up from the
sea? Or the town ramparts angling up the hill? Or Aurélie sitting beside

the road, sketching, as she had so many years before? Awash with feeling, Anna reflected on that earlier time, and her youth.

She was almost eighty-one now, she wrote, time passed all too quickly, and she could not get around so easily anymore. What a shame, for

> I would still love to run through the hills at dawn. It gave me such pleasure to pass the whole day there, collecting plants and sketching. But time destroys all, leaving of our dear pleasures only sweet memories! I am no longer that alert tourist, braving every obstacle, climbing nimbly up craggy rocks and great ravines. My dear children and I, untiring walkers, managed our long trip from Nice to Genoa as nomads do, stepping into the unknown, fearlessly. . . .

Daughter Aurélie, by now in her fifties, made first a pencil sketch, then a watercolor, of Noli from the southwest, sighting along the arc of the little bay toward town. The painting survives: we see the ancient convent, the proud Tour du Canto, the campanile of the cathedral, the sinuous line of ramparts marching up the mountain to the château at its crest, all in warm sepia tones. A few boats. A peasant or two. Upon rocks by the water's edge sit mother and daughter, sketching, just as they had in 1853. Noli looks much as it did then. . . .

But not entirely. Off to the left in Aurélie's watercolor, tiny, at first invisible against the hill behind it, set back a little from the sea, a dark broken line slashes across the paper—linked rail cars, seven of them, led by a locomotive, black smoke streaming from its stack, chugging down the coast toward Nice.

The *rattachement*, just seven years after Anna de l'Épinois's first visit to Nice, brought in its wake the railroad. And the railroad changed everything.

∞

At the time Napoleon fell in 1815, Europe had suffered twenty-six years of war and revolution, the harvest of a feudal eighteenth-century world strange and unfamiliar to us today. But by the time the railroad reached

Nice in 1864, just half a century later, Europe had firmly stepped into the modern era. Historian Paul Johnson contends that the first decade and a half after Waterloo brought with it "the birth of the modern." After 1830, the newborn grew up fast: Marx and Engels's *Communist Manifesto* appeared in 1848; Flaubert's almost blasphemous *Madame Bovary* in 1857; Charles Darwin's *Origin of Species*, with its transformative ideas of evolution, in 1859.

Politically, it was an uncertain time. Europe sought new stability on the wreckage of the old order. Mostly, it maintained a fragile peace; the Crimean War, which broke out in 1853, was one notable exception. But the social and political fabric had been badly rent. People hungered for basic rights and democratic institutions; unrest simmered. In 1830 and 1848, especially, it bubbled up into bloody insurrections across the Continent. Meanwhile, new nations—Greece, Belgium, Italy, and others— were struggling to be born. By 1864, Italy had assumed something like its modern form. Germany was emerging from a confusing welter of three dozen individual states. In England, Queen Victoria was still on the throne she'd assumed in 1837. In France, the limited monarchy restored after Waterloo became a republic under Louis-Napoleon, Napoleon's nephew; but in 1852, he proclaimed himself emperor, Napoleon III, ushering in two decades of resurgent French chest-thumping and grand public-works projects.

It was in industry and technology that the modern era took its most familiar form. The Enlightenment of the mid-eighteenth century extolled reason, applied it to religion, politics, morality, and everything else. Science flourished. Now, in the first half of the nineteenth century, came technological and economic payoffs. The telegraph—"the Victorian Internet," one writer has called it—bound Europe together and, through transatlantic cables, to America. The Bessemer process held out the promise of cheap and plentiful steel. Smoky steam engines supplanted human and animal energy, pumping water, powering looms. And, of course, driving trains of rail cars across the countryside.

When it finally reached Nice, the railroad was no longer a new technology, but the product of half a century's development; the first steam locomotive went back to 1804. By 1860, rail's peculiar smoothness compared with horse-drawn locomotion, its annihilation of distance, its dominion over the landscape, were already taken for granted. Europe was interlaced with a large network of rail lines. England had ten thousand miles of track—and a three-class fare structure that left even the poor able to travel. France was slower off the mark, with only the most rudimentary system by 1840; but by 1860, it had more than five thousand miles in place.

The *chemin de fer* reached Marseilles in 1855, and Toulon in 1859. The emperor himself had authorized P.L.M.—the Paris-Lyon-Méditerranée rail company—to extend the line to Nice, as a "welcoming gift," it's been said, for joining France. By 1864, with the Var spanned by a six-arched stone bridge, the railroad was ready to roll into Nice.

∞

But *where* was it to roll? Where, exactly, would the new station go? From a spot high atop the Château Hill, the story is told, the emperor pointed to a spot—on the Paillon's right bank, about a mile back from the oceanfront; a great boulevard would connect it to Place Masséna, in the city's heart.

Not so fast, some objected.

After unification, one historian has written, "heads turned to Nice, and the maddest hopes were born." One such hope was rebirth of the city's port, cruelly devalued by Nice's Sardinian rulers; the imminent opening of the Suez Canal could make it a busy waystation between Paris and the Orient, perhaps one day to rival even that of Marseilles. But that depended on its ready access to the railroad. So the new *gare*, or station, had to go near the harbor, practically down by the water's edge.

No, said other Niçois, the city's future depended on tourism. It was not goods you wanted the new railroad to deposit at its front door but people—wealthy travelers now just a day's journey away. These *hivernants* didn't want to arrive midst a busy port's dirt and commotion. No, the train should drop them near the gracious Croix-de-Marbre district, on the right bank of the Paillon. But not *too* near its hotels, cafés, and promenades; you didn't want soot and noise from the trains to sully their days in Nice. The railroad should get them to town, then vanish—

only to reappear, five restful winter months later, when a carriage would drop them at the station.

Tourism won out; the *gare* would go on the right bank, though not so far back from the sea as the emperor had first suggested, only about three-quarters of a mile. Even this seemed too far to some. *"Lou cousu es vengat fouol, a mes la gara au mitan de la campagna,"* the Niçois grumbled in their dialect: "The mayor's gone mad; he's stuck the station in the middle of the country." But the mayor probably figured little in the decision, it being made in Paris, by the P.L.M. company in consultation with the imperial government.

The *gare* went up, all arches and red stucco, an agreeably scaled affair that an otherwise stern critic of Nice architecture termed "the only edifice of our period halfway elegant." On October 18, 1864, the first train pulled in, bringing Nice within twenty-three hours of Paris. Three days later, Tsar Alexander II arrived on a special train; on the 27th, it was Napoleon III; on the 30th, the future Leopold II of Belgium. Nice was stitched into the world as never before. From this moment on, visitors' accounts almost never tell of any trouble in getting there; normally, they don't mention the trip at all.

In the end, a few blocks' difference in the location of the *gare* probably mattered little; it was the arrival of the railroad itself that counted. For a century, Nice had dwelt in the imagination of Europe; now, on an impulse, Northern Europeans could get there the next day. And get there they did. In 1865, a hundred thousand people got off the train at Nice; by 1874, annual patronage had tripled, amounting to almost a thousand people a day.

Among those arriving at the new station was Sarah Putnam, of Massachusetts. "We started at 7 o'clock for Nice, our resting place for the winter, in the cars," she wrote in her journal on January 5, 1866. "The cars," of course, were the rail cars that bore them along the hundred or so miles of track from Marseilles. Sarah noted of the journey only the orange trees and grapevines visible after Fréjus, and vistas marrying blue sea with snow-capped Alps.

On February 7, while staying at the Hôtel du Nord with her family, she went to have her portrait taken at the photography studio of

Pierre Petit. Monsieur Petit posed her—her fine hair collected into a chignon and dressed up with a pretty ribbon, hoop skirt ballooning out around her—with pen in hand; Sarah was an inveterate diarist, and a skilled maker of pen-and-ink drawings. The journal in which she wrote about Nice, begun two months before in Paris, was the "Eighth Volume of My Life." She was sixteen years old.

Monsieur Petit was not the only Niçois to make his living from Sarah and her family that winter. Tourists had become the city's mainstay; their economic weight could be felt on every page of Sarah's diary.

From the Hôtel du Nord, the family could see the sea and, across the bed of the Paillon, the Public Garden. But the Nord was not ranked among the very best hotels in town; according to one guidebook, it appealed mostly to "Russians and commercial travelers." That night, the Putnams found their four-room suite a trifle chilly. So, the following afternoon, they looked for another place, found one to their liking, and that evening advised the Nord of their intention to leave. Not to worry, *madame et monsieur,* a new stove will be installed in your rooms *tout de suite;* that afternoon, the men were at work.

While in Nice, the Putnams bought flowers to keep their rooms fresh and cheerful.

They bought preserved pears pierced by little sticks, like American candy apples.

They hired a one-horse carriage and rode up to Cimiez, where they saw the ruins of the Roman amphitheater.

One day, after a month and a half in Nice, Sarah went shopping and for ten francs brought a wood box, "to remember Nice by," inlaid with a scene of a woman on a donkey—the old Nice, the Nice fast disappearing.

The Putnams attended balls. They went to the theater. They and the hundreds like them rolling into town each day made Nice prosperous. It was Economics 101, supply and demand, all over again: With the coming of the railroad, demand for all Nice offered—hotels, photographers, preserved pears—rose precipitously. Supply couldn't keep up. Prices soared.

Elsewhere in France, the franc maintained more or less constant buying power during these years. In Nice, however, a market basket of food valued at fourteen francs in 1860 cost twenty-five in 1870. One French wit observed that, "to live in Nice, it's no longer enough to be a *poitrinaire*," a tuberculosis patient, "you must be a *millionaire*." Meanwhile, a tourist guidebook noted in 1866, Nice hotels had become "as expensive as those in the largest capitals in Europe." This despite an orgy of hotel-building. In 1867, the right bank of the Paillon was home to forty-three hotels; all but ten of them had been built within the past seven years.

Mostly, the new hotels were run by outsiders, including Swiss, Polish Jews, Alsatians, and French from beyond the region. More grist for the old canards about the Niçois, their laziness and lack of enterprise? "The Niçois is no worker at all," insisted one guidebook in 1888. "If he sells sun and flowers, it's because nature kindly furnishes him with an abundance of both. He need not weary himself preparing them on his own." But the Niçois were competing with all of Europe. French law favored the growth of *sociétés*, large corporations, which could bring bigger money to bear on big projects—land development, hotels, electric power, trolley-car lines, casinos—than could small-time local investors.

Pulling in money from across Europe, Nice was caught up in a fever of land speculation—a word some then viewed more benignly than as a synonym for "greed." Many speculators were leading figures in French political and business life who themselves wintered on the Riviera and saw its potential up close. Bankers like Baron Rothschild and Henri Germain, founder of Crédit Lyonnais; or Baron Haussmann, then reshaping Paris to his magisterial will, who kept a villa on the heights above the city. They came to Nice each winter, met in its social *cercles*, and brought a little of Paris and London—a spirit of enterprise, a belief in the transforming power of capital—to this once-sleepy Alpes-Maritimes town.

Land prices shot up. Before reunification, one French franc could buy five square meters of prime undeveloped land in Nice—the size of, say, a large walk-in closet.

By 1863, after reunification, on the eve of the railroad's arrival, the same one franc would get you a plot about as big as a newspaper page.

By 1885, it would buy a piece of the Promenade des Anglais the size of a business card.

"Who can foresee what Nice will become" when the railroad links it to the rest of Europe? asked the city's mayor in 1861. Well, Joseph Dessaix could. Dessaix, president of the local historical society back when Nice belonged to Sardinia-Piedmont, collaborated with an artist, Félix Benoist, on an 1864 book that caught Nice on the very cusp of change. Down along the beach by the old town, Benoist sketched fishermen mending nets or sleeping at midday in the shadow of their boats, while their wives, in big skirts and cone-shaped *capelines*, washed clothes; their rustic dress, wrote Dessaix, would soon be "only a tradition." Meanwhile, the fine terraced gardens that graced Cimiez villas would, Dessaix was sure, succumb to speculative fever, yielding to "cut stone [and] . . . an army of workers"; the land was becoming just too valuable. "Too bad for some of these beautiful gardens; let's pay them a nod of farewell and regret."

"The railroad whose entry to Nice will soon be a *fait accompli*," Dessaix declared, "is going to change the face of the country."

As indeed it did. In 1883, a story in the local paper, *L'Éclaireur*, noted that Nice's prosperity now rested on apartments, villas, hotels, and shopping; no mention of such traditional mainstays of the economy as anchovies or olive oil. When, early in the next century, someone totted up the number of Nice jewelry shops, the total came to 160; that made it, in all of France, second only to Paris.

O Nizza!

Marie Rattazzi, the bright, eccentric, high-living granddaughter of Napoleon's brother Lucien, and a sharp observer of Nice high society, saw the great change taking place around her. Her book, *Nice la Belle*, captures the town at almost the last moment when the old ways still roughly balanced the new.

It was 1868, just four years after the arrival of the railroad, and it struck Rattazzi that now there were two quite distinct ways to live in Nice. It was still true that nowhere could you better live a life of peace, quiet, and calm. But, she noticed, many *hivernants* now "lead all-consuming social lives. They're always going out. For nothing in the world would they miss the four or five balls invariably given each evening; in the morning, they're still dancing." Or else they were gambling, attending concerts, viewing parades. "Nowhere can you amuse yourself better, or as much, as in Nice." No winter of quiet pleasures for these new visitors; they were out for a good time.

Marie Bashkirtseff surely was. The daughter of a Russian aristocrat whom her mother had left when Marie was still an infant, "Moussia," as her friends knew her, first came to Nice in 1870, at the age of twelve. She was no ordinary adolescent and would blossom into no ordinary young woman. She taught herself Latin and Greek. She read Plutarch, Dante, and Zola, aspired to become a singer, wished above all to leave a mark on the world. "To marry and make children! Why, any washerwoman can do that!" she wrote in her journal. "I want glory." Around 1874, she developed tuberculosis. She gave up singing, turned to art, studied in Paris, and ultimately produced hundreds of accomplished paintings; a life-size self-portrait hanging today in a Nice museum shows her, trim, in a black dress with white lace ruffle at the neck, with small cherry lips, deep-blue-gray eyes, artist's palette in hand.

It was not art, however, that brought her immortality, but the journal she started keeping around the time she moved to Nice. Frank, intimate, capricious, filled with fantasies, flirtations, acerbic asides, it went on, through eighty-four handwritten exercise books, until her death in 1884; she was only twenty-five, but she'd lived a life worthy of ten ordinary women. Published soon after, her journal became the talk of Europe. In it, she captured the resort city she'd visited eleven times and loved with all the ardency of her temperament.

Moussia was not immune to Nice's quieter charms. Mornings, she'd leave her family's vast, many-roomed villa and stroll along the Promenade des Anglais, often deserted during these hours, enjoying the sea and the lush gardens set back from it. Sometimes she'd take a book to read. Sometimes she'd take the dogs.

But more often Moussia drank deeply of Nice's more formal pleasures and amusements. She'd go by horse out to the new racetrack for opening day, where she'd find *tout le beau monde niçois*, all of Nice high society, on hand. She'd attend charity balls. She'd visit the Russian and French naval squadrons in Villefranche. She was always shopping—fine fabric on avenue de la Gare, hats at André Médecin on rue du Pont-Neuf, belts at Matton Brothers on the Cours Saleya. She attended the French theater and the Italian opera; one reader of her journal judged her "more aware of the spectators, and the effect she produced, than on the artistic value" of the performances. Moussia was a social animal, and Nice had become a frenetically social city.

When, in 1877, she was admitted to the exclusive Cercle de la Méditerranée—inspired by Paris's Jockey Club, site of concerts, balls, and theatrical matinees, and *the* place to be seen—Moussia was thrilled, and flattered. "The Secretary of the Cercle gave me a little speech at the time of my admission. He said this was a good time, [the Cercle's] membership large yet select, but that there'd been a gap—one waiting for me to fill."

The other leading social institution catering to the city's *hivernants*—and, like the *cercles*, created for them—was the casinos. In principle, these were just large halls devoted to music, dancing, and other social activities, but in time they came to *mean* gambling, as they already did at spas like Vichy, Dieppe, or Biarritz. In 1867, residents of Nice unsuccessfully petitioned the government to get gambling banned in Monaco, whose Monte Carlo casino had already become a powerful tourist draw. Pressure mounted in Nice for a casino of its own that might prove "the biggest, the most beautiful of the casino-cathedrals, a sparkling vision that would attract pleasure-seekers and high-rollers from afar." A vast Crystal Palace of an idea ran aground on just where it might go. But, finally, after fire destroyed an earlier incarnation of it, the Casino of the Jetée-Promenade, to give it its proper name, built of iron on stilts driven into the seabed, opened in 1891 across the street from the Public Garden and adjacent to the Promenade des Anglais.

It was a massive, Moorish-inspired affair that looked as if it had stepped out of Baghdad, garish and ornate. It would invite derision as well as praise, yet become a fixture of every picture postcard and tourist poster, a constant presence in the life of Nice for half a century, a public icon to rival Paris's Eiffel Tower. Wherever you went in Nice, you saw it. Whatever you did in Nice, you wound up there. From ten in the morning to midnight, it swarmed with activity, with singers, comedians, dancers. It was a place to admire lavish carriages as they returned from the races, to observe the goings and comings of neighboring hotels. In 1908, gambling was finally admitted to its roster of amusements, its east gallery set aside for baccarat and other games. Of course, by then Nice had no fewer than five casinos.

They and Nice's *cercles* were to countless visitors—men, women, and often children, too—a scene of savored moments. Of being seen with the right marquis or duke. Of watching the little ball settle into a coveted slot on the roulette wheel. Of hearing a famous singer perform. Opulent places to gather, among those like yourself, and—no mystery about it—have a good time.

Of course, the *most* fun, Marie Bashkirtseff wrote in 1879, when she was twenty, was to scream out to Englishmen in the crowd, "Your wife is cheating on you!" Or else go up to people she'd never seen before and tell them they were faithless lovers, that she would wreak revenge on them yet. Moussia was writing of Carnaval, and at Carnaval you could do whatever you liked. One time, she and her brother Paul dragged some poor Russian into their carriage and fairly assaulted him with silly and outlandish pronouncements, at the end of half an hour leaving the poor man perfectly befuddled.

An ancient pre-Lenten tradition in Roman Catholic countries, Carnaval was a time unshackled from the bonds of ordinary life. In Nice, it dated back at least to 1294 and featured costumes, masks, balls held in the public squares, candles lit in the windows of houses lining the crooked little streets of the old town. Noisy, raucous, and rude, its excesses each year prompted the bishop to issue new edicts and prohibitions for the following year; no one took them seriously. Carnaval, someone once said, was a festival "not given to the people but that the people give to themselves."

But then came the wrenching French defeat in the Franco-Prussian

War of 1870, and the bloody days of the Commune—a kind of second French Revolution that spread fear of violence and disorder across Europe. Nice officials worried that a too-clamorous Carnaval might frighten off visitors. Especially so after Alexandra Fyodorovna, whose royal visit in 1856 had helped interest the Russian nobility in Nice, chose to spend the winter up the coast in San Remo. Carnaval, felt the city fathers, needed to be reined in, order and safety made top priority, the *hivernants* reassured.

The year after the city took Carnaval in hand, a mayoral edict made it *interdit*, prohibited, to throw at a person, carriage, or house any object that might hurt someone, or dirty or damage his clothes, including eggs, oranges, fruit, cereal, plaster, or beans; all, we may be sure, had enjoyed spirited use before. Henceforth, no one in mask or costume could insult or provoke anyone, or publicly sing dirty songs or, for that matter, any songs that, even if otherwise benign, "contain offensive descriptions."

Carnaval became a centerpiece of the city's efforts to lure visitors. Each year it became more elaborate, better publicized, with grander floats, prettier women, more ludicrous masks, noisier fireworks. Had it lost, along the way, a little of its nervy bite? Maybe so, but you wouldn't know it from the bravado of Marie Bashkirtseff and her brother.

In 1868, with the opening of its new racetrack, Madame Rattazzi observed that "Nice has completed the ensemble of key amusements winter society demands. Neither numerous balls, nor the theater, with comedy and opera, nor blue sky, nor sparkling waves, suffice for vacationing tourists." They demand something more, something to shake them up, rouse them from their lethargy. And now, with the new Hippodrome, she was saying, Nice had that, too.

Many, indeed, would look back to the Nice of the late 1860s, say, up through the 1870s, as altogether ideal, the balance just right. During these years, writes one scholar, "tourism booms . . . [yet Nice] retains the marks of a small provincial city." When, in 1913, author Robert de Souza looked back wistfully to this period, he graced his book with a photograph taken from the heights of Mont Boron one morning in 1880; it was a time, he wrote, when Nice's homes and gardens boasted "graceful proportions," and Nice as a whole, "already a big city, had the most harmonious municipal form."

Nice was poised on a knife edge between its somnolent rustic past and its cosmopolitan future. It was all things to all visitors, the two Nices—or, rather, Madame Rattazzi's two modes of enjoying it—in a kind of equilibrium. But it was an unstable equilibrium, one that couldn't last.

∞

In 1866, a British guidebook warned visitors to Nice of "extortion even in some of the first-class houses," of a "want of attention and of ordinary civility," of bad food even where the prices were higher than in Paris or Rome. Best rent a private home for the whole season, it advised, rather than be left to the mercy of avaricious hotelkeepers. Wrote one wry French observer, "The business of fleecing the English is better than cultivating jasmine and tuberoses."

Around this time appeared a book entitled *Life in Nice: Advice and Directions for Our Winter Guests.* Its author, Léon Pilatte, cautioned visitors that they were "exploitable material, the bountiful source from which flows a measure of prosperity" for the locals. The Niçois was not always out to fleece you; but neither was he, ready smile or not, your intimate friend. The best advice? *Take care.*

Had Pilatte stopped here, we might judge him laudably solicitous of the tourist's well-being. But what he added later, read warily, renders his "advice" suspect. "You will come back" to Nice, he promised his readers. Come back no matter how badly burned or egregiously cheated? Didn't much matter, he seemed to say, "because this sky, this sea, this sun, these mountains, exert an allure whose force you will feel when you are away. You will come back."

Nice was becoming a little full of itself. It needed to watch out, warned the British guidebook quoted earlier. If not checked, its excesses and abuses would "drive foreigners to other more favored sites, and thereby render this prosperous and agreeable city comparatively deserted as a winter residence."

It was a lesson the Niçois would have to learn again and again: there was always some other pretty town down the coast—or, later, across the world—to strike ever-fickle tourists as fresher and more appealing than itself, some new saucy little thing eager to draw admiring eyes to its own lithe and seductive form.

Premier among these new competitors was Cannes, whose story properly begins in September 1834, when cholera broke out in Marseilles. Two months later, the authorities declared an epidemic. Along the Var, then still an international boundary, the Sardinians established a *cordon sanitaire;* every foot of the frontier fell under an armed soldier's gaze, and at the bridge, the normal guard was doubled. Cholera did finally reach Nice. But these forceful public-health measures reduced the number of deaths, and historians would view the Sardinian policy, even in hindsight, with approval. From the point of view of Riviera tourism, however, it had permanent repercussions. In late December 1834, one of those stopped at the Var on his way to Nice was the former lord chancellor of Great Britain, Lord Brougham.

Henry Peter Brougham—like Smollett, like so many before and since—had been driven to Nice by exhaustion, mental and physical. His official duties had left him drained; he spent seven hours each day in court, never got to bed before two in the morning. In six months, he'd written two thick printed volumes' worth of formal judgments. His brother had recently died. His daughter, who joined him in the great six-horsed carriage that brought them to the Sardinian frontier, was ill. Nice, he hoped, would do them both good. Yet here they were, at the Var, after crossing all of France, and border guards in the service of His Sardinian Majesty dared bar their way.

Brougham was not used to being barred by anyone. He was the embodiment of British *hauteur*—eccentric, incalculably rich, an august political figure who had helped abolish slavery in the British Empire, exposed flogging in the army, created the University of London. If ever there was a Great Man, Brougham was it. Yet *still* they turned him back.

It is a legendary story after that. Brougham retraced his steps west and put up for the night at a simple *auberge,* where a first taste of bouillabaisse moved him to ecstasy. The next day, he went to Antibes to inspect a house where Napoleon had stayed, and vowed to buy it. But public outcry—sell it to an *Anglais!?*—blocked the sale. So Brougham went to Cannes, bought for a pittance a plot of land on the Fréjus road, built there the Château Eleonore, named for his daughter, and lived there for the next thirty years.

Every passing traveler, it seems, contrived to see Brougham's villa, a columned mansion that looked out over the Mediterranean, its gardens set off by fine iron-and-stone fences, terraces of orange and almond trees rising up the hill behind it. Brougham, of course, loved it, but not everyone else did. One traveler commented on its "rather cockney taste in the stuccoing and painting." The French author Stendhal in 1838 lamented that it was "so bourgeois, so denuded of all that speaks of the imagination." No matter. It was big, it was extravagant, it was Brougham's, and that was enough to draw the gaze of English aristocrats to Cannes. The town got rail service in 1860, four years before Nice. By the time Brougham died there, eight years later, it had become Nice's chief Riviera rival.

Cannes's newcomer status was precisely part of its charm, gave it just that sense of freshness Nice had enjoyed a century before. When Prosper Mérimée, a celebrated historian and writer, visited Cannes in 1856 after two weeks in Nice, he reported that, though he'd been "amused" in Nice, "there were too many people, too many English, too many Russians." Cannes, on the other hand, seemed natural and new. Compared with Nice—and for stylish people who could afford to divine slight differences among fine things and choose among them, comparison was all—Cannes represented rest, quiet, and less intrusive pleasures.

Another Nice rival, this time to the east, beside the Italian frontier, was Menton. And it was another British doctor, J. Henry Bennet, who helped make it one. The town, until 1860 part of the Principality of Monaco, seemed to him blessed by better climate even than Nice. By the time the third edition of his book, *Winter in the South of Europe*, came out in 1865, Menton counted six hundred winter residents. Many, as years before in Nice, were ill. "The most wretched little spot," an American called it, its invalids enough "to give one the blues." But their money was as good as anyone else's, and when the railroad reached

Menton in 1868, a flood of visitors followed. By 1871, with construction money furnished by Swiss, British, and German banks, Menton boasted thirty hotels. By 1877, according to a guidebook appearing that year, it was "vying with Nice as a place of winter residence, claiming to have still a softer and more equable climate."

Climate—the same wondrous climate that the rest of Europe envied—figured in the competition among the Riviera towns: to listen to champions of this town or that, the climate *wasn't* the same. Menton's groves of lemon trees attested to its "peculiar mildness," wrote Dr. Bennet. Edwin Lee had baldly asserted that Villefranche, around a little cape from its larger neighbor, "possesses a much warmer climate than Nice." The practice extended even to neighborhoods *within* Nice. William Farr, whose 1841 guide to Nice included a chapter entitled "Medical Topography," recorded that the most humid part of the Nice suburbs was along the road to Villefranche, the next-most near a particular hotel, and so on. Of course, he allowed, locally available instruments couldn't measure the difference. "We are daily expecting others from Germany," he assured his readers, "which are [more] highly sensitive."

Now, weather *could* differ in nearby coastal places. You could sit out on the veranda of a villa in Beaulieu, under blue skies and warm sun, listening to the waves gently scour the rocks below, and yet sometimes *see*, a few hundred yards away, rocky promontories lost in cold, thick clouds. But partisans of one town or another, playing up small differences for competitive advantage the way they might detergents today, were making much of little. The fact was, the railroad had eclipsed climate as a competitive factor. The railroad anointed some places, denied its imprimatur to others; the former enjoyed prosperity, the latter lost out.

Among those denied the railroad's favor was Hyères, fifty miles down the coast, practically in the lap of Toulon. Hyères had long been a rival to Nice as a winter travel destination. Back in 1775, Sulzer passed through, decided it did his health good, and resolved to stay the rest of the year there; he changed his mind and set off for Nice after encountering a spell of wind and snow. But Hyères lay nearer the Rhône, with its easy river access, and avoided extra miles and days of travel. For years it grew almost in parallel with Nice. Grew in parallel, that is, until the railroad passed it by; pretty soon, the city fathers were fairly hawking Hyères as a bargain vacation site.

Nice's chief rival to the east was Monaco, where gambling, in its Monte Carlo district, was the big draw. Ruled by the same family for seven hundred years, the tiny principality, fifteen miles up the coast from Nice, had until recently been a shabby little town indeed.

> Two or three streets on perpendicular rocks; eight hundred wretches dying of hunger; a decayed castle; a battalion of French troops; a few orange, olive, and mulberry trees scattered over a few acres of land, themselves scattered over rocks; such is, pretty nearly, the picture of Monaco,

at least by one late-eighteenth-century account. In 1856, threatened by bankruptcy and hoping to mimic the success of Northern spas, Monaco's royal family authorized the building of a gambling casino.

But the little fiefdom was hard to reach. An 1858 illustration shows three croupiers peering through binoculars and telescope toward a lone carriage coming from Nice, literally *searching* for gambling business. Such business failed to materialize until the arrival of the railroad in 1868. "Crowds of people," by one account, "poured out of the trains and into the gaming rooms." Monaco's fabulous new casino, now in the hands of the veteran roulette concessionaire François Blanc, virtually minted money—profits of two million francs in 1868, ten million in 1879. The sumptuous Hôtel de Paris went up beside it. By 1877, *Morford's Short-Trip Guide to Europe* could note that Monaco was "taking the place of Baden-Baden as the central resort for fashionable gambling."

Stories from the gaming tables of fortunes lost and won, suicide born of desperate ill-luck, and the sheer gilt-edged glitz of the place became the stuff of legend. And in the glimpses they granted of moral degradation set against worldly opulence, the tables fascinated even those who didn't bet; they became a tourist attraction themselves. In 1896, an American visitor, Adelaide Hall, first strolled across the

casino's manicured grounds, finally resolved to venture inside with a friend and, "for the first time in our lives, see a gambling table." The scene struck her as joyless; the gamblers were "as businesslike in their play as if they were bank clerks engaged in routine work." Another American visitor wrote of

> earnest, absorbed people . . . putting their gold or silver on various spots, watching anxiously the croupier as he dealt the cards or rolled the ball. . . . I saw young girls playing there not yet out of their "teens," old women rouged and powdered, their wrinkled hands fairly trembling with eagerness as they clutched their winnings.

"Let Nice take care," one observer warned in 1861, "fashion has its caprices. Such neighboring towns as Menton, Monaco, Antibes and Cannes" threatened it. Of course, in favoring them all, the railroad made them all a little alike, too. In his study *The Railway Journey*, Wolfgang Schivelbusch noted that towns touched by a railroad "were no longer spatially individual or autonomous. . . . For the twentieth-century tourist, the world has become one huge department store of countrysides and cities."

Along the Riviera, a whole string of pretty places geography had kept apart through all of history were now less than an hour apart, and equally within reach of Northern capitals. They were each separate towns, mindful of their competitors; yet they were also, collectively, the Riviera. Nice had lost a little of what made it unique.

The Riviera as a whole had lost something, too. Margaret Maria Brewster could find Nice, compared with Cannes, too gentrified for her taste, too rife with fashionable lounges, balls, theaters, shops, and smartly dressed men and women. "At Cannes we have country quiet." But that was 1857. After the railroad came, less country quiet remained in Cannes or, for that matter, anywhere on the Riviera. Prosper Mérimée found Cannes crowded with "Englishmen and unpleasant Russians. This avalanche of foreigners," coming on the heels of the railroad, had "spoiled this beautiful country. I need to find some other se-cluded place as warm as this but less overrun by civilization."

The railroad made many wistful for a more serene and simpler past. Just six years after it reached Nice, a writer recalling Smollett's visit a century before, W. J. Prowse, could cast the Scottish physician's trans-portation problems in a roseate glow and bewail this new technology that left Nice a day's travel from London. Though it was tedious, he wrote, "many of us might nowadays prefer his style of traveling." These days, "you can be whirled away from London to Nice so rapidly that the whole thing seems like a dream." (There was just no satisfying some people: once the trip to Nice took too long; now it was over too fast.)

Consider the ride south from Paris—"a close, hot, muggy night, with a fat Frenchman on one side of you, and a fat Frenchman on the other side of you." Lyons, before dawn. Then Marseilles, which "means that you are dreadfully weary," and on toward Nice. "You pass through some of the most exquisite coast-scenery in the world, and through a no-ble range of historical hills; but you are jaded, and beaten, and fagged."

At last, Nice. "You have 'done it,'—you have come a thousand miles without resting. Next day, if you feel a little tired, you had better send for a doctor; for in plain English, you have done too much."

In 1903, Alexander Innes Shand returned to the Riviera after forty years away. In the old days, by *diligence*, "you scaled height after height, glad to stretch your legs, and you lingered at each zigzag to look en-tranced over the expanse of sea, to gather wild-flowers, to catch butter-flies, to examine some fragment of ruin." Why, the road, wrote Shand, "had seemingly been engineered for the delectation of the tourist." But now, by rail, you tunneled through mountains, clung snakelike to the low ground, missed the best scenery.

To some, plainly, it was Nice *before* the railroad that attained what one French scholar has called "a kind of tranquil and serene perfec-tion"; it all went downhill, in other words, from there. In 1872, Alexan-der Brown complained of many Riviera hotels'

social medley of nationalities, tastes, and dispositions, from which it is impossible always to exclude many specimens of the rising generation, a state of things that ill assorts with the wants of those in quest of health, and little calculated to add to happiness or comfort. The bedroom arrangements are still less flattering. As a rule the apartments are small, the maisons undergoing a subdivision consistent with the largest return in profit for the season; the partition walls are seldom thick enough to bar one's own expressions of uneasiness and quite thin enough to be constantly reminded of your neighbour's.

Listen to enough of this and you'd conclude what every generation of elite traveler always concluded: the tourists were ruining everything.

Of course, it was not their numbers alone that were so offensive; it was who they were.

PARIS IN WINTER. THE WIND BLOWS THROUGH THE CHESTNUT TREES
in Madame's garden. The flower beds are mantled in ice. Toward three
in the afternoon, darkness settles in, and the city's lamps are lit. "An icy
mist invades the streets. The gas lamps flicker with a smoky red glow
that barely peeks through the blue disks of fog around them." A cold,
desolate darkness.

All this Madame suffers in Paris. And all this she will leave behind
her, writes Henry de Montaut in *Voyage au pays enchanté*, published in 1880.
Fictional "Madame"—we imagine her as in her thirties, she and her
husband comfortable, though not rich—is bound for that "enchanted
country," the Riviera. There "sun and roses await us, the gentle warmth
of springtime, the perfumed fragrance of the flowers, and the salty, in-
vigorating breath of the sea." Eighteen hours and she'd be there. *C'est
bien le moment de partir*, it's just the right time to leave. . . .

Ah, but not quite yet. Because first, Madame—de Montaut now
addresses her directly, in the second person—you must secure the as-
sent of your husband. He can be two-faced, one moment smiling, gracious, and eager to please, the next sullen and disapproving; and over
the years, this *wanting-to-say-no* side of him has gained force. But, "happily, you are a woman, which is to say a diplomat of the first order."

The wintry chill and overcast skies have left your husband glum.
"He sits in a corner by the fireplace, in front of the fire of your little
salon. He pokes at it with impatience." You've been sitting across the
room, stretched out on the *pouffe*, a big round backless couch, observing,

waiting for just the moment to make your move. Finally, you draw a chair up close to his, and purr: "Oh, how lovely it would be in Nice. How we'd enjoy the pure blue sky, the warm air, the radiant sun."

You expound on Nice's attractions, pleasures, festivals. . . . But with restraint, Madame's mentor advises: "Too much enthusiasm could pique his resistance."

You confide in him, too, that your doctor has advised that, whereas the harsh Parisian winter could harm your fragile health, Nice would restore your bloom.

But no military strike, which is how de Montaut styles it, forever goes unanswered, and, sure enough, your husband protests: no, not this year—too expensive.

But you're ready for this, and can demonstrate that your trip expenses won't exceed your budget. "Work them up," de Montaut advises, "*your* way."

Your box at the opera? You can sublet it; some friends are ready to take it off your hands. After all, you smile sweetly at your husband, "every little bit helps. . . ."

Still resistance? It is time, writes de Montaut, to throw in the reserve battalions. "The doctor advises," you tell your husband with utmost delicacy, "that certain hopes too long and vainly cherished could find, in a winter passed in Nice, the best conditions for being fulfilled."

An instant's incomprehension . . . and then your husband's face erupts with pleasure. . . .

Nice, Madame, is yours.

Now, it would be easy to dismiss this little soap opera, sure to make any latter-day feminist cringe. Yet one suspects that something like it was, during these years, being played out all over Europe. It was no longer just the wealthy and well-born who fled the dark and cold of the North. More and more, Nice's guests included those, like our young married couple, who needed to watch their expenses, keep household budgets in balance.

By the time de Montaut conceived his guileful Parisian heroine, Nice had taken on a more egalitarian tinge. Yes, the city had numerous grand hotels, he wrote, but "to small fortunes, Nice presents more modest dwellings, perfectly acceptable low-cost pensions. There is something for every pocketbook, every taste, every desire." The same went for getting around town—magnificent carriages for the wealthy; modest rentals for the less affluent; bus, tramway, saddle horse, or donkey "for pocketbooks still less well furnished."

So, rich or not, de Montaut invited his readers, they should come to the Riviera. "Come to Cannes, come to Nice, come to Monaco and to Menton, you who can! And if you cannot remain for more than a season, come anyway!" De Montaut was scarcely wooing society's dregs, but his appeal acknowledged that the door to the Riviera had now swung open wider.

Thus far, it is plain, our account has weighed heavily on the side of French chancellors, Russian aristocrats, and British lords and ladies. But by the late nineteenth century, the railroad and other transportation improvements had reduced the cost of travel, made it faster, more convenient, less dangerous. Wealth was piling up, and spreading out, across Europe and America. Travel and leisure were becoming available to more people—and to a broader *range* of people.

Among the legions of travelers arriving in Nice, as elsewhere in Europe, many were still aristocrats and *rentiers*, men and women on whom inherited wealth, rooted in vast estates, bestowed boundless leisure.

Some, too, were newly minted millionaires and others who prospered from the new industrial economy—the "conquering class," someone once called them. These *nouveaux riches* had money, enjoyed spending it, and were growing in number.

Others among the new travelers were yet more ordinary folks. Not the poor; not manual workers, farmers, or laborers. But, rather, people a little like that modest *Français moyen* we met earlier, Monsieur Paccard—only more *moyen*, more average, yet.

In 1866, the *Murray Handbook for Travellers in Northern Italy* (which still took in Nice) noted the fewer *diligences* and many more rail lines traversing the region. Then it turned to the costs of travel, an issue easier to address "now that people of all classes are obliged to adopt the same means of locomotion, railways." The author supplied prices. He advised budget-conscious English travelers to patronize the *table d'hôte*. He suggested that single men might content themselves with hotels of the second rank. "Ask the price of everything beforehand," he went on, "and never scruple to bargain." This violated "our English tastes," but in Italy it was the custom, and you were deemed an inexperienced traveler if you did not. Local innkeepers were inclined to foist upon you needlessly elaborate meals, a practice you were advised to discourage firmly.

What is so telling about these travel tips was their preoccupation with costs. One book published a few years later in America was blunter yet; it was entitled *The Economical European Tourist: A Journalist Three Months Abroad for $430*, and aimed at "Americans of limited means or plain habits." Meanwhile, through organized tours, international travel was reaching those of means more limited yet.

Back in 1841, an English cabinetmaker and temperance advocate named Thomas Cook began chartering trains to bring working-class people, at reduced fares, to temperance meetings. This, in embryonic form, was the first of the modestly priced, minutely organized "Cook's tours," which proliferated through Britain and then, after the 1860s, throughout the Continent. By the time *Cook's Handbook to the Health Resorts of the South of France, Riviera and Pyrenees* appeared in 1905, Thos. Cook & Son was furnishing its customers railroad timetables, reserving them sleeping-car tickets, exchanging their currency, selling them insurance, supplying them letters of credit and certificates of identity.

One set of tours brought travelers across the Channel to Calais and thence to Paris, down to Lyons, Marseilles, Cannes, Nice, Monte Carlo, and on into Italy, before returning through the Alps. Each tour was specified by number. Travelers were allowed so many pounds of free baggage, offered "travelling coupons" to one of three classes of hotel. Fares included lodging, meals, carriage drives and excursions, fees, tips, and guides, and came to one pound, one shilling a day. In Nice, they could stay at the Métropole, the Grand, and the Beau-Rivage, among other hotels; an extra charge applied to stays during Carnaval.

A Cook's tour didn't just cut the cost of travel; it reduced travel's uncertainty, annoyance, confusion, and risk. And these were functions that tour guidebooks like the red-bound *Handbook for Travellers* series

John Murray started in England, or Karl Baedeker's in Germany, performed as well. These guidebooks, well established by the 1860s, did not treat Nice as had Smollett or Sulzer; their journals had recognizable literary styles, were leisurely, digressive, and stocked with the authors' own experiences. The new guidebooks were more utilitarian; a French scholar who has studied their treatment of Nice over the years, Jean-Louis Potron, pictures the excursions they featured as "squared off, measured, timed, and priced."

Before 1840, by one reckoning, fewer than half a dozen guidebooks to Nice had appeared; one told of celebrated artists and savants from the town, neighborhoods the traveler might visit, and a few local sites worth a trip, but nothing of hotels or restaurants. Over the next twenty years, however, Nice guides multiplied, a new one appearing every other year or so; from the *rattachement* to World War I, the pace quickened to two a year. History and climate lost space, relatively speaking, while itineraries, listings of useful information, alphabetical indexes, and other tourist-useful trappings proliferated.

The *Murray Handbook* for 1866 described some of the Hôtel Chauvain's rooms as "gloomy," Cimiez's Hôtel de l'Orangine as enjoying "a fine bracing air and . . . lovely view." It directed readers to a real-estate agent on rue du Paradis; castigated Nice restaurants as a whole, but noted the passable ones; advised readers they could find Mr. Hall, an American dentist, on Place Masséna. . . .

Improved roads. The railroad itself. Tourist agencies like Cook's. Good hotels. Servants, chefs, concierges, and other skilled hotel staff eager to please. Established amusements like Carnaval and the Hippodrome . . . This flourishing tourism infrastructure, together with Murray, Baedeker, and other tourist guides, was helping to make getting to Nice, and having a good time there, easy, efficient, and almost routine.

And not just for Europeans.

∞

She stood on the deck of the twin-funneled German steamship *Fulda* and watched the dock recede slowly away. She was thirty years old, embarked on an eight-month trip to Europe with her sister and a friend, and overcome by powerful feelings. From earliest childhood, Laura Libbey, American, had longed for Europe. She'd "dreamed of it, built air castles about it," but always it had seemed impossible. So that now, on Saturday, February 6, 1892, as the boat inched away from the dock and her friends on land waved farewell, it was hard to believe her dream was coming true.

Out at sea, she and her companions would go up on deck, hunt down the steamer chairs they'd rented for the trip, then snuggle under rugs, veils, and caps, mummy-style, and chat amiably for hours, all the while "enjoying to the full the long roll of the ship as she slowly mounted the waves . . . and watching the gulls as they circled in our wake." It was a happy time, despite her tiny second-class cabin, which probably cost about two-thirds of one in first class. She wrote, good-naturedly, about how her blanket came in a cotton bag that served as sheet; she started to remove it, but then saw how dirty it was, and promptly restored it to its cotton shell.

On her first morning at sea, Libbey was wakened by a band tramping through the ship's passageways, belting out hymns—the voyage's only concession to Sunday piety, despite the presence on board of several clergymen bound for the Holy Land. Later, the *Fulda* passed so close to the Azores she could see individual trees on its hillsides. Another time, "the air was so balmy and the moonlight so beautiful" that the captain held a dance, ordered the deck dressed up with flags and pennants, and fireworks to light up the night sky. At last they docked in Genoa, where, after only a few hours, Libbey had to gather up her bags and board the train for Nice.

Every detail of long-coveted Europe seemed to her curious and strange. She noted the "funny little cooped up carriage" of the train that bore her and her traveling companions to Nice, set up like an old-fashioned coach, seats facing one another; the tiny windows, pulled up and down by a strap, that slid down into the doors; the copper boxes mounted on the floor beneath their feet, filled with hot water to warm the compartment, but never renewed before they grew cold.

Joining them in their compartment was an Italian gentleman who broke out a parcel and—with fanfare, one suspects—unfolded it to reveal broiled chicken, rolls, and a bottle of wine. Laura and her traveling companions "looked at each other with dismay." They'd eaten nothing since early morning, had supplied themselves with no provisions, were quite famished, and had to watch Signor lay into this ample lunch.

Hurtling toward Nice, they passed through pretty little villages, oohed and aahed at mountain-and-sea vistas. For a while, the tracks hugged the shore, and "the spray from the waves dashed up against the windows of our car." They saw quaint churches, and ruins, and houses frescoed with trompe-l'oeil designs of porticoes, windows, and painted blinds; at one, a faux-cat sat beside a faux-window. Finally, at seven that evening, they reached Nice. A quick check of the Baedeker and a long carriage ride through town brought them to the Hôtel des Princes. There, wrote Laura Libbey, "a most welcome and well cooked dinner was in readiness to refresh us after our long fast!"

They had arrived in darkness. The next morning, Laura woke, stepped to the window, and gazed out at the sun sparkling on the blue waters of the sea.

∞

After the Civil War, Americans began visiting Nice, as they did the rest of Europe, in large numbers. Around the time of Nice's reunification with France, scarcely any *hivernants* were American; by 1870, one in seven was. Enough were visiting the Riviera by 1880 that de Montaut could make American women, right alongside Riviera visitors from Italy, Russia, and England, the butt of one of his canny verbal caricatures:

> I like nothing to bother me.
> I like to do what pleases me.
> I dream of total happiness:
> To be free, with a big, fat purse.

When, in 1877, travel writer Henry Morford issued the ninth edition of his *Short-Trip Guide to Europe*, he was still pounding away at what seemed to him the skewed notions Americans had about visiting

Europe. Once, he noted, such trips were inconceivable for all but the wealthy few. Unfortunately, that myth lingered. Falsehoods propagated by those who *had* traveled were partly to blame; some just couldn't resist exaggerating the costs, as well as the imagined peril, of their trips. His, Morford's, duty was to disabuse his readers of such error. Steamships had not yet entirely supplanted sail, but a trip to Europe, he was saying, need not take so long, or cost so much.

On Benjamin Silliman's first trip to Europe, in 1805, he traveled aboard what was then reckoned a large sailing ship, the *Ontario;* it got him safely across but then sank, with all hands, on the trip back. In the 1851 trip that brought him to Nice, he took the *Baltic,* a paddle-wheel steamer. The *Baltic* was safer, Silliman realized, simply because it speeded the trip, leaving its passengers more briefly vulnerable to the perils of storm and sea. "Only a very small portion of mankind can ever travel abroad," wrote Silliman. But that portion was growing larger, thanks to safer, more comfortable Atlantic crossings, some of which took just six days.

Swifter crossings made briefer stays in Europe more possible. In 1854, a handbook for American travelers in Europe by an American college president—he dismissed Nice as "a town of no great note"—had observed that, although a year scarcely sufficed to see Europe, most travelers would "limit their tour to one season, of six or eight months." In 1877, however, Morford was endorsing much briefer trips. Even six *weeks* let you glimpse "a little fragment of the Old World," he wrote; you'd at least see London and Liverpool before rushing back across the Pond. Beyond four months, he conceded, "the phrase 'short trip' may be said to be exhausted," but that could get you to the Italian lakes and the south of France, including Nice. The cost? About fourteen hundred dollars.

Now, fourteen hundred dollars was quadruple what a common laborer in the United States made in a year, double that of a skilled worker. Still, those Morford called "that class of people standing midway" between lowly steerage passengers and the truly wealthy could manage it. Then and later, many grumbled that the hoi polloi were taking over Europe; in Paris, sometimes, the *arrivistes* were virtually shunned. But mostly, these American provincials managed to have a good time.

On June 8, 1867, thirty-three-year-old Mark Twain, not yet a celebrity author, boarded the paddle wheeler *Quaker City* in New York, for a six-month voyage across the Atlantic to Europe and the Holy Land; his sixty-five fellow passengers were almost all Americans, almost all virgin travelers. Twain's wry account, *The Innocents Abroad*, fairly skewered his sometimes rough-hewn and credulous traveling companions (as well as their *too*-well traveled counterparts, who "prate and drivel and lie" about their exploits abroad). In Marseilles, Twain left the *Quaker City* for a side trip to Paris, then rejoined it in Genoa, to which it had steamed directly, bypassing Nice; so posterity is deprived of anything he might have said about Nice or its visitors. On the other hand, Nice got plenty of the sort of novice travelers Twain poked fun at. Case in point: John Thomas Toof.

An Iowa-born preacher his friends knew as Thomas, Reverend Toof traveled to Europe in 1889, bound for the Holy Land with his mother, wife, and daughter. His first sight of the Mediterranean "filled my soul with unexpected pleasure," the pious gentleman wrote. "I feel like JERUSALEM, with CALVARY and MT. of OLIVES, and all the treasures of PALESTINE, are not so far away. God be merciful to me."

From Marseilles, Reverend Toof and his wife took the train for Nice, keeping the windows open the whole way: "Air so salubrious, could not get enough of it." The many tunnels through which they passed stirred in him a theological reverie: A tunnel *seemed* dark, you see, but wasn't; there was light at both ends. But the traveler, with his sadly imperfect vision, could not see it. Likewise, mankind, especially skeptics and atheists, plunged into darkness after the Fall. But "the light of truth," Toof noted hopefully, still shines on those "morally entunneled in our midst."

In Nice, Toof and his party made the usual tourist rounds. Like everyone else, he was struck by the sight of hundreds of washerwomen at work beside the bed of the river he called the Paraglione. "No [wash] board such as we use, and no tubs; only their hands, a board, some soap," and river water. He visited graves and historic places, strolled along the Promenade.

It was at the old town's domed seventeenth-century Sainte-Réparate Cathedral, whose inscriptions he recorded and where he made a charming little sketch of a bell, that Reverend Toof went astray. COUNCIL OF NICE, he wrote in the neat block print he sometimes used: he wouldn't be surprised if it was right here, in this very church, that the great Council was held. His landlord seemed to corroborate that Nice was its site, moving Toof to a number of "wholesome suggestions and meditations," which he duly set out in his journal.

Perhaps language miscues fed Toof's credulity. Or maybe the landlord was enjoying himself at the expense of the American minister, or else was himself confused. In 325 A.D., the Council of Nicaea established an orthodox belief system for the early church known today as the Nicene Creed. Nicaea, however, was not medieval Nice but, rather, lay in today's Turkey, a thousand miles east across the Mediterranean. Reverend Toof's blithe assertion—"NICENE CREED. Originated in and disseminated from Nice"—was nonsense.

Toof's wife made spiritually less of Nice than did her husband, but perhaps emotionally and sensually more. Roses were in bloom, as were daisies and buttercups, all heedless of the calendar; it was mid-January. Back home, she was sure, her friends were freezing. "Oh," she wrote after their drive along the Promenade, "this has been a grand day."

On January 8, 1890, Henrietta Maria Schroeder didn't have such a grand day. "I am *FURIOUS!!!!*" she confided in her diary. "I was never so angry in my life!!!" The whole page looked like that, slashed with underlinings and rows of angry exclamation points like the raised pikes of a Roman legion. The opening page of her European journal warned it was Strictly Private Property—and then, as if that were not enough, "Nobody on the face of this earth has any right to read this book without my permission, except my best and most beloved friend, Caroline Bowen Wetherill." Miss Schroeder, a fair, thin-featured Boston girl on the cusp of womanhood, was fourteen years old.

After two months in Paris, where they'd scarcely seen the sun, she and her family caught a train from Gare de Lyon to Marseilles from which, one morning a few days later, they started for Nice. The scenery moved her the way it did everyone else. She wrote of the

> rough, wild rocks, with here and there a tiny inlet with some strong fort or noble castle on it, and the water dotted with beautiful lateen sails, the *bright* blue sky with a tiny woolly cloud sailing in it, the warm, warm, sun, and the warm breeze gently stirring the palm leaves, the waves quietly smashing on the rocks below—oh! it is perfect Paradise!

They ate dinner at the Grand Hôtel. They walked along the Promenade des Anglais—so called, she wrote, "because English and Americans are always to be seen promenading" there. They climbed the Château Hill, marveled at the view, then headed for Monte Carlo.

And it was there, the day after their arrival in the tiny principality, that Miss Schroeder's adolescent angst erupted. "Well! I never! Of all the blankety blanked blanks I never heard of, this is the *worst.*" And do you know what provoked her outrage? Miss Henrietta Maria Schroeder of Boston had been denied entry to the gaming rooms of the Monte Carlo casino. "*Me, me,* the aged *me,* too young to go into a casino!!!!!!!!!!!! Oh! I tell you what, you just wait till I grow up! Won't I be a terror though!!"

For all his sniping at Americans of whose hopeless provincialism he was so avid a student, Mark Twain saw virtue in their travels. "Travel is fatal to prejudice, bigotry, and narrowmindedness," he wrote in a pensive moment near the end of *The Innocents Abroad,* "and many of our people need it sorely on these accounts."

Margaret Fuller, literary critic of Horace Greeley's *New York Tribune,* had back in the 1840s conceived an early typology of American travelers.

Of her three types, one was the thinking American—with whom, we may suppose, she and her readers were supposed to identify. This enlightened species learned all he could from the Old World, took home all that might take root in American soil, and returned home freed of "baseless notions and crude fancies."

But Fuller had to acknowledge, too, those Americans of coarser sensibilities. There was, for example,

> the servile American—a being utterly shallow, thoughtless, worthless. He comes abroad to spend his money and indulge his tastes. His object in Europe is to have fashionable clothes, good foreign cookery, to know some titled persons, and furnish himself with coffee-house gossip.

Then there was the conceited American, who saw nothing of worth in Europe, for whom all was stupid, silly, or revolting. His big, raw backcountry hands fit only for steam engines, "he seizes the old Cremona violin, makes it shriek with anguish in his grasp, and then declares he thought it was all humbug before he came, and now he knows it."

∞

Veteran travelers might be forgiven their distaste for such bumptious creatures, as well as for others of humble caste that cheap travel unloosed on Europe. For Nice regulars, the town could seem anonymous now, less exclusive. As one historian would have it, visitors had grown "too numerous to know one another and to mingle comfortably. Nice had become a great city . . . a little Paris from which intimacy had disappeared."

Some among the *nouveau-riche* crowd in Nice were just plain unsavory. "The character of visitors and winter guests in Nice has considerably changed," griped one German, a Herr von Helle-Wartegg, in 1883. Good families no longer felt at ease in Nice. It had become "infested with a swarm of fashionable idlers, Bohemians and ladies of questionable reputation . . . camp followers for the wandering European aristocracy."

For Henry de Montaut, the modern sleeping car best embodied the loss. Once, if you were getting to Nice by train, it was in a sumptuous *coupe-lit*—just the two of you on a plush sofa where you could sleep as snugly as in your bed, and where you need never fear an intrusive porter shouting, "*Vos billets, s'il vous plaît*," Tickets, please. But since 1875, reaching the Riviera normally meant a sleeping car—de Montaut used the English term—with its skinny corridor and gaudy wood compartment, where you had to rub up against who-knows-whom. It reminded him of nothing so much as "a traveling menagerie, containing various species of wild animals."

You didn't need to be an out-and-out snob to be troubled by the changing face of the Riviera. In a talk he gave a few years after de Montaut's book came out, J. C. Harris, the British consul, who'd practically adopted Nice as his own, described with scorn and sorrow what he saw going on around him. His talk appeared as a pamphlet in 1884, a time when Nice stood near, or so it might seem later, its touristic zenith. His title? "Nice's Decline as a Winter Resort."

Sounding like a physician diagnosing a patient's illness, Harris asserted that the quality of visitors to Nice had declined over the past fifteen years—that is, since the coming of the railroad. Once, "you'd recognize many well-known people. Nice was Europe's center of fashion and celebrity." Its well-bred visitors lived with simplicity and grace. They picnicked, took day trips into the countryside, reveled in the fine art of conversation.

Now all that had changed. Many of the old-style visitors went to Cannes instead. And those still loyal to Nice didn't even stay long enough to rent a villa for the season. When they came, it was for the races, or regattas; once these were over, they left. "They stay for just a few weeks at the vast, mostly over-priced American-style hotels which have appeared suddenly among us."

For some of the new visitors, Harris could not entirely hide his contempt: "I do not want to say, thank God, that there are not still many respectable people in Nice; but it is also true that you see here quite a number of captains of industry, people of both sexes of more or less blemished reputation, people who affect titles to which they have no right, hiding their true, sad selves" from public view.

Part of the problem was neighboring Monaco, with its gambling; many drawn to it stayed in Nice, the nearest big city, bringing with them too much money, too many women, too base a character. Prosperity? Yes, but it was a tainted prosperity. Ask any hotelkeeper, any shopowner, wrote Harris, and he'd tell you how each year he faced more losses from visitors who simply walked away from their bills.

A magazine much read in London, he went on, had pointed out that Nice was building up so fast that the once-rustic lanes that lent it such charm were disappearing forever. Replacing them were broad, dusty avenues flanked by houses that were but a pale, provincial imitation of Paris.

To listen to Harris, even Nice's vaunted climate was at risk: those broad new streets, when they ran north-south, served as channels for cold mountain winds like those that had pummeled the city so mercilessly the previous December. "Does it pay Nice," he asked, "to sacrifice part of its climate for the sake of being a big city?"

Harris's solution was to develop Cimiez according to English tastes. Give it a post office and a telegraph, an Anglican chapel. Insulate it from the dirt of town and the mix of people encountered there. Recreate up on the Cimiez hill, in short, the countrified Nice of old. Do that, and the British would return. These days, the architects and city planners were making right angles of everything, extending the city into the countryside and destroying "the true country that every Englishman seeks above all."

They were turning little Nice into a big noisy city, and this Englishman, for one, hated to see it happen.

NICE WAS BOOMING DURING THESE YEARS, OF COURSE, AND MR. Harris's concerns might seem unduly peevish. The decades before 1914 were prosperous ones, with Nice in fullest flower as a tourist mecca— a magic moment in the life of the Season, when the city was all it ever had been, and all it ever would be, only better.

One of its visitors was Victoria, Queen of England, Empress of India, who came to Cimiez each year, for five years, near the end of her life. The first time was in 1895, when she stayed at the newly built Grand Hôtel de Cimiez. Later, she favored the Excelsior Regina, across the street from the Roman arena, its great white frontage looming over Nice from high atop the Cimiez hill, tropical gardens gracing its entrance, flags flying from its turrets.

The queen, by one account, always "showed childish excitement at the thought of exchanging Windsor for the Mediterranean. On arrival she behaved more like a girl of seventeen than a Sovereign in her seventies." She liked nothing better than to have her carriage hitched to two white horses and be driven out into the country; the locals would line the route, hoping for some of the coins that, in a little ceremony at each stop, she'd dispense. She'd visit local festivals, enjoy their rustic stalls and throngs of visitors. She'd be driven across the grounds of local villas, along garden paths shaded by eucalyptus and olive trees. Once, she was taken down to the Promenade des Anglais, for a parade of French troops. Another time, on a fine spring day in 1898, she went up the *corniche* road, past the Observatory. As she described it later in her diary,

EXCELSIOR HOTEL REGINA

NICE-CIMIEZ

the view was "marvellous, on the one side the snow-clad Alps and on the other the sea"—a royal insight indistinguishable from those of the common herd of Riviera journal-keepers. On her final visit, in 1899, two years before her death, she was driven down the coast to Beaulieu. It was, she sensed, her last outing "in this paradise of nature. . . . I shall mind returning to the sunless north, but I am so grateful for all I have enjoyed here."

At a time when gardeners made three or four francs a day, and a woman at a Grasse perfume factory one, the queen's two months in Nice depleted the royal coffers of eighty thousand francs. She would leave England aboard the royal yacht *Victoria and Albert*, escorted by torpedo boats, royal bed included in the royal baggage. Her private rail car, which each season brought her to the Mediterranean, its walls lined with silk padding, was furnished with Louis XVI sofa and chairs covered in blue silk. Her personal staff numbered sixty, and included servants, dressers, and a French chef.

Each year, just before her return to England, she would bestow gifts and royal honors on those who'd served her; one hotel manager was peeved that he got only a bust of the queen, not an official honor whose initials following his name would redound to the prestige of his hotel; visits of royalty *mattered* to the Riviera tourist industry. An 1896 guidebook listed no fewer than twenty-three sovereigns who'd visited Nice since the Crimean War. Those of Sweden, Norway, Denmark, Holland, and Portugal were among them. So was Leopold II of Belgium, who bought a vast estate on Cap Ferrat, the spit of land on the other side of Villefranche from Nice.

Nice newspapers heralded the arrival of kings and princes. Local authorities fussed over them. And why not? They lent to Nice a luster that could not be bought at any price. And they bore just those trappings of untrammeled wealth that marked the age.

∞

These were the years when Nice luxuriated in civic self-confidence, flaunted its excesses, snuggled up to decadence. These were the years when Nice and its neighbors along the coast together became "La Côte d'Azur"—courtesy of a minor poet named Stephen Liégeard.

Liégeard's 1887 book of that name was dedicated to, and addressed to, Xavier Marmier, an aging member of the Académie Française who lived in Paris, and suffered its cold winters. Soon "the dark season comes," the author warns Marmier. Might his dear master wish to accompany him "to the coast of light, of gentle breezes, of mysterious and perfumed woods"?

"To the Orient?" comes the imagined reply.

No, and not Italy, either, exactly, but rather the Mediterranean coast from Hyères to Genoa.

Gradually, seductively, indulging in flights of lyricism and inflated rhetoric, Liégeard leads Marmier on their imagined voyage. "Come! We will say adieu to the mists of the Seine." They will leave behind sadness, and cowardice, and the insanity of politics. They will explore. They will visit Marmier's friends and fellow eminences along the way.

"Oh, tempter . . . !" Marmier interjects at last. He is bewitched by the idea, yes. But at his age "one lives on memories, and these memories are better for the soul than the most vivid realities. . . . Leave me to my old house on this small square, to my gutter on the rue du Bac." He cannot go, but Liégeard, with his blessing, should go—and return to write of all he has seen. "In so doing, you will have served your reader and earned my friendship."

And so Liégeard sets out on his trip, and his book. "I have studied sea and sun," he concludes his book's introduction. "I have interviewed men and stones. I have listened to the breath of the wind and the murmur of the tide." Marmier could not accompany him? Well, then, he tells his readers, let us set out on this voyage, this book, together. "Let us taunt the returning winter. Our ship's deck is strewn with flowers, the sail is full. . . . Let us sail along this *Côte d'Azur*."

Some have speculated that the Côte d'Or of his native Burgundy gave Liégeard the idea for the name. Or else the Côte de l'Argent, near Biarritz. In any case, the name stuck. Today, Americans mostly refer to Nice and environs as "the Riviera." The French call it "La Côte d'Azur."

It was probably a few years before Liégeard's book appeared that an anonymous artist took a boat out into the Baie des Anges, dropped anchor a little ways offshore, and from there sketched a panorama of the Nice seafront; or so the final illustration gives us to think. From out in the bay, looking in toward shore, we see a magnificent wall of hotels lined up shoulder to shoulder along the seafront. First, the five-story frontage of the Hôtel Victoria, which became today's West End; then, marching west to east, a whole succession of pensions, villas, and hotels, including the Méditerranée, the Hôtel des Anglais, the Hôtel d'Angleterre, the Hôtel de la Grande Bretagne; set back a little from the sea, along the Paillon, the Hôtel de France. This was Nice circa 1880.

In the twenty years or so after the arrival of the railroad, Nice's wealthiest visitors still mostly stayed at their own parklike villas—more like châteaux, really—surrounded by acres of lush plantings. Like Villa

Diesbach on the Promenade des Anglais. Or Villa Acquaviva, also on the Promenade des Anglais, where Marie Bashkirtseff stayed with her family. Or the steeply mansard-roofed Villa Valrose, completed in 1870 by the builder of the Russian railroad system, Baron Paul Derwies. Valrose had a five-hundred-seat theater that made it Nice's musical hub for a decade. Its magnificent park was filled with palm trees and rosebushes, statues, grottoes, and waterfalls. It had taken the labor of eight hundred men three years to build it. You didn't erect a place like that unless you planned to come back again and again, for most of each winter.

But the railroad technology that supplied Baron Derwies his fortune reshaped the very rhythms of Riviera vacationing. At a time when the total number of visitors to Nice was perhaps a million a year, someone determined that those passing the winter there numbered just thirteen thousand French, six thousand English, twenty-five hundred Russians, and a like number of Americans. The discrepancy lay in a definition of "passing the winter" that counted only those staying at least two months. It was just such season-long stays that the railroad was making passé. When it still took two weeks to get to Nice, you weren't about to go for just a few days; with the trip taking two days, you very well might. The railroad, in short, left travelers more apt to make the trip—*but,* on average, more apt to make it a short one.

Too short, typically, to justify renting a place for the season. Replacing the villa as lodging of choice was, especially after 1880, the great hotel "palace." More visitors, many of them wealthy, but each staying briefly? The solution, during this age of machine-as-metaphor, was a factory of opulence—one that treated guests, one after another, in turn, to all the comforts of their own villas. The era was capped by the opening in November 1912 of the fabulous Negresco, with its great oval ballroom, the product of a Romanian Gypsy chef's untrammeled fantasy. Today any mid-range hotel offers what once was billed as "every modern comfort"; but back then a telephone in every room, central heating, and private bath represented real luxury. Modern technology was helping to coddle tourists.

Late in the century, Cimiez became the new node for fashionable hotels. After 1881, the old Cimiez road had been joined by a wide, new boulevard de Cimiez that barreled straight up the hill, and opened it up to development. To Cimiez's two hotels in 1884 were soon added the Riviera Palace, which began four-times-a-day carriage service down the hill to Place Masséna and the seafront. Then came the Excelsior Regina, whose inaugural season Queen Victoria graced in 1897. And the Alhambra, the Winter Palace, and others. They were grand and glorious and, like dinosaurs, would mostly not survive beyond the brief window in time during which they flourished.

The Belle Époque, they called it later, referring to the three or four decades preceding the Great War. Looking back from across that bloody divide, Europe could seem like an Eden of well-born people living beautiful lives. In Nice, the high-living heart of it, along with the Promenade des Anglais, was the avenue de la Gare. This broad swathe of boulevard—it began at Place Masséna and shot straight out from the Paillon toward a point just east of the train station—was lined with music halls, brasseries, restaurants, and cafés, thick with lively crowds at every hour. London House, a few steps off the avenue, aswarm with gloved and monocled dandies for lunch. Garden House, dear to the gourmets. Maison Dorée for late-night revelers.

The era lives today in its *affiches*, or publicity posters—today collector's items or, in cheap reproductions, the staple of college-dorm rooms—which first served the railroads, later hotels, festivals, towns, and whole regions. One, from about 1910, promotes a musical revue: It is night. Stocky, boutonniered gentleman, indecent smile plastered across his face, out on the town. Slim, sex-proud woman in flowing, feathered hat, bare arms, shoulders, and breasts bathed in the nighttime glow. With an inviting wave of the arm, she gestures toward the luminous Jetée-Promenade, site for the evening's revelry. The legend, in English, draped across her fringed dress: "VERY NICE."

Propelled by new printing technology, the *affiches* constituted a new art form. And almost from the start, they helped to sell the region, touting visions of exquisite countryside, sparkling skies, exotic vegetation, and beautiful women. One poster, from 1907, shows a Niçoise in native dress, red-striped skirts and *capeline*, one arm cradling a basket of flowers, the other planted appealingly on her hip. She stands astride a

topographic map of the region that shows the route of the Paris-Lyon-Méditerranée railway: the Côte d'Azur, the name emblazoned across the top, just thirteen hours from Paris.

These were the Riviera's glory days, the gold standard against which all subsequent eras would be measured: here was how tourism *ought* to be. Nice, queen city of the Riviera, was not merely established; she was in her magnificent prime. Elegant, cosmopolitan, and mature, she was no longer that saucy little thing of the 1840s or 1850s, her natural charms the sole source of her allure; now she complemented her good looks with jewels, ornament, and artistry.

Of course, viewed in quite another way, she could seem, well, *put to-gether*—like a slightly older woman, dependent now on makeup and finery, a bit *past* her prime.

⊗

When you remember a rose in fullest flower, when you recall its velvety softness, its fragrance reaching up to your nostrils, drowning them in dizzying aroma, you are thinking of it just before it fades, and as it never will be again.

Nice, during the Belle Époque, was probably the fastest-growing city in Europe. During the twenty-four-year period that ended in 1872, the city's resident population rose from thirty-seven to fifty-two thousand; that was respectable enough. But by 1886, the figure had shot up to seventy-four thousand. By 1901, to 105,000, and by 1906, to 134,000; in five years, it grew faster than much larger Marseilles, and added to its population half as many people as did Paris, which was twenty times its size. A local booster might laud such figures, along with the evidence of its new hotels and bustling *gare*, as proof of Nice's health. And yet they were symptoms of malaise, too; its very growth left Nice less appealing. Stumble upon the right bits of evidence and you might think that J. C. Harris, that curmudgeonly naysayer of 1884, was on to something. . . .

In February 1896, a Chicago woman, Adelaide Hall, who twitted herself as "an old maid . . . a bit nervous, cranky, and very ambitious," wrote to her sister Jane. Did she remember how, as children together, they'd dreamed of traveling to Europe? Well, in a few weeks she and a friend would board the *Kaiser Wilhelm* in New York, and do just that.

At the dock early the following month, she and her friend found the ship "throbbing and straining at the cables which bound her to land." In their stateroom they were greeted by fragrant bouquets of roses, lilies, and carnations, by letters and telegrams wishing them *bon voyage.* Soon the signal was given for visitors to return ashore, lovers embraced for the last time, handkerchiefs fluttered in farewell, and they were under way.

Once they'd landed in Italy, a train bore them east toward the Riviera, inspiring in Hall the usual rhapsodies: "The rocky arms of the coast reach out into the deep purple of the sea, embracing stretches of sandy beach as clean and inviting as the finest of marble baths. . . ." Then they arrived in Nice. Later, she'd describe its hotels and broad boulevards, their drive along avenues "shaded by plane trees and bark-shedding eucalyptus." She'd tell of day trips to the hilltop-perched town of Èze, and their adventures at the Café de Paris in Monaco. But Nice itself? It left her cold. "We were disappointed," she declared, "to find Nice so much like a modern city, and lacking the wilder beauty of the smaller towns to the east."

Nice—*Nice la belle!*—had failed to seduce.

In 1898, a writer noted how, forty years before, Nice, Villefranche, and Menton were "little old Italian towns," a trip east from Nice offering fine views, picturesque little ports, local color. Now, though, "from the Esterel to San Remo all that has been ruined by barbarous hordes from the north, who build on each promontory and in every bay American hotels and Parisian boulevards." The railroad had destroyed coastal vistas, brought in its wake "thousands of unsightly hotels, high walls, pompous villas, and big Paris-style streets, which annihilate all trace of the past."

Nice's once-enchanting mix of city and country was being ravaged. "Few of the dear old mysterious Italian gardens of the past still survive in Nice; the land is too valuable, and bricks and mortar more remunerative than peaceful walls and wild unrestrained flower-beds," wrote one observer in 1912. The old St. Augustine Church where Martin Luther preached and Masséna was baptized? Torn down. So were quaint old inns like the Chapeau Rouge, where cardinals may once have stayed.

The German philosopher Friedrich Nietzsche had no use for the new Nice, either. He preferred its old town, the Italian section, making him a harbinger of tastes that would not take hold until the next century. He did return regularly to Nice, living on next to nothing, working on *Thus Spake Zarathustra*. But he reviled much of what he saw: "I cannot stand the French part of Nice," he wrote. "It constitutes a stain on all the splendor of the south." It was tasteless and too polished.

From his earliest visits, part of the Englishman's delight in Nice, recall, was that it was *not* Nice, but Italian Nizza. And it was this Italianness—or the rusticity imputed to it— that now was fading. Passing through the Riviera in 1775, Johann Georg Sulzer had observed, "National characteristics must be studied only in the country, where the inhabitants follow without embarrassment Nature's ways. In the big cities, men are all about the same, and education makes all of Europe in some sense a single nation." Well, Nice had become one of those big European cities, its Niçois spark dimming. An 1895 photograph shows the domed pleasure palace that was the Jetée-Promenade sitting low over the water near where the Paillon spilled into the sea. In the foreground, sunk into the pebbly beach, stood rows of ramshackle wood-and-string contrivances, drying laundry draped over them. The caption, in a book throwing a backward glance at the era: "Meeting point for two civilizations." One of them was dying.

Some visitors tried to hold on to what was passing away before them. You can see this on almost every page of Mary Tothill's *Pen & Pencil Notes on the Riviera and in North Italy*, which appeared in 1880, a book of deft drawings each annotated with a brief caption. Laid out half a dozen of them to the page, it has some of the lightness and charm of a modern comic book.

In the first frame we see the four travelers, three women and a man—the family relationships are unclear—in an English drawing room: "A family conclave. We must go somewhere—but where?" reads the legend.

In the next, two of the women pore over books: "The Riviera is decided on and the latest editions of 'Murray' procured and studied."

Then it's the Channel crossing, Paris, the Louvre, a sketch of "Parisian bakers discussing the morning's news," a chilly night on the train, the Rhône, and, finally, after Avignon, "first sight of the Mediterranean." Then the Esterels, Cannes, Nice, and Menton.

What draws Mary Tothill's eye are the rural scenes, the local peasantry, the beguiling breach between the big city London they know and an indigenous Riviera life fast disappearing.

Here are "agricultural laborers," in their *capelines.*

A barefoot girl in a skimpy little dress proffers flowers: *"Voulez-vous des fleurs Mademoiselle?"*

A "good-tempered merry Italian" sells them souvenirs of Cannes.

In one drawing, a peasant woman, babe in arms, turns back to glimpse two of Miss Tothill's party sketching by the side of a trail. "What," she's made to think, "can they be doing?"

Though she took time to sketch its Promenade des Anglais—the sweeping arc of beach dotted by walkers, the ubiquitous palm trees— Mary Tothill and her party probably spent little time in Nice itself. The Riviera that drew her was not that of Nice, but the surrounding countryside. It was as if her trip constituted a last chance to "study" it, capture it on paper, before it faded away forever.

∞

It is but slight exaggeration to say that, by century's end, there was no room in Nice for anything *but* tourism. It was as if a single biological species had first colonized, then taken over an island ecosystem. This spelled trouble; island ecosystems are notoriously fragile, being vulnerable to disease and other environmental insults. Tourism, too, is fragile; travelers are a fickle lot, little tolerating threats to their safety, comfort, or pleasure.

All it took to disenchant one Massachusetts woman was a single spell of bad weather. Eliza Homans had arrived in Marseilles after stops in Avignon and Arles, finally reaching Nice on a day when, meteorologically speaking, everything went wrong. "A raw, damp chilly morning ripened into a hot uncomfortable noon, and died in a raw, damp, chilly evening." That, in 1875, was enough to sour her on Nice. "Nice *ain't* one bit what I thought." She'd read all she was going to read about blue water, orange groves, olive trees, and palms; up close, Nice had let her down. "Nothing," she concluded, "I want to see again." And in many subsequent trips to Europe, she never did.

Nice's prosperity had always been a brittle and precarious one, and still was. Following the big winter season of 1862–63, local proprietors too eagerly hiked their prices; the following year, tourists stayed away, and the season was a disaster. A smallpox scare in Nice sent tourists packing in 1879. Cholera did the same in 1884. And early one morning in February 1887, just hours after the end of Carnaval, an earthquake rattled the Riviera. Buildings crackled and creaked like coffee grinders. Inkwells danced across tables. Thousands, half dressed and frightened, fled into the streets. That "will give the coup de grâce to the Season," wrote Friedrich Nietzsche, staying in Nice at the time. And it did. Just five people died, but the earthquake emptied hotels up and down the Riviera.

In 1861, before the railroad, Nice counted nine winter visitors for every hundred permanent residents; twenty years later, the figure was fifty. Nice had become a town where every business decision, every act of government, turned on whether or not it was good for tourism. The needs of the visitors diffused like a gas—was it noxious? benign?—all through the city.

Many scholars have studied this diffusion. One, Nicola Mallet, wrote how, despite incessant demands by the locals, the Paillon was channeled underground only in 1883. Why? Because that "receptacle of putrefaction, [that] oven of pestilence," as a local paper called it, was odious only in summer. In winter, when the *hivernants* were around, it flowed through town freely, clearing out its bed, cleaning away the refuse of the previous summer. In other words, since it didn't much bother the tourists, it didn't need to be fixed right away.

An American, Charles Haug, found that the city's tourist economy warped its whole social fabric, leaving it more stratified between the tourist districts on the far side of the Paillon and the old town. Once, the *vieille ville* had been more diverse, home to every occupational grouping, including business and professional people. But during the forty years of fevered growth ending with the Great War, the new *hivernant* quarters drew off Nice's most favored classes, leaving the old town a working-class ghetto.

As the century neared its end, lengthening shadows darkened Nice's sunlit façade. Promoted as an oasis of leisure and loveliness, Nice had surprisingly little public green space. It was inundated by professional beggars each winter. Its native inhabitants, four in ten of them, were abysmally housed.

Jean Lorrain, a French poet and playwright, saw the Riviera as a madhouse, one a little like the corrupt Berlin re-created in *Cabaret*. "All the crazy people of the world, all the lunatics and hysterics, meet here." From Russia and America they came, from Tibet and South Africa— emperors' former mistresses, croupiers married to Yankee millionaires, deposed and reigning kings. "The Riviera," he wrote, is their

> undeserved fatherland; nowhere else will you meet such a collection of young hundred-year-olds and ornamented ostriches. . . . Some evenings at the Nice Opera there are intermissions where the room seems macabre with the weight of centuries in the crowded loges. You'd think the cemeteries weren't closed at night and that the corpses had all escaped.

Nice's glitter masked ugliness and corruption that were physical, social, and moral all at once.

Even the palms that lined the Promenade des Anglais bore a breath of falsehood and unreality; like much other Riviera vegetation, they were not native. *Phoenix canariensis*, the Canary Islands palm tree, was introduced to the Riviera only in the nineteenth century. Soon its showy fronds and proud, scaly trunks became a fixture of every wealthy *hivernant*'s garden. By late in the century, it was being planted up and down the avenues, squares, and parks of Nice and other Riviera towns and had become as ubiquitous as pretty girls in Riviera tourist posters. As one student of the subject, Daniel Gade, has noted, the municipal authorities sought strains apt to survive occasional killing frosts—and to produce the lush, persistent, year-round foliage that *meant* mild winters, cried out Tropical Paradise.

In fact, wrote Robert de Souza in 1913, the palm tree never quite belonged on the Riviera. It was "only decor, and false decor at that."

∞

Thirty years after J. C. Harris warned of the "decline of Nice as a winter resort," de Souza, one of the most ardent critics of the new Nice, took up kindred themes in *Nice: Capitale d'hiver,* winter capital. Today, his 518-page tome might be seen as an environmental treatise. Rabid development ruled by narrow interests and heedless of history and beauty, he wrote in the preface, had left cities across Europe "spoiled, trampled, massacred." Nice—more than Paris, more than Rome—offered "the most lamentable and significant example."

Take the city's gargantuan hotels. Products of a virtually unregulated industry, many were grossly out of scale with their surroundings, monopolizing sun and views for themselves; locals, and many visitors, too, were relegated to what amounted to *"maison-casernes,"* barracks houses. Everywhere, nature had been despoiled. The lovely many-acred estates that adorned the *collines* above the city were being broken up. The natural grace of Nice and its verdant surroundings was being destroyed.

Nice had about 180 hotels, ten thousand rooms—a growth of onethird in ten years. But at least by de Souza's stern gauge, only four ranked as top-notch, offering American and British amenities like private bath, flush toilet, and full electric lighting. Despite charging higher prices than those in Switzerland and Italy, the average Nice hotel failed to offer what some ordinary workers in Britain and America enjoyed in their own homes. Nice's hotels were living off the past, maintenance and restoration going ignored. The great Hôtel Excelsior Regina, where Victoria stayed? Yes, it offered a memorable façade—at least from the south. But from the north, the side you didn't normally see, it was raw and unfinished.

For some years, de Souza wrote a column for the local newspaper, *L'Éclaireur,* the bully pulpit for his aesthetic and environmental ideas.

Fond of the old Sardinian city planners, the Consiglio d'Ornato, he was horrified by the rampant, speculation-fed building he saw reducing Nice to an unlovely barracks of a place. Why, just look at the Municipal Casino, on Place Masséna; it ought to be instantly razed.

De Souza felt that the casinos actually harmed tourism: they stripped visitors of their purses before they'd gotten a chance to see anything but the Jetée-Promenade or the other casinos, sent them packing prematurely. "So here you are on the Riviera!" he remembered greeting one friend.

"Yes, I'm heading back this evening."

"Already? How long have you been here?"

"Three days."

"You go two thousand kilometers in order to stay three days?"

"What can I tell you? I planned to stay two weeks, hoping the four thousand francs I'd set aside for the trip would be enough. . . . Well, I stopped with my wife at the Jetée, and we went in. Bad luck. Then, in the afternoon, at the casino, we figured to catch up. More bad luck. So all we can do now is head back."

De Souza wrote with anger, a sense of foreboding and deep loss, but also with love. Cimiez and its Roman remains awakened in him particularly strong feeling. When he was a child, he wrote in an untypical aside, "breaking up clumps of red soil would deliver, like old forgotten piggybanks, handfuls of coins." Now Cimiez, too, was being ruined. Forty or fifty years before—that is, before the railroad—wealthy *hivernants* had created magnificent enclaves up there. Their heirs, though, had to look at "the hideous buildings that surround their gardens and that have saddened the final years of many an old man."

For tourists themselves, de Souza felt disdain; members of their species, he complained in one of his *Éclaireur* articles, would not, back home, "take two steps in their spare time to visit some [local] monument. Aesthetic exaltation is not to them a daily felt need. Travel to them is more distraction than emotion. Any artistic beauty they discover remains for them a simple 'curiosity.'" In other words, tourist as philistine.

De Souza was not, however, so far above the common herd that he rejected tourism outright, or failed to see value in it. If you wanted to keep the tourists coming, he was saying, keep Nice beautiful and control its growth; otherwise, its very success, unchanneled and out of control, would kill it.

Blinded by the annual influx of foreigners, the thin-skinned Niçois couldn't admit their fair city had problems. They placed constructive criticism in the same camp as vicious attacks by rival tourist interests. To listen to de Souza, they couldn't see what was going on before their eyes. They appreciated neither the region's natural beauty, nor the economic value it represented. Why, La Côte was desecrating itself with advertising posters. And who were the worst offenders? The casinos and hotels who had most to gain from keeping the Riviera beautiful!

Nice, de Souza as much as said, had little going for it but its natural beauty and its climate. And each year, it faced new competition. Opatija, on the Adriatic. Merano, in the Tyrol. Pau, in the Pyrenees. Winter sports, encouraged by the automobile—the *automobile*, at last the automobile!—represented an unexpected new development. Alpine resorts were recording explosive growth at the Riviera's expense. When, a few years before, Côte d'Azur *hôteliers* went, name by name, through lists of visitors to a Swiss tourist area, seven in ten were known to them as former customers.

The cover of de Souza's opus carried the Nice coat of arms— proud eagle, feet planted on two shores—beneath the bold blue letters of the book's title. One didn't need to agree with his diagnosis in every respect to appreciate that he was fighting the good fight. That he'd unleashed his indignation in the service of a place he loved.

But de Souza's concerns were aesthetic and environmental. He did not see the darker clouds. *Nice: Capitale d'hiver* appeared in 1913. The following year, in August, the first guns roared, armies clashed, and every dream for Nice, all hope in Europe, was stomped down into the blood-soaked mud of the Great War.

THE TENSE MONTHS OF THREATS AND ULTIMATUMS PRECEDING THE outbreak of the war had left all Europe on edge. So, when the mobilization orders finally came, some greeted them with relief. The boys would be home by Christmas, you could hear it said in England, but four Christmases would pass before the killing stopped. Nothing in the history of warfare had prepared Europe for the devastation wrought by machine guns, poison gas, tanks, and artillery. The first August battles involved two million men. Before the year was out, France had suffered almost four hundred thousand battle deaths.

The fighting was six hundred miles away, but touched Nice almost from the start. The city's hotels, so comfortably distant from the front, were pressed into service as hospitals; eighteen of them were requisitioned by year's end, twenty-seven by early the following year. By the end of September, just two months into the war, Nice harbored forty-five hundred wounded soldiers, and was already overtaxed. The authorities had initially asked the Alhambra, one of Cimiez's hotel palaces, to make 25 beds available; then 50, 115, finally 250. Convoys of sick and wounded were taken to the Casino de la Jetée-Promenade, the city's icon of *hivernant* good life, now christened Depot of the Wounded. In Nice, clean sheets grew scarce.

It was not only wounded soldiers who descended on Nice, but refugees from shattered villages in northern France and Belgium left homeless by the war; the first convoy arrived on September 11. By the end of the month, four hundred refugees had arrived; by the end of

October, more than two thousand. Most had lost everything, came with only their clothes and a few bags. Twice a day, groups of them went down to the basement of the Municipal Casino to be fed. Some, surveying this Riviera paradise miraculously untouched by war, could not hold down their bitterness. "Here," they'd say, "you would doubt there's a war at all." They complained of unfamiliar southern food, scant coffee and wine, the ill-will of the locals. Yet many were staying at hotels, perhaps in beds, that not long before had borne the coddled bodies of wealthy tourists.

At first, simple patriotism, and the grim sight of refugees and crippled soldiers, evoked only sympathy; indeed, some *hôteliers* didn't wait to be asked and actually volunteered their facilities. But whereas the soldiers were immune from criticism, the refugees came to be seen as lazy, dirty, and demanding. One group of them, put up at a Cannes hotel, had refused to help in the kitchen, or so the story got around. And for the sake of these ingrates the region's tourist industry should suffer?

So new voices began to be heard over the patriotic din. Maybe, some hotel owners suggested, theaters, skating rinks, or garages could be used to shelter war victims, not just hotels. That idea didn't get far, but it was a start. Why had mostly the city's *best* hotels been requisitioned? the hotel association complained to the Chamber of Commerce early in 1915. Why not "find more modest places, though just as suitable, which would satisfy the same goals but cost the state less"? Nice's hotels were being put to a use for which they'd never been intended. They weren't being kept up. Furniture from one hotel would wind up, willy-nilly, in another. Hotel rooms and corridors smelled like the hospitals they'd become. Owners had received no account of what they might be due in recompense.

German and Austrian visitors, of course, had vanished. The Russians couldn't get money out of their country. Would-be visitors from neutral countries were understandably reluctant to seek repose in a nation at war, however distant the fighting was supposed to be. With its swarms of ragged refugees and bandaged soldiers, Nice could present a mournful sight. Meanwhile, Spanish and Italian resorts reminded anyone who'd listen that *their* countries were at peace, *their* casinos open. Come for

"Winter in San Sebastián," one magazine advertisement urged; the Bay of Biscay resort offered a "delightful and healthful climate, a most pleasant stay."

Though the Nice tourist industry was not about to capitulate, advancing its interests was rhetorically delicate: Business-as-usual while France bled? Shamelessly lure fat-pursed foreigners to the Riviera sun even as French soldiers shivered in trenches up north? Impossible. If there was to be a "Season" in Nice, a French officer wrote in to the paper, let it be "A Season of the Wounded," the city's doors opened wide to them. Early in the war, some campaigned for reopening the sidewalk cafés. Never, replied Nice's military governor: "While our brave officers and men are killed heroically on the field of battle, a parade of idle rich . . . in the city's sidewalk cafés would constitute an intolerable indecency. Let us speak no more of it." That's what proponents of tourism were up against.

Yet, even early in the war, they found ways to make their case. No one, said a city official, sought a true Season in Nice; but to maintain an island of repose for war-ravaged Europe—that was something else again, and, he implied, entirely honorable. The city's largest daily, L'Éclaireur, noted that, though Nice must avoid noisy, festive amusements, it might embrace those appropriate to wartime, such as classic tragedies. Rousing Nice from its economic doldrums was not just necessary but "a patriotic duty," since tourist revenue supported charities, paid taxes, protected the property of the combatants.

One Nice official wrote how it was necessary "to combat discouragement in the economic realm." A healthy tourist industry would help "sustain the terrible struggle in which our country is engaged."

"Nice doit vivre," the city's other major paper, Le Petit Niçois, declared: Nice must live. "Faithful to its traditions, Nice must receive its guests with a smile of welcome. Nice must attract, and keep, all its old friends and clients. Nice must summon up all its customary seductiveness and charm." Indeed, the city's noble work would be a kind of "prayer," yes, a prayer that, reaching high into Nice's boundless blue heaven, would promote the success of French arms.

Always that thin line. Always the grim-faced nod to the war, the patriotic sentiments. But always, too, the economic realities: "To open our hotels and receive our winter guests," declared a city official, "is not to blunt the painful anxiety which grips us. It is simply to affirm our unswerving confidence in the future."

High-sounding rhetoric that masked raw avarice? Perhaps not entirely. In fact, there was only so much the war-weary could bear. Ultimately, the natural human need for respite—from grim war news, from austerity, from unending calls for national sacrifice—needed answering. Ultimately, writes an historian of the period, Ralph Schor, "the thirst for pleasure grew."

Attempts were made to reclaim the Season; the regional hotel association mustered thirty-two thousand francs for publicity. The minister of foreign affairs advised French consulates that, save for big, showy festivals, the Côte d'Azur was all it ever had been. French ambassadors abroad were encouraged to get out the word. Brochures were printed, articles sent to the Parisian press, travel agencies, railroads.

Even that first year, Nice limped a little back to life. The Municipal Casino would remain closed for most of the war, but soon the coal and vegetables it had stored were carted off elsewhere; it became a war-information center and site for charity balls on behalf of soldiers and widows. Carnaval, too, was suspended for the duration, but the Eldorado, the Excelsior Regina, and the Gaieté-Cinéma and other movie theaters reopened. So did the Casino of the Jetée-Promenade; the wounded were directed elsewhere. The hotel association found money to promote a Season "adapted to today's situation." Women dressed soberly, but the uniforms of French and English officers supplied some of the missing color. Entertainment returned to the Jetée. "A diversion of thought is permitted," a writer for L'Éclaireur contended in January 1915, when moved by "moral feelings of an elevated order," such as those bestowed by good music or a fine show.

Still, the 1914–15 winter season came to little. Half as many tourists arrived as did during the last year of peace. Hotel revenue, depressed further by lower room charges, ran about a third of prior years. The

man who held the chair-rental concession for Nice's public gardens, one of those many little businessmen who lived off tourists, pleaded for a reduction in his license fee, and got it.

∞

For four years the war ground on. The arrival of convoys laden with wounded became an everyday sight. Taken off the train, the soldiers were borne on streetcars fitted with stretchers, or by ambulance, to hotels; there they stayed, on average, a month and a half. The stream was steady enough that some of the hotels—like factories, mirroring how once they'd served streams of pleasure-seeking tourists—specialized: the Grand Hôtel got the most gravely wounded; the Imperial those needing physiotherapy.

Prices shot up; a kilogram of beef costing three francs in 1915, cost eight in 1918. To conserve fuel, streets were lit but feebly. Gangs of lawless youth roamed the streets of the old town and of working-class neighborhoods. The use of drugs like opium and cocaine spread. Nice's social and economic fabric was unraveling.

Still, its tourist industry tried to make the best of things. Before America's entry into the war, in 1917, it made efforts to draw American visitors, promoting train service from Bordeaux to the Côte d'Azur intended to mate up with new steamship service between New York and Bordeaux. Hotels requisitioned early in the war reopened, including the Negresco, the Winter Palace, and the Ruhl. So did theaters, though war forced discretion on their offerings. Photo and painting exhibitions continued, often with the war as their subjects.

By the winter of 1917, Nice had a real Season, even to hints of Belle Époque excess. Jacques-Henri Lartigue, a slim, bright-eyed twenty-three-year-old painter, photographer, and *bon viveur* who'd been coming to the Riviera with his wealthy family since he was two, witnessed it close up. He stayed at the Hôtel Atlantic on boulevard Victor-Hugo, but went often to the Ruhl, on the Promenade; in his journal he called it the "beehive for all the pretty women and the chic world," aswarm with guests and visitors coming and going for tea, lunch, and dinner.

One evening, he ambled over to the restaurant of the Hôtel Savoy, feeling "rather chic," savoring the sight of authors and celebrities he knew or recognized. It could have been prewar Nice.

To some visitors, Nice seemed insufficiently serious about the war. A British writer, Herbert Gibbons, recalled how, at the height of the Verdun offensive of 1916, with Paris threatened and France's fate uncertain, "in Nice there seemed to be no mass instinct of national danger, no sickening anxiety." Pedestrians on the avenue de la Gare scarcely glanced at newspapers with their war dispatches. Maybe, he speculated, Nice hadn't been French long enough; it was fewer than sixty years since the *rattachement*. Or maybe tourists and other temporary residents diluted French identity.

What *was* the proper place of leisure, pleasure, and amusement in a nation at war? Sometimes, during these years, Nice civic life seemed like one unending debate of the question. Plays, sidewalk cafés, art shows, gambling, and other frothy fare all provoked controversy. In the fall of 1916, for example, a writer for one journal defended the return of gambling to the Municipal Casino. Gambling was immoral? Well, then, maybe horse racing and cabaret were, too, he argued. That summer, Nice had hosted, "under the name 'revue,'" what seemed to him "pornography spiced with scatology." *That* a casino could freely offer! Yet, if, right upstairs, a few rich people sat in a private room playing cards for money, this was somehow immoral, even when charity got a cut of their winnings.

But it was difficult for any rhetoric, however nimble, to bridge the chasm between visions of heedless pleasure on a sunlit Mediterranean shore and those of muddy trenches thick with poison gas and strewn with the dismembered and the dead. When a Paris newspaper insinuated that the Côte d'Azur thought more of pleasure than war, a local publication, the *Économiste du littoral*, got the message: Paris's response "demonstrates that the little that has been done [to promote tourism] is all that can be attempted. . . . A country cannot be at once at peace and at war."

On the whole, war won out. Visits to Nice did increase from that first winter's low. But the Bordeaux-Nice train service lasted only a month; no one took it. Early in 1917, the sound of tangos and waltzes could be heard wafting from hotel lobbies; the bands that played them were promptly barred from doing so. Near the end of 1917, hopes for the Season were shattered by rail-transport problems, which kept visitors away, and hotels short of sugar to satisfy the palates of their guests and of coal to heat their baths.

There was little to do but look ahead, to the *après-guerre*, the afterwar years. In the future, the conviction grew, tourism would have to be managed more efficiently. Its success, one business journal observed in 1915, needed "money, coordination of effort, a single organization." A *départemental* office of tourism was established. So was a school of commerce and industry, a section of which was devoted to hotels. Hundreds of thousands of American tourists, it was said, would visit French battlefields after the war. Some, surely, would stop on the Riviera. All one could do was prepare to welcome them properly.

∞

The United States entered the war in March 1917, and General Pershing's million-man army helped force German surrender a year and a half later. The first American wounded reached Nice in June 1918. But long before, American authorities had designated Nice, along with Riviera towns like Cannes and Menton, a prime leave center; a month before war's end, the word went out that in Nice hotels, taxis, *tabacs,* and barber shop prices were to be posted in English as well as French. Employees of large department stores took crash courses in English.

"Nice is full of Americans," one American wrote home in December 1918. "All the officers come down here on leave." That winter, some seven thousand Americans visited Nice; the Jetée-Promenade, metamorphosed once again, was now their welcome center. American jazz could be heard in Nice night spots. Before they left in May of the following year, some sixty-five thousand "Sammies," as the French called Uncle Sam's boys, had tasted Nice, as well as other Riviera towns up and down the coast.

One was Rob Welsh, who, at the time he'd entered the U.S. Army, was a twenty-six-year-old farmer from Califon, in rural New Jersey;

Califon was just forty miles west of Manhattan Island, but might as well have been four hundred. Inducted in May 1918, Welsh had landed at Brest in October. Soon, with about twenty others in a special Quartermaster Corps unit, he was tending horses and hogs near Nevers, in central France.

On January 27, following the Armistice, he learned he was bound the following morning for a week's leave to the south of France. He and some of his friends caught an afternoon train to Chagny—"rode first class," he wrote in his journal—and late the following day arrived at Marseilles. After a night on the town there, he boarded another train, which, skirting the sea, brought him through Cannes, Nice, Monaco, and, finally, to his home for the week, Menton. There he was put up at the Hôtel Venise, "a large place and quite 'high-toned.'"

The following morning, he hiked across the border into Italy. Then, in the afternoon, a little mountain-climbing—"strenuous work at that," he noted. A vaudeville show at the YMCA that night. The next day, Monte Carlo and its casino, "the greatest gambling house in the world." He took the cog rail fifteen hundred feet up to La Turbie, where he saw Augustus's monument to the might of Rome. He visited the monastery at Laghet. And the palace in Monaco. Next day, Nice. First he saw the château, then "spent the rest of the day looking the town over," before returning that evening to Menton. He saw prehistoric artifacts at the museum in Monaco. Attended a boxing match at the Y. Climbed steep paths up to the Menton cemetery. Then, at last, it was over: "Our seven days are up, and we have to leave Menton tonight."

Later, in August, after traveling a little elsewhere in Europe and being promoted to sergeant, Rob Welsh returned to the States. He ran a turkey farm, served as a milk inspector, and died, at age seventy-four, in 1966. Into that week on the Riviera, he'd crowded the experiences of a lifetime.

On the Riviera around the same time was Ella Fife, a Red Cross nurse from Charlottesville, Virginia. She'd been at a nursing facility near Paris when the Armistice came. "Nobody," she wrote her mother a few days later, "will ever know the sensations I had when those first guns went off announcing 'Peace' to this war-sick old world. . . . I lay there and wept for one solid hour." The cathedral bell began to peal, and didn't stop for forty-five minutes. "That old bell seemed to be sounding down through the ages all the wars and troubles these poor French people have had for generations." They were already evacuating her patients, she noted, which would leave her with more time. "I want to see some of the country. . . . They may send us to the south of France."

A month and a half later, she was at a hotel in Cannes. "I wish you could see this lovely place," she wrote her mother. She could look out the window "and see the sea for miles, so blue and beautiful, dotted with little white sail boats." Their palm-studded lawn was full of "bright flowers blooming out of doors here in December—roses everywhere." The next day, she was taking an automobile excursion to Nice, then over the *corniche* to Menton.

The Riviera, she wrote, was "like the beautiful stories and pictures I've read and seen about such places, but never dreamed I'd go to one of them. . . . Couldn't think of anything more ideal," she added, "than spending a summer here."

That, of course, was a bizarre idea: *summer* on the Riviera?!?

12

WHEN "THE SEASON" BECAME SUMMER

NICE, THE WHOLE WORLD KNEW, TEEMED WITH VISITORS DURING winter, but lay empty in summer:

> Great deserted streets, stores padlocked, furnished apartments with their shutters closed tight, flags above empty boutiques, their displays gone, swarms of bluish mosquitoes buzzing against their windows . . . Wide sidewalks, cooked to whiteness by a torrid sun. And on one's shoes, white chalky dust, smelling like vanilla.

That was Nice one summer in the 1870s. Another summer around the same time, the teenaged Marie Bashkirtseff got trapped in Nice. There was no one around, nothing to do, and the mosquitoes picked at her mercilessly. "I feel exhausted, listless, unable to do anything. . . . To pass summers here is death! It's losing half your life!"

A 1912 guidebook listed Nice hotels down the side of the page and, beside each, along with room prices and the like, when it received guests. For the six-hundred-room Grand Hôtel, it was November 1 to the end of May. Which is about how the rest of the page looked, most of the city's hotels shutting down for summer. The Season was winter, summer a wilderness, period.

The reasoning was simple: You visit balmy Nice to escape the cruel winter of the North; but why stay once the cold and damp back home yield to spring blossoms? And, of course, it would be ludicrous to *pick* summer to visit Nice—which, being warmer in winter, was sure to be unbearably hot in summer. Tobias Smollett, who mostly prized Nice's climate, wrote how, "from the month of May, till the beginning of October, the heat is so violent, that you cannot stir abroad after six in the morning 'till eight at night." So hot you couldn't go out! *Violent* heat!

Foul smells probably also helped close down Nice for summer. With the Paillon mostly dried up, stinking sewage, little diluted by rain or freshwater streams, trickled through town and into the sea near the Promenade des Anglais. Nice's presumably unbearable heat, American scholar Charles Haug has suggested, was in part a polite surrogate for the stench.

Many well-off Niçois left town for the summer, heading for neighboring mountain villages like Saint-Martin-Vésubie or Peira-Cava. Others looked to the off-season as a chance to have the city to themselves. Or to repair roads and renovate hotels. It was a time, in any case, when they needn't bow and scrape before their guests.

Nice hotel owners often owned spas up north, or hotels in Normandy, or in the Alps, which all winter stood closed; mid-April meant it was time to ready them for summer, which was *their* high season. Each spring the day would come, an old *hôtelier* recalled years later, when the hotel's whole staff, desk clerks to chambermaids, would gather, pile into sixty or seventy carriages, and abandon Nice for summer work in Vichy, Évian, or elsewhere up north. All over town, posters would go up on hotels and shop windows: RELOCATED FOR THE SUMMER.

And yet, heedless of the evidence, a bullheaded corner of the brain, blinded by today's crowded beaches, cries out: It cannot be. People come *now* to Nice in summer; why didn't they *then?*

In fact, a few did. Early stirrings of a summer season go back to at least 1857, when some hoped Russia's dowager empress might forswear Rome for the summer and stay instead in Nice. A bathing pavilion was built for her and for Helene, the grand duchess. Influenced by a local doctor who wrote glowingly of the health benefits of sea bathing, Helene did remain in Nice. Her stay prompted the prediction that ahead lay "an era of double prosperity . . . conferring on [Nice] for the whole year a cosmopolitan character it could until now claim only in winter."

The grand duchess's summertime visits didn't catch on, but the Riviera wasn't *wholly* deserted come summer. *"Ouvert toute l'année,"* open all year, Nice's Hôtel Chauvain advertised in 1873. Among Riviera towns, Saint-Raphaël regularly got summer guests. So did Monte Carlo, thanks to its gambling. When Boston physician Arthur Howard Nichols visited the Riviera in 1894, he noted, "Monte Carlo, unlike the other fashionable resorts of the Riviera, is thronged in summer as well as in winter." One advertisement vaunting the principality's hotels, casino, and shops, summer and winter alike, touted "the sea breeze which constantly refreshes the atmosphere." In Riviera publicity, now as then, the sea breeze *always* blows.

"It's often been proposed, without success, to add to the winter season a summer season," a Nice guidebook observed before the Great War. "It's not impossible; you'd need only the will to do it." The heat posed no obstacle; those breezes wafting in from the sea or down from the mountains often left Nice more pleasant in summer than London, Paris, or Geneva. All that really stood in the way was expectation, habit, and routine—the dead weight of tradition.

And after the war, tradition retreated on every front.

∞

The war left nothing as it had been; it was like the foot-thick steel door of a bank vault that seals off everything on one side of it from everything on the other. The 1920s were a fluid, restless time when social mores, dislodged from well-worn prewar grooves, slipped and slid across an unsettled postwar terrain. Europe quivered with change. Nice's genteel world of rich *hivernants* had broken up.

The Russians, for example, were a shadow of their prewar presence, thanks to the fall of the tsar and the Bolshevik Revolution. Even before war's end, one Nice visitor remembered in 1931, "the center of the Russian colony was a soup kitchen on a side street, presided over by princesses and served by beautiful million-heiresses of the old regime," now reduced to working as governesses or stenographers. After the war, it was said, the Russians sold first their jewels, then their furs, then the furniture of their villas, then the villas themselves. One Niçois later recalled a family of Russian nobles, accustomed to a palace hotel in Cimiez, begging the authorities for a license to sell ladies' and children's hats.

"No more grand dukes," declared one writer, Charles Graves, of the postwar period on the Riviera, "no more Baltic barons, no more German princelings, no more Austrian archdukes." A pitiless inflation would destroy vanquished Germany's remaining wealth. By 1918, Henri Negresco, who a few years before had launched the fabulous hotel palace that bore his name, realized his old clientele had disappeared. He sold the hotel and moved to Paris, where cancer killed him two years later.

But postwar change cut both ways. Ordinary French soldiers, sent to the Riviera to convalesce, had gotten a whiff of lemon and mimosa. So had Belgian refugees and American doughboys. As a source of visitors, Europe's aristocracy had dried up; but their place had been filled by people less well born but more numerous. The war had reshuffled the tourist mix.

Participatory sports like golf, tennis, polo, and skiing were big among tourists now, old-style pleasures on the wane; one prescient observer suggested in 1923 that hotels offer gymnasiums, like today's fitness centers.

The German and Swiss complexion of many large hotels was gone.

Many skilled workers never came back from the war at all; the city's dead numbered four thousand.

Nice's hotel school, formed in 1916, took up some of the slack; the Niçois themselves were learning to be better hosts.

On every front, then, change. Sometimes beneficial, often not, but in any case change. And it was in this freshly turned postwar soil, where almost any seed might take root, that the greatest change of all took place: during these years, "the Season" became summer.

❧

One day in 1927, the photographer Jacques-Henri Lartigue—we met him ten years ago, in Nice, enjoying himself as if there were no war— takes an early color photo of his first wife, Bibi, in Cannes. She poses for him sitting on a large rock jutting up from the sea. The sun skims

low, piercing the still shallows that surround her perch, sparking under-
water glints of copper, azure, and gold. A parasol thrown over one
shoulder, she looks up at the camera. She wears a light, filmy dress that
leaves arms, legs, and thighs entirely bare. Another Lartigue photo, this
one black and white, captures a young woman lying on a rattan mat on
a Riviera beach, drinks tray set on the sand beside her. Her short blond
hair is swept onto her neck. Her bronzed back is bare. The fleshy white
mound of her buttocks spills out from the briefest of shorts.

Make no mistake: these were new kinds of images, and new sensibilities. A generation earlier, the women in posters, photos, and paintings wore flowing dresses with flowers, ruffles, and folds of fabric. And
they were covered not for modesty's sake alone but to protect them
from sun, wind, and water. The last thing you wanted was brown,
weathered skin that recalled peasants toiling in the fields under a relentless sun. Or fishermen who spent their lives on the water. Or, worse
yet, one of European colonialism's dark-skinned subject peoples. Men
and women of high station did not wish to look like *that*, coveting
creamy white skin instead. You might occasionally welcome the sun's
warm glow on your face, but not your whole body.

Likewise the heaving swells of the sea; for most of the centuries before World War I, the ocean was deemed no place for fun and frolic.
When painters depicted the Promenade des Anglais, they typically
sighted down its length, filling their canvases with finely dressed men
and women, the neighboring sea a peripheral element.

At least since the Middle Ages, water, bathing, and the seaside generally held little appeal for Europeans. "As late as the sixteenth century,
bathing as a hygienic protocol was quite unthinkable," write Lena
Lencek and Gideon Bosker in *The Beach: The History of Paradise on Earth.*
"Cleanliness was manifested in clothing, not the body." This, they write,
led to "a generalized horror of the beach." This horror softened in time,
but to step freely into the sea for the sake of health or pleasure, much
less cavort in it, remained an outlandish idea.

For women especially. Stepping into the water from a Nice beach
much frequented today by sunbathers, Tobias Smollett savored the sea

back in 1763. But from doing as he did, he advised, "the fair sex must be entirely excluded, unless they lay aside all regard to decorum; for the shore is always lined with fishing boats and crowded with people." Conceivably, a woman might have a tent pitched on the beach in which to change clothes. But she could hardly wade into the water without attendants at her side. Best that she forget the beach entirely, he as much as said, and have "sea-water brought into her house, and make use of a bathing-tub."

Gradually, though, things changed. Early-nineteenth-century Romantics made something of a cult of the beach. Sea bathing came to be seen as good for your health. Oceanside resorts cropped up all over Europe. By 1853, the Nice police were issuing regulations that set aside a stretch of beach near Les Ponchettes for women, and barred nude bathing. Bathing establishments, with *cabines* set periodically along the beach, appeared. Among those frequenting them in the 1870s was Marie Bashkirtseff, who, from off the back of a boat, would jump into the surf, float lazily on her back, or swim at her ease.

By the 1890s, three beach clubs enjoyed a measure of summertime chic, their multicolored cabins arrayed along the shore for three hundred yards. Vendors circulated among them selling cream puffs. In 1894, an anonymous writer took his readers there. He showed people waiting for a *cabine*, relaxing after a swim, or enjoying the spectacle afforded by the other bathers. Here, wearing his pince-nez, a gentleman steps into the sea. There a young woman pauses decorously as she emerges from the bath. "She has beautiful hair," we learn. "She's attractive—and she knows it all too well."

By the eve of World War I, new relationships among sun, sea, and the human body—a new world of summertime leisure—were evolving. In history's long sweep, these changes could seem abrupt, especially to Niçois raised on seemingly immutable seasonal rhythms and unnerved by any departure from them. But in fact, they played out more gradually than did those of, say, the railroad; well into the twenties, winter still ruled the Riviera.

In the early days, the summer idea was so new that mass publications

offered cautionary little tales. "So powerful an agent as the Riviera sun cannot be used immoderately," England's *Spectator* advised in 1928.

> The rash bather who lies for an hour with his bare back in the sun on the first day of his arrival will probably spend the next three days in bed with the skin off his back, a high temperature and swollen limbs.

Go easy, the advice continued.

> If you or your party give yourself too much to do, too many engagements, too many amusements, too much motoring on hot, dusty roads, then, indeed, you will find the Riviera too hot in the summer.

In time, the change took hold. "The hotels of Cannes, of Antibes, of Nice, and of Mentone, once silent and deserted at this time of the year," now enjoyed new prosperity, wrote John Strachey, in an August 1928 article entitled "The Riviera in Summer." British tastes had changed. "We have learnt to like real heat, for we have learnt to live, to dress, to eat, to sleep in the right way and at the right times to meet it."

It was quite simple, it was as if he threw an arm around his reader to say: "One simply spends the time in the sea, or, if not actually submerged, at any rate lying clad only in a bathing dress upon its margin." The idea carried all the force of revelation.

☙❧

"Le Soleil Toute l'Année," "Sun Year Round," read one tourist poster in 1931; it showed a woman in trim bathing suit, arms held out, as if in prayer, to a radiant, Art Deco–inspired sun. Another from 1935, *"L'Été sur la Côte d'Azur,"* "Summer on the Côte d'Azur," featured palm trees and yellow-striped beach umbrellas. Neither beach scene looks remotely like Nice.

Back in 1889, a *L'Éclaireur* editor had prophesied that one day Nice would, as a summer resort, hold its own against all of Europe, thanks no doubt to some "new Smollett." But no Smollett-like personage figured in summer's ultimate dominion over Nice. Most of the action during the twenties, in fact, took place outside it. Nice was a follower, not a leader, in the great transformation.

We are on Cap d'Antibes, the little spit of land that projects into the Mediterranean between Nice and Cannes. It is the summer of 1922, and the American songwriter Cole Porter has rented a château. Porter invites the expatriate Americans Gerald and Sara Murphy to join him. The Murphys fall in love with the area, buy a villa, and prevail on the owner of the Hôtel du Cap, the fabulous Belle Époque hotel at the tip of the cape, to remain open for the summer. Soon the well-connected Murphys are host to luminaries enough to make the whole *cap* glow, including Picasso, author and art patron Gertrude Stein and her companion Alice B. Toklas, and actor Rudolph Valentino. Ernest Hemingway and his wife come. So do F. Scott Fitzgerald and his.

On to Cannes. It is 1923, and, following a Mediterranean cruise, fashion designer Coco Chanel arrives, sporting a deep tan. The sight of her—"brown as a cabin boy," someone described her later—causes a sensation. By the end of the 1920s, write Louis Turner and John Ash in *The Golden Hordes,* a suntan has become visible proof that its bearer has the wherewithal to escape to the Mediterranean—"a fading trophy [that] . . . becomes a mark of class distinction just as the aristocratic 'milk and roses' [complexion] had been."

On to Juan-les-Pins, a little town with a sandy beach on the far side of Cap d'Antibes from Nice. Inspired, the story goes, by a film featuring a Miami beach party, a Nice restaurant owner transforms Juan's little casino into a fashionable summer resort. American millionaire Frank Jay Gould buys the casino and in 1927 opens a two-hundred-room hotel. Soon Juan-les-Pins teems with scantily clad cocktail-sippers. They call it "Pajama Land," an American, Eustace Adams, writes a little later; he refers to loose-fitting beach clothes, not sleepwear. "You go back to your hotel and have lunch in your pajamas, have tea in them and, as night falls, change into your evening clothes. It is all very pleasant. And the lessons in anatomy you learn!" Summer on the Riviera, he's been told, *means* Juan-les-Pins, which is reputed to have "the best beach on the coast."

The best beach: Juan is *in.*

Nice is not.

Credit Coco Chanel and Frank Jay Gould, then, for drawing the spotlight off Nice and leaving it with only a peripheral role in the changes taking place on the Riviera? Hardly. Nice's faded appeal, its tardiness in adapting to summer, went deeper. And one factor was the automobile.

In the spring of 1905, a nineteen-year-old New Jersey woman, Anna Wilcox, reached Nice about midway through a three-month European trip with her husband and young daughter; they had taken the *Deutschland* to Naples, then worked their way north to the Riviera. Mrs. Wilcox's diary had preprinted pages headed "Places I Have Visited" and the like; but she breached its sterile categories with tart gibes about, for example, "horrid English people" she'd met and Germans who were even worse. From Nice, they took a day trip to Grasse, in the hills behind Cannes, where they toured the obligatory perfume factory. As side trips go, Grasse was unremarkable. Notable only was that she and her party got there by car.

Friends they'd met in Nice, it seems, had a "fine new auto," which they first took over the *corniche* to Monte Carlo: "How we ran. Such fun. Then returned to Nice by the coast road." That was Friday. The next morning, it was off to Grasse, by a road that wound through the hills and offered "ever-unfolding new scenery and views." On the way back, they got a flat, but still reached Nice in plenty of time to pack for their departure the following morning for Paris. It had all been so *easy.*

Almost from the beginning, the automobile reached into the traveler's imagination. An 1898 *affiche* for the Paris-Lyon-Méditerranée railroad celebrated Carnaval with the usual images of beautiful women, masked revelers, and lively drinking; but we see also, in the cloud of dust it kicks up, the rakish silhouette of an automobile. Two years later, the Michelin tire company issued the first of its tourist guides, precursors of the red and green ones ubiquitous today. "Having a motor car in this landscape is magical," wrote Jacques-Henri Lartigue. "The drive to Cannes along the narrow, deserted little road which follows the coastline via Golfe Juan is wonderful."

But deserted little roads grew fewer; even by 1913, you could see hints of a more congested future. In that year, Robert de Souza reported that the seaside road from Nice to Villefranche no longer suited lazy promenades but had become a "great" 'artery of circulation.'" In 1908, Nice authorities began monitoring auto traffic near the port. One February day a little later, they counted 1,338 automobiles—up from 934 two years before. Bicycles, though, were fewer; the glut of cars discouraged them.

For automobiles and their owners, the twenties and thirties were like the early days of an ultimately rocky relationship when the new lovers still enjoy one another. Travelers could still savor the automobile's speed, its delicious wind-in-the-face freedom. "All one need say," wrote Lartigue, "is *I'd like to be in Cannes, I'd like to be in Monaco,* and you're there." The automobile took you *wherever* you wanted to go—unlike the railroad, which manacled you to steel rails and fixed schedules. "The motorcar has restored the romance of travel," Edith Wharton wrote in *A Motor-Flight Through France.* "It has given us back the wonder, the adventure and the novelty which enlivened the way of our posting grandparents." It got you, in other words, off the beaten track.

And Nice was *stuck* on the beaten track.

The width of the Riviera's touristic strip had always best been reckoned in hundreds of yards, not miles (though in Nice it reached back a bit farther, to Cimiez). The automobile, however, helped open up all the mountainous backcountry behind Nice, as well as shore points the railroad didn't serve. Now you could almost as easily drive up to L'Escarène and Sospel, and up into the mountains to Peira-Cava, or out along the twisting road of the Loup Valley, as get to Nice itself. Le Cannet, near Cannes, spun into popularity. So did Roquebrune, near Menton. The automobile didn't change things all at once. But it had as profound an impact as the railroad, only in reverse: it sapped Nice, whereas the railroad had nourished it.

In emerging as a modern city before World War I, Nice had lost

some of its youthful freshness. Now, as haven for a moneyed class wistful for the great days of the Belle Époque, it could seem a worn, creaking holdover from the corrupt *other* side of the great divide that was the war. Magdalena Samożwaniec, the thirtyish daughter of a Polish painter, passed the winter of 1924–25 in Nice. She enjoyed the sight of men in white flannel suits and women in gay springtime outfits adorning wicker chairs beside the great hotels. But on the Promenade, where *tout le monde* met, she saw decadence, too. She saw rich American women who dressed up as *gamines.* And "chattering old ladies with hats of light blue and pink, white capes with ermine collars, huge cut diamonds and pearl earrings, clutching the leashes of their Pekinese and Scotch terriers." On their arms, often enough, were "sad, wan, tragic gigolos." To many, a specter like this, of dandies and the decrepit, was how Nice seemed after the war.

Many fashionable travelers now spurned urban centers in favor of unassuming retreats where they might enjoy rustic dress and simple pleasures. "To know a country and its inhabitants," one prewar book aimed at European travelers advised, "one must make contact with the natives and soak up the local setting as much as possible." Some artists had been doing that since long before the war. Back in 1905, Henri Matisse had settled for the winter in Saint-Tropez, then a remote fishing village; he and artists like him were dubbed the Fauves, or wild ones. In their canvases, writes one critic, "the artifice of art, the practices of tourism, and the fiction of national character all passed themselves off as natural." Now, in the 1920s, this turn to the fresh and natural took on the force of fashion—one favoring out-of-the-way Edens, not cities of decadence like Nice.

Nice was losing all vestige of nature's wild potency. Posters and picture postcards that sang Nice's song to foreign tourists, one journalist noted in 1927, still displayed flowers in showy profusion—"climbing roses, wisteria, bougainvilleas winding along the building façades, entangling their clumps and clusters of brilliant red on the smallest projection." There was just one problem. Nice didn't look that way. He saw no raucous floral explosions, just "neatly tended flower beds that tolerated not the least luxuriance." Nature *tamed.*

One day late in the 1920s, an American couple, Louise and Donald Peattie, in search of sun—and, after the death of their daughter, hope—took the luxurious Blue Train down from Paris. They checked in to a Nice hotel, came down for lunch, and sat out on a terrace by the sea, weighing their options. Resolving to rent a Nice villa, they had the concierge send real-estate agents their way. But soon they were being shown a succession of what felt like "alien houses that were not home, dusty with ghosts of other tenants who had worn this stair carpet and broken that fauteuil and stained these faded brocade hangings." No, they didn't want that.

A day later, they were in a taxi, still grappling with what to do, but intent, in any case, on driving *somewhere.* "Oh, get us out of here!" Louise finally cried to the driver. "Anywhere, anywhere out of the noise and the streets and the people." Soon they were in the foothills outside of town. "Nice was behind them now, and well lost."

This was Nice to cultivated travelers during the twenties. In 1920, it is true, the Shah of Iran stayed in Nice; and in 1924, Queen Marie of Romania. Isadora Duncan, a revered icon of modern dance, was in Nice in 1927 when her scarf got caught in the spokes of the sports car in which she was a passenger, killing her, prompting mournful headlines in Nice and around the world. But by and large, the *most* beautiful people were elsewhere on the Riviera, lying out on the *plage* somewhere, baking in the summer sun, not ambling along the Promenade in Nice.

As it slipped from favor during the twenties, Nice was faulted for doing too little to encourage summertime visitors. Where, critics asked, was the clean-up of the beach that would make seaside bathing more appealing? Why not open up the Jetée-Promenade, which closed each year by May, to summertime guests? Why not bigger *fêtes* during summer to lure visitors? Just look down the coast, at Juan-les-Pins—some by now call it the Deauville of the Côte d'Azur—and you'd see how far Nice was being left behind. Nice lay stuck in its Belle Époque groove; some Niçois could not even bring themselves to talk of a summer "season"—the very idea was heretical—only of a summer "period."

Still, by fits and starts, Summer did come to Nice.

One inspiration came right after the war, from American soldiers on leave. In May 1919, when the Riviera Leave Zone closed down, local hotel owners held a Fête France-Amérique at the Hôtel Ruhl. The American commander of the zone thanked the French for their hospitality, noting that thousands of Riviera-sampling American soldiers would "take with them an indelible memory of the beauties of France." But the Americans had left behind memories among the Niçois, too—of young men splashing in the Mediterranean's warm waters, heedless of the summer sun.

To many of those soldiers, inured to sultry American summers, Nice's seemed downright mild; its midsummer temperatures were about like those of Atlanta or Washington, D.C., but the air was drier and more comfortable. So they flocked to the water's edge just as they would have in Atlantic City, New Jersey, or Brooklyn's Coney Island. The sight of them, healthy and free, had planted the idea of summer among the Niçois, a local chamber-of-commerce official later asserted, spurring a challenge to assumptions "until then respected with incomprehensible rigidity."

In 1920, the *Économiste du littoral* claimed that efforts to fashion a summer season in Nice were already succeeding. "During the hottest months," it reported of the previous summer, "our city no longer seemed deserted. Our streets and avenues always bustled." (Of course, it added, Nice in summer would "never be anything but a pale reflection of Nice in winter!") Two years later, the chamber of commerce insisted its efforts permitted it to declare, "Nice is a tourist city all year."

This was an expression more of hope than of fact, of course, but ingrained attitudes *were* slowly changing. Plainly, an *Éclaireur* writer reminded his readers in 1923, Paris's prejudice against the heat of the Côte d'Azur was not shared by everyone—witness the Spanish, Scandinavians, Swiss, and, especially, Americans who came to Nice.

Summer gambling came to the Jetée-Promenade. The Negresco, the Ruhl, and other big hotels announced they would remain open in summer. For 1926, Nice set in motion a major tourism push, sponsoring concerts, parades, and dances. *And* a gala at the Jetée that tourists could attend in beach clothes; this was the ultimate concession to summer. That same year, a tourist guide insisted:

> Nice is an all-the-year-round resort, and apart from the closing of a few of the palatial hotels and luxurious shops, the town presents much the same aspect in all seasons, for the streets are always thronged. There is ample amusement through the summer.

But wishful thinking was still at work, as a final comment attests:

> Nice in summer is certainly more natural than during the winter, when the great cosmopolitan crowds are found within her gates. One gets to know Nice better in summer time, for one has more leisure in which to admire her charms.

More natural and more leisured, of course, because it was so much less busy.

"Less busy" gave summer a leg up that once, back in the early 1800s, Nice had enjoyed year-round: low prices. Winter was high season, summer still cut-rate. Seashore resorts in the south of France, a French-

NICE   Hôtel et Pension Funel

government tourist office advised in May 1924, wouldn't be so busy as those up north. So villas would be cheap, living "very reasonable"; the same went for good hotels in Nice and elsewhere.

All through the 1920s, the Nice summer season remained a curiosity. Indeed, if the almost suspect tone of one 1926 newspaper article is to be believed, the Niçois themselves weren't quite sure it would pan out. A reporter went out onto the beach and asked a local celebrity, author Guy de Téramond—he posed, standing beside his daughter on the beach, in an odd, shoulder-baring, one-piece bathing suit—what he thought about the idea.

Oh, summer could work in Nice, he replied. It was not too hot, and resorts like Trouville, up north, seemed to grow colder year by year; people would *have* to come south. Could Nice in summer become anything like Nice in winter? Yes, but "it will be necessary"—*il faudra*—"that shops and other establishments remain open." The rest of the interview was littered with these *il faudra*'s: It would be necessary to schedule summertime concerts. It would be necessary to open halls for public events . . . to organize advertising . . . to clean the beach . . . to put up modern bathing facilities. All, so taken for granted today at any summer resort, were necessary if Nice was serious about welcoming summertime visitors.

Early in 1929 came the long-awaited opening of the Palais de la Méditerranée, a new luxury casino fronting on the Promenade des Anglais, air-conditioned throughout, and stocked with gambling rooms, dance halls, bars, and a pool; it was financed by the syndicate that had made such a big success of Juan-les-Pins. The main gaming room, almost two hundred feet long, offered a magnificent view of the Baie des Anges. Later that summer, Nice held a succession of regattas, swim meets, fireworks, concerts, bicycle races, and other *fêtes*, culminating, on Bastille Day, in parades and fireworks over the Quai des Ponchettes.

Over the course of the 1920s, summer revenue from the *taxe de séjour* imposed on hotel receipts tripled; that for the traditional winter season climbed, too, but not nearly so fast. Summer in Nice was taking hold but, until after the next world war, its dominion would remain incomplete.

13

NEW HAPPINESS

A FAMOUS ROBERT CAPA PHOTOGRAPH SHOWS PABLO PICASSO IN shorts and open shirt on a Riviera beach with his mistress of the moment, the young and fetching Françoise Gilot. She is caught midstride, wearing a big beach hat and shell necklace; her face glows with joy. Picasso, barefoot in the sand, trails after her, like a servant, screening her from the sun with a big fringed beach umbrella. They could be any two lovers on vacation.

Picasso and other celebrity visitors to the Riviera would come to be seen as Beautiful People, leading privileged or otherwise magnified lives, far removed from those of ordinary folks. In fact, most of the artists and writers who, during the twenties and thirties, preceded Picasso to the Riviera were hardworking people who wanted what other people wanted. Much separated them, as artists, from the common herd. But their need for pleasure, relaxation, and release made them a lot like other tourists.

Henri Matisse first came to Nice in December 1917, during the last year of World War I. Later, he'd buy an apartment on Place Charles-Félix, high over the Cours Saleya, and become a Nice fixture, but for now he was just a visitor. He was almost fifty, already a renowned artist, widely exhibited around the world, with a permanent home in Paris and a studio in a suburb outside it. He'd come down sick with bronchitis and his doctor had directed him to Menton. But he wound up in Nice instead, at the Hôtel Beau-Rivage.

Matisse had a south-facing room so long and narrow that between bed and window there was room only for a shabby armchair. A tall, shuttered window, a recurring feature of his paintings from this period, looked out on· the Baie des Anges. In Matisse's earliest winter days there, rain imprisoned him indoors. But, inevitably, the sun returned. "When I realized that every morning I would see this light again, I couldn't believe how lucky I was."

Mostly, Matisse stayed in his room, posing models in front of the *persiennes*, ignoring the world outside, using what he called the peculiar "luminosity of the daylight" to create an aura of enchantment. He'd write of "the light as it came in through the shutters . . . from below, as if from footlights at the theater. It was all fake, absurd, amazing, delightful."

Matisse's Riviera, writes art historian Kenneth E. Silver, is largely

an interior place, a world of rooms——in hotels and apartment houses——all of which give onto the Promenade des Anglais and the sea. Matisse's is a tourist's view par excellence, a tourist whose greatest pleasures are derived from his lodgings and his vistas, from the distance he keeps from the place he visits.

Likewise for other artists visiting the Riviera between the wars. With a few exceptions, writes Silver in another article, they

shared the experience of most other tourists on the coast: they went for a more-or-less brief period of time, usually ranging from a week to several months; they enjoyed the pleasures of the Riviera while inhabiting hotel rooms or rented houses; and then they left. . . . The work these artists made on the Riviera remains, whatever its intentions, marked by the tourist experience.

The artists were preoccupied with issues of joy, play, and pleasure. And many of the scenes they painted could have appeared on picture postcards: Antibes in the morning light from out in the Baie des Anges, by Paul Signac; a festive Jetée-Promenade at night, by Raoul Dufy.

Writers visiting the Riviera during the twenties explored leisure in their work, too, much as they might have war, or business, in other settings. W. Somerset Maugham sets "The Three Fat Women of Antibes" in a Riviera beach club. His "The Facts of Life" tells of a boy's coming of age in the gaming rooms and hotels of Monte Carlo. F. Scott Fitzgerald's *Tender Is the Night* is a Riviera romance in which no one does much but talk, drink, carouse, and lie out on the beach.

In *A Voyage to Pagany*, William Carlos Williams's fictional protagonist, Dev, travels through Europe much as the author himself had in 1924. On a Riviera-bound train from Marseilles, skirting the sea, Dev's companion, Lou, spies "her first mimosa tree in blossom," as if it's something she's read enough about to anticipate.

> Look, look, Lou kept saying, now darting to the sea side of the car . . . now to the other. Olive trees and cactus and low palms; the sun caught in the protecting mountains; the pale blue sea— and Lou was all delight. . . . So this is the Riviera!

They pass through Cannes, with its crowds, its English and American faces; and Nice,

> a smooth indentation of the coast line, the great hotels backing away from the town upon the hills, glass and bright towers. It was all a brilliant confirmation to Lou of her newly awakened insights into happiness.

Finally, they get off on the other side of the hill, in Villefranche. Tramping down to the old fishing village, they pass small shops, a few steps down from the street, "with strings of onions and peppers—in the Italian style—hanging outside before them. The place was full of smells." They meet men who wear round blue caps and look like sailors.

In fact, they're not sailors; their knowledge of ships extends only to the rowboats on which they take tourists into the sheltered harbor. But awareness of this artifice dulls Lou's pleasure not a bit. "Oh Dev," she says, "how wonderful it is just to be here."

❧

In *Côte d'Azur: Inventing the French Riviera*, Mary Blume describes the Nice of the twenties, when it struggled with new summer sensibilities and lost cachet to its Riviera rivals, as "good only for shopping." Maybe you'd go to Galeries Lafayette, the big department store on Place Masséna, to buy an outfit for a costume party. But "it was like going to town," one of her informants told her. "Nobody lived there."

"Nobody," however, referred only to a thin slice of *le beau monde.* In fact, *plenty* of people were coming to Nice; the city was less fashion-able—but more visited. Arrivals at the Nice *gare* tripled in the ten years ending in 1929. In 1930, the city counted 305,000 tourists, up from 134,000 eight years before. All through the twenties, people came more than ever—for the gambling, for Carnaval, for their health, for the sun, for a good time, for mostly the same reasons the bons vivants, artists, and writers did.

One July day in 1927, Jennie Reizenstein and her sister, of Balti-more, on a nine-week European tour, found themselves on a Nice-bound afternoon train from Avignon, sharing a compartment with other Americans. As the train chugged along, they compared notes. *Staying in Nice, are you?* one of the other Americans inquired. *Just back from several months there ourselves. Stayed at a wonderful place, Pension Sollar.* . . . It was a lit-tle outside the center of town, but just five minutes back from the Promenade des Anglais, graced by a broad, gently curving grand stair-way bordered by bushes and plants. The Reizenstein sisters had sup-plied themselves with the names of several hotels, but opted instead for this new find. "We are lucky mortals to have found such a place," Jen-nie wrote in her red leather journal the following morning, as she sat in the garden, under the shade of palm trees, awaiting her sister for break-fast.

The ensuing days were full of good eating and walks along the Promenade; Jennie was mesmerized by the sea's infinite variegations of blue. Once, they stopped at the Negresco for a criminally overpriced orangeade; at least one waiter in Nice, she wrote, would look in vain for a tip. They shopped at Galeries Lafayette. They saw Cimiez and its villas. They drove along the winding roads of the Gorges du Loup. They bought Chanel No. 5 in Grasse. The following day, a bus took them along the *corniche*. As it circled round the mountains, they reached "dizzying heights," from which she could see "the irregular and picturesque coast below," with terraces of stone walls that flanked ripening grapes, and palm trees and cacti growing wild along the road. "It can't be humanly possible," wrote Jennie Reizenstein of Baltimore, Maryland, "to spend a day of more glorious sights than those we saw today."

About the same time Reizenstein visited Nice, so did Nina Murdoch, a thirty-seven-year-old Australian children's-book and travel writer on her first trip to Europe. "I lie exquisitely at ease with but one thought singing through my mind," she wrote on her first day. "'I am in France! On the Riviera! At Nice!'" Murdoch gushed over *everything*, from the polished wood coat hangers in her closet, to the large porcelain basin in her bathroom, to an electric light so placed "that a man can see to shave without cutting his lip, and a woman can make up without looking as if she had cut hers."

One Sunday morning, wisps of guitar music and a soft baritone voice filtered up from the garden—"a rich little song of love, swelling with passion." Murdoch went to the window, flung open the shutters, and looked down to see a dark, slim, mustached figure. Over the wrought-iron railing, she dropped a one-franc coin. Her serenader replied "with such a superb sweep of the hat that fancy sees him clad at once in velvet and silk, scented and beplumed—a gallant catching the rose from his mistress' bodice."

Mrs. Murdoch, nine years married but traveling in Europe alone, saw the Riviera through a soft, pink, plainly eroticized haze. At lunch, she basked in the never-wavering stare of a Frenchman at the next table. She even enjoyed her treatment by the waiter, who "pours my humble glass of water as if it were an oblation. . . . Like all his compatriots, he is an artist who demands from life form and colour and a flowing graciousness"; the prospect of a generous tip, or simple professionalism, presumably figured not at all.

In this woman's reveries, the waiter, the man at the next table, and the mustached minstrel seem to have no purpose but to please her.

Whether or not this qualifies as touristic narcissism at its worst might be worthy of debate. What's not debatable is that Mrs. Murdoch had a very good time.

Soon, though, many fewer people—fewer artists, writers, Americans, Australians, fewer of everybody—were having a good time on the Riviera.

∞

"It was not for a couple of years that the draught made itself felt," observes Somerset Maugham's narrator in his novel *The Razor's Edge,* referring to the world economic depression prefigured by the stock-market crash in October 1929.

> Then an estate agent told me that on the stretch of coast that reaches from Toulon to the Italian border there were forty-eight thousand properties, large and small, to be sold. The shares of the Casino slumped. The great hotels put down their prices in a vain attempt to attract. The only foreigners to be seen were those who had always been so poor that they couldn't be poorer, and they spent no money because they had no money to spend. The shopkeepers were in despair.

The whole Riviera was in despair. Conditions worsened in 1931, when the British devalued their currency, making travel for them prohibitively expensive. Nothing to fret about, a Nice optimist said in 1931: "We operate here in the upper international strata, where business setbacks are scarcely felt. Keep smiling!" But the French tourist industry had little to smile about; the number of foreign visitors plummeted from more than two million in 1927 to fewer than seven hundred thousand by 1936.

Nice, where by late 1931 hotels and shops had cut their prices by a third, suffered even more than the rest of the Riviera. In part, because it had further to fall. In part, because it had responded less nimbly to the changes of the twenties. "Nice . . . has remained more '1900' than the rest of the Côte d'Azur," wrote French diplomat Paul Morand in a 1938 book reflecting his frequent visits to the Riviera. Though "covetous of two yearly harvests of visitors, Nice has accorded seabathing only the secondary importance it was accorded in 1900." And, he went on, "the bare back, the pajama, and feet in espadrilles are not well thought of there." Morand wrote approvingly of this resistance to fashion, yet was depicting stagnation. A 1930 magazine ad showing the Promenade des Anglais crowded with women in the little round hats and slim silhouettes of the 1920s bears a distinct prewar flavor. To Nice, the ad asserts in its stilted English, "worldknown celebrities foregather every winter, eager to enjoy life in this inspiring azure kingdom." As if the world hadn't speeded up. As if the Riviera hadn't discovered summer. As if nothing had changed.

But with the Depression, which would grind on until World War II, sap the economies of Europe and America, and leave millions without jobs or hope, everything changed. Casino revenue at the new Palais de la Méditerranée dropped, in just three years, from twenty-one million francs to six million. As for that other engine of the Nice economy, its hotels, they were in trouble, too, especially the Belle Époque palaces. Most were almost half a century old by now. They were too big, cost too much to maintain—and were out of step with the simpler tastes and cleaner lines of the day. The Splendid, a two-hundred-room hotel on boulevard Victor-Hugo, saw receipts drop almost in half from 1929 to 1930, then plummet another 40 percent by 1935. It survived, but many other large hotels went under, or were turned into schools or hospitals. All told, thirty-one hotels, with 3,150 rooms, vanished between the two world wars, most of them after 1930. Hôtel Polonia, London Palace, Savoy, Grand Hôtel de Cimiez, Majestic—each a grand name, each shuttered by 1937, each a blow to the economy.

More than the prosperous twenties, the tremulous times of the thirties woke the Nice tourism establishment from its long sleep. Nice had responded only grudgingly to the postwar era, prosperity masking its problems; the depression doldrums, on the other hand, lent urgency to them. So did the competition for tourist business from Fascist Italy, which took every opportunity to point up scandal or social disruption in France. In response, and in ways familiar to us today, Nice became more commercially aggressive.

One Nice representative in Paris kept a big cardboard-covered book that recorded his success at landing favorable mentions in European newspapers. Like, for example, the photo in England's *Daily Mail* in August 1931 that showed half a dozen smiling, lightly clad women lounging on the beach, the glow of their bodies apparent even through the coarse halftone printing. The caption reads:

> Thousands of holiday makers are revelling in the sunshine of the Riviera. [Here we see] an animated patch of the beach at Nice, where this year the summer visitors have been more numerous than ever.

Once, travelers' letters, or their effusions after having returned home, had been about the only means by which Nice's charms could become better known. Then Tobias Smollett wrote his *Travels.* Other books followed. Railroads commissioned colorful posters. Now, in the 1930s, ad writers set out deliberately to burnish Nice's image.

"Nice in Summer is as Lovely as in Winter," asserted one postcard-sized ad that ran three times in London's *Daily Telegraph:* "The Blue Sea, the Mountains, Yachting, Alpine Climbing, Hotel Prices Greatly Reduced." In English, it was "Nice in summer . . ." In the Netherlands, in 1932, it was "Warme Winters, Droge Zomers." In Germany, in 1935, it was "Nizza im Sommer." "Vacation time approaches," an ad in a French-language newspaper in Switzerland reminded its readers. "Perhaps you still hesitate about your choice of vacation spot? Look no further. Nice invites you to enjoy the perfect summer stay. . . ."

In 1932, the Nice hotel association established a Maison de Nice in Paris, to handle publicity and hotel reservations. Three years later, Nice Mayor Jean Médecin cut the ribbon on a big storefront office on boulevard des Capucines, and later that year arranged a conclave of mayors to coordinate publicity efforts along the Côte d'Azur. Early in 1933, he sponsored an international tourism conference that drew 250 delegates from across Europe. But in the short run, at least, none of this amounted to much; the city's new assertiveness could make scant headway against global depression.

✺

In February 1934, as he did each year, Zurich antique dealer Albert
Meyer, thirty-eight, visited Nice and patronized its night spots. One
Tuesday evening, he went club-hopping and met a girl named Jacqueline—except that at three that morning, when he brought her back to
his hotel, she registered as Marie Faivre, twenty-eight.

The couple didn't call down for breakfast until the following afternoon.

Later that day, toward midnight, Meyer ordered up drinks from the
bar. Whiskeys. Four of them.

It was a little later, while they sat on the edge of the bed looking at
pictures of his children—or so he told police later—that she noticed
the revolver in his bag on the nightstand.

How does it work? she asked.

When he took it out to show her, she grabbed it and pointed it
at him.

"Deeming this rather dangerous joking," he explained, "I pushed
her arm aside." The gun went off, twice. Meyer was hit in the chest, the
impact driving him down onto the bed.

Certain she'd killed him, overcome with remorse, Jacqueline, alias
Marie Faivre, put the gun to her right temple and, the way Herr Meyer
told it, shot herself dead.

A few years earlier, filmmaker Jean Vigo had pictured Nice as a sink
of depravity. His black-and-white documentary, *À propos de Nice*, at first
shows waves rolling onto the beach, sidewalk cafés being tidied up, and
other reassuring images. But then a dark, surreal note intrudes. A
woman reappears, repeatedly, in different clothes; then, finally, nude. A
man sits in the sun, emerging not bronzed but blackened and burned.
We see an elderly, mustached man in a suit too tight and too short,
asleep, more dead than alive; a woman reading an English newspaper,
skirt risen unbecomingly to her knees. All bizarrely juxtaposed with
wild dancing girls, incinerator stacks, painted lips, the corruption and
decay behind Nice's exquisite façade laid mercilessly bare.

Now, as the Depression persisted, the incongruity of a tourist town devoted to pleasure at a time of widespread human misery became ever more starkly highlighted; people looked at Nice with new eyes. "The city charms—and it repels," Herbert Gibbons wrote in 1931.

> You have been drinking in its beauty and its fascination. Then, suddenly, something sordid, ugly, disgusting, breaks the spell. On the Promenade des Anglais sewage greets the eye as well as the nose. Not vicious women and poor little dolls alone, but cruel and weak faces, shifty and vapid faces, self-centered and morose faces, leech faces, pig faces of well-tailored men . . .

What besides money, he asked, distinguished these wretched princes of the Promenade from back-alley brutes?

For France's left wing, the Promenade was injustice incarnate, embodying all the worst of capitalism, a place where servile, underpaid workers abjectly pampered the idle rich. In 1935, when it judged Mayor Jean Médecin unduly preoccupied with luring tourists and insensitive to the city's impoverished and unemployed, the regional communist paper, *Le Cri des travailleurs*, dubbed him "Jean of the Promenade des Anglais."

In February 1936, *Le Cri* sent a reporter, André Lapauve, to Cimiez to survey the damage the Depression had wrought. "Cimiez la Morte," the article was called, "Dead Cimiez." The Excelsior Regina, that ultimate symbol of Belle Époque extravagance, where Queen Victoria had stayed, was closed. So, at the other end of boulevard de Cimiez, was the Majestic. "And we are at the height of the season!" The palaces had had their day before the war. A brief prosperity afterward had brought some jobs. But now the jobs were gone. Cimiez was gone. Places like the Regina, wrote Lapauve, must be handed over to the workers who'd built them.

"Ah," he went on, as if in the throes of a fevered dream, "how lovely Cimiez will be someday, under the socialist regime, when bustle and life will be restored to it by workers who, as part of their *congés payés*"—their paid vacations—will flock there for their health.

Paid vacation?

In the national election of 1936, as France seethed with industrial and political unrest, a new Popular Front government, comprising three left-wing parties including the communists, was swept into office. On June 11, 1936, a two-week paid vacation for most workers was voted into law—and with scarcely a murmur of dissent; the Front's right-wing foes saw in *congés payés* a way to quench the flames of revolution by promoting, in the words of one scholar, "a classless leisure and a common culture of pleasure."

Although offering no bar to translation, the phrase *congés payés* is so deeply rooted in its time and place that it doesn't "want" to be translated. But back in 1936, the very idea of a paid vacation was unfamiliar to most French workers; white-collar civil servants might enjoy them, but few others—maybe fifty thousand ordinary workers nationwide. France had lagged behind both Great Britain and Nazi Germany in responding to the strains and anxieties of the regimented twentieth-century workplace.

But even with *congés payés* as law, some workers didn't quite know what to do with it. On vacation, you wake up whenever you like? Well, that first Monday morning, many woke up just when they always had. Others simply didn't believe that, when they returned to work, their jobs and their pay would be waiting for them. It was, after all, the middle of the Depression, when, as one scholar has written, "free time conjured up not so much leisure . . . as unemployment, the workman's dread."

Besides, who had money to travel to places of his dreams? For many, even getting to the coast of nearby Normandy was an impossible expense. Few could afford a car; indeed, it wasn't automobiles but tandem bicycles whose sales surged during this period and became a symbol of freewheeling delight. But as for a longer trip, such as to the Côte d'Azur, who could afford *that*?

Enter Léo Lagrange. The new undersecretary of state for leisure and sports, just thirty-five, held ideas that seized the imagination of France. He was no writer, but gave interviews and radio talks that promoted his views on a subject few had thought much about. *Loisir?* Leisure? It came from the Latin *licere*, he instructed an interviewer for *France-Soir-Dimanche* soon after taking office, meaning "it is permitted"; quite literally, then, leisure meant *free* time. Lagrange took such ideas with utmost seriousness, propagated them with evangelical fervor, and became such a symbol of leisure and sport that stadiums and gymnasiums across France would one day bear his name. "We want," he concluded one radio address, "that the worker, the peasant, and the unemployed should discover in leisure a joy in life and a sense of their own dignity."

And this was the man who, in the brief interval before the first *congés payés*, urgently called a meeting of the directors of France's railroads. What he had in mind, he explained to the men before him, was train tickets for workers and their families at 40 percent off the normal fare.

The rail-company directors, most of them much older than he, sat around in a circle, silent, severe, scarcely moving. Yes, one of them said at last, it was true they had signaled a willingness to make a gesture, but . . .

A gesture, declared Lagrange, wouldn't do.

But, Monsieur le Ministre, one of them replied, they could hardly be expected to carry so many passengers at a loss; surely that much was evident. Lagrange was mounting a fatal strike against the rail companies of the French nation.

"We're finished," thought his wife, Madeleine, who was there for the meeting as his aide. "We carry no weight with these people." But her husband persevered. Later, she'd be unable to recall what he said to them, only the passion with which he said it. Finally, he posed the question in the starkest terms: "Gentlemen, is it Yes or No?"

A hushed conference. Then, the way Madame Lagrange remembered it, the railroad spokesman replied, "It's Yes, Monsieur le Ministre; in four days, you will have *le billet Lagrange.*" And that was what they called it from then on—a ticket cheap enough to let a worker, who all his life did just as he was told, travel to the far corners of France and feel that same delicious "it is permitted" as did the idle rich.

The labyrinthine stipulations governing *le billet Lagrange* would be familiar to anyone buying an airline ticket today. You had to show written proof you were eligible for *congés payés*. You had to be traveling at least two hundred kilometers. You had to be away at least five days, but no longer than thirty-one. The tickets were good for every train until the end of September—except not on, uh, certain days. The ordinary *billet Lagrange* got you 40 percent off the usual fare. But ten people traveling together got 50 percent off. And special trains to particular destinations reduced the fare further; Paris to Nice, round trip, could be as little as 175 francs. At a time when a hotel employee, say, might make seven hundred francs a month, this was low enough for some families to manage.

Beginning that August and during the last five months of 1936, 550,000 Lagrange tickets were sold; the figure almost doubled the following year. Sales offices were set up in factories, because workers in outlying industrial suburbs would find it difficult to get into town to buy tickets. Aside from soldiers, many Frenchmen had never traveled any distance on their own and wouldn't even know where the train stations *were*. Labor unions organized group trips, in part because many workers didn't know travel's most elementary how-tos.

The big top-end hotels were out of reach for most of the new vacationers. But as a Communist Party newspaper noted a few years later, *congés payés* profited small and mid-range hotels, and helped make summer the new high season more than all the publicity by the established tourism authorities. Many workers stayed at youth hostels or camped; a *hôtel du plein air* was, of course, a tent. Many, too, found themselves thinking fondly of relatives they hadn't seen for a while; you'd "remember your Auvergne cousins, your Breton uncle, or your army buddy who catches oysters on the Arachon coast."

On July 31, 1936, virtually every factory in France shut down for fifteen days. Tandem bicycles loaded with young couples and their few belongings whooshed through the streets of Paris. Crowds packed the train stations. "I'd never noticed until then," recalled someone charged with helping the new vacationers find their trains at the Gare de Lyon,

to what extent travelers on the great express trains seemed so blasé, and affected such indifference. Whereas the ones we

helped made us think of a village wedding: They cried with joy.
They sang. They said such sweet, innocent things, like "Long
live life!"

Trente-six, they'd call it later, 1936, a year raised to the same place in
the memory of some as 1789, the French Revolution. The song sung in
those heady first days of '36 saluted happiness, light hearts, and love. It
was called "Allons au-devant de la vie," or, roughly, Let us go off in
search of life. And that's what they did. They set off for the mountains.
For the countryside. For the Côte d'Azur.

The scene at the stations drew much press attention. The trains
whistled, smoked, and heaved. The crowds thronged. A reporter for *Fi-
garo*, Georges Ravon, boarded an afternoon train to Nice and, much as
author Tom Wolfe might today, fixed on the revealing surfaces of his
working-class fellow passengers. He observed

> red ties, scarlet handkerchiefs, wild roses lost in masses of well
> brushed suits, cardigan sweaters buttoned right up to their cel-
> luloid collars. The women, too, had made commendable, often
> pleasing attempts at elegance. There were berets, and flowered
> hats, and feathered hats. . . . But also a sportier look—of knick-
> ers, and bulky wool jumpers embroidered with their wearers'
> initials. . . .

One photo shows young men and women on the point of departure, hanging out the windows of a crowded train compartment. From
down at track level, we gaze up at them, almost reverently; the sun
makes halos of their hair. *"La mer au bout des rails,"* reads the caption, the
sea at the end of the tracks. Actually, most workers, especially families
with children, never got near the sea. They stayed close to home, using
their *congés payés* to sit back and relax, or else to make short trips into the
country to visit family. Still, tens of thousands *did* reach the Riviera.

The day after leaving Paris, four hundred of them on that first train
arrived in Nice. At the station, the local association for popular
tourism, brass band and all, welcomed them. A reporter wrote of "ex-

clamations of wonder from the crowd at our vaunted blue sky and bright sun." After posing for pictures in front of the station, they were directed to small hotels and pensions where special accommodations had been made for them. Arranged for them, too, were show tickets, shop discounts, and bus trips.

A children's book written later, by Roger Bordier, captures the excitement of that year when banners and placards filled the streets, strikes swept the country, the "Internationale" rose on every worker's lips, and *congés payés* reached deep into French life. *J'étais enfant en 1936*, it was called: I was a child in 1936.

"You know, Pierrot," Papa tells the young narrator as Uncle Louis's train pulls away from the platform in Paris, "we too will soon take the train, for our first vacation. Where would you like to go?"

Over the next few days, the family confers. Papa likes the southwest, Mama the beaches of Brittany. Seduced by visions of palm trees, little Pierrot, still small enough to sit on his father's shoulders, holds out for the Côte d'Azur.

Too expensive, says Mama. Besides, "we haven't the clothes for a place like that."

Says Papa: "We'll manage." The Lagrange tickets will help. Côte d'Azur it is.

After a long night on the train, they reach the shores of the Mediterranean. There they buy clothes of a kind they've never needed before. Light shorts and a mauve *capeline* for sister Gisèle. For Mama, a flowered dress. For Papa, a cloth cap and white short-sleeved shirt. And for Pierrot, a blazer so big on him he has to roll up the sleeves.

At one point, they sense hostile glares, hear people whispering among themselves: "Who *are* those people?"

Papa turns abruptly toward them: *"Salopards!"* Bastards!

But soon they're laughing it off. "Why be angry with them?" Pierrot thinks later. "Victory was ours. And so was the sea."

They sit on a bench beneath palm trees along the sea wall, balancing picture postcards on their knees, writing friends back home. Pierrot has picked a card showing steps leading down to the shore, beach umbrellas, the sea gently lapping the golden sand. He gropes for what to say, dashes off a few words, looks up. And then, for a long time, he just sits there "looking at the palm trees and, through the palms, the glowing red sun, shining on our new happiness."

And it *was* a new happiness. New for him, for his family, and for millions who'd never before traveled. "Thanks to *congés payés*," a leftwing journal observed in 1939, "the French worker has had a chance to know this paradise long perceived as inaccessible to the common people: the Côte d'Azur." By one estimate, two hundred thousand *congés payés*—the phrase was sometimes applied to the people who took them—enjoyed the Riviera in 1937. For six straight hours, one August day that year, trains pulled out of the Gare de Lyon every twelve minutes, most of them bound for La Côte.

For the most part, the new vacationers tried to fit right in. Many of the women, like Pierrot's mother, bought *capelines*, the traditional Niçois peasant hat (though that only proved they weren't really Niçois). The *congés payés* didn't demonstrate. They didn't wear placards. Mostly, they were trouble to no one. That first summer, an official noted, there'd been complete calm on the Riviera. "The police have not pointed up the smallest problem." In short, they behaved themselves.

The revolution in leisure had revealed deep fissures in French public opinion, leaving some to worry they would *not* behave themselves, that the Republic might not survive ordinary workers taking off on vacation. "In opening the way to the red trains," noted a right-wing publication, referring to their revolutionary cargo, "we close it to the famous Blue Train" and its more genteel passengers. One cartoon showed an old lady, complete with lorgnette, looking out at the proles frolicking in the sea: "You don't think, do you, that I'm going to go into the same water as these Bolsheviks!"

Just as most workers weren't used to the idea of paid vacation, most Nice *hôteliers* weren't used to catering to them. Since the war, Nice tourism had turned upside down, what with summer supplanting winter, hotel palaces shutting down, small family-operated hotels springing up. Thousands of visitors of modest means didn't stay at hotels at all, but in furnished rooms let by enterprising Niçois. *Congés payés* represented yet one more blow.

Robert Viers, who headed a group of small hotelkeepers and championed the summer season, saw Nice's future dependent on a *tourisme moyen*, or Everyman's tourism, coexisting with the traditional *tourisme de luxe*; the group's slogan was *"Nice pour tous,"* Nice for all. But to *hôteliers* who'd come up serving the wealthy and well-born, this was a hard pill to swallow. It was bad enough when their Russian aristocrats had vanished. Now they were to welcome metalworkers and shop clerks?

Beneficiaries of *congés payés* worried whether they could expect even ordinary respect in high-toned places like the Riviera. "Who will protect us against being cheated in the auberges and the hotels?" was a question posed in one socialist newspaper. The reply came back: *You will.*

> Be our information agents everywhere you go, and say it loud during your stay. Make hotelkeepers and merchants understand that it's in their interests to satisfy their new clientele. Because next year, based on information you gather, we will recommend hospitable establishments to our million members—and we will boycott the others!

The new tourists *were* sometimes treated shabbily. *"Interdit aux congés payés,"* at least a few Nice shops advised: If you're one of *them*, don't come in. A metalworker's wife recalled how the staff at one Riviera hotel was surprised she and her friends knew how to use a fork. And some of the barbs greeting *congés payés* were downright wicked. One cartoon grotesquely caricatured Popular Front leaders gathered at a seaside resort junked up with liquor bottles, trash, and Lenin posters.

Harvey Levenstein, a scholar of American tourists in France, writes how, even by the mid-nineteenth century, "middle-class Americans traveling in Europe who did things that were routine for upper-class tourists in the first half of the century" were tarred with "the shameful term 'tourist.'" Those new to exotic places and beautiful things, it seems, *always* get the cold shoulder from those who have enjoyed them all along. The French factory workers were no exception.

Back in 1896, at the very height of Belle Époque dissipation and excess, Charles Lenthéric concluded a history of the Riviera this way:

> In this France of ours exists a region specially favored by Nature, but which private speculation has turned till now into a domain . . . reserved for the benefit of a few people fortunate in possessing this world's goods, most of them wealthy foreigners. It is desirable, it is indeed no more than just, that this land and this sun should be accessible, if not to all our fellow-countrymen, at least to many more than now enjoy it.

Forty years later, the first trains from the Gare de Lyon brought ordinary workers and their families, piled onto rude wood banquettes in third-class compartments, to the Riviera. The gravelly shore below the Promenade des Anglais rang with the joyful noise of vacationing workers and their families. It was *Trente-six,* and something like Lenthéric's dream had come true.

14 HÔTEL EXCELSIOR

IT IS ONE MORE IN A LINE OF GUIDEBOOKS GOING BACK TO THE early days of Riviera tourism. This one's called *Nouveau Guide touristique de la Côte d'Azur*, 1940 edition. It is published by Nice's largest newspaper, *L'Éclaireur*, and sells for eight francs. Its cover is bright red, save for an inset that stylishly integrates the region's icons—palm trees in the foreground, the arc of the shore, the blue of the sea, a village clinging to a precipice, and, rising above the whole tableau, jagged Alpine peaks. . . .

But *this* old guidebook, from *this* year, sears your fingertips. For 1940 was the year France fell; when the Nazis occupied its north; when Jewish refugees fled to the Riviera to escape their persecutors. Some of them, certainly, clutched guides such as this. *Maybe this one.*

From 1940 to 1945, Nice's hotels, restaurants, nightclubs, parks, theaters, and casinos became a stage set for tragedy. During the First World War, Nice had been six hundred miles from the front. During the Second, Nice *was* the front. Not for the whole war, and not for pitched battles like Normandy or Stalingrad. But in Nice, the Gestapo tracked down men, women, and children and sent them to their deaths. In Nice, Allied bombing raids took civilian lives. Resistance fighters fell. And just a few miles down the coast, in mid-August 1944, the Allies invaded southern France. In five years, control of Nice passed from France's Third Republic, to the Vichy regime, to the Italians, to the Germans, and finally to the Americans, before being restored to France in 1945. During these years, hotel rooms where once people made love or

silently contemplated the sea became military command posts, torture chambers, or temporary asylums that reeked with fear.

❧

In September 1939, after Nazi Germany invaded Poland, France and England declared war. The impact on the Riviera was swift. Railway companies that fed travelers to Nice from Lyons, Avignon, and Marseilles, their rolling stock requisitioned by the military, drastically cut service. The first Cannes Film Festival, set to begin the same day as the invasion, was canceled. Overnight, Nice hotels lost half their business. The same went for the big department stores, where sales of jewelry, perfumes, and other luxury items dropped 70 percent.

In May 1940, German armies swept into Belgium and France. Within weeks, Paris fell. By the cease-fire terms, Germany occupied the northern half of France. The other half, *l'État français*, a French State with its capital in Vichy, remained unoccupied, though at Germany's sufferance; "Vichy" became forevermore a synonym for spineless collaboration with a cruel enemy.

Nice and the rest of the Côte d'Azur lay in unoccupied France, to which hundreds of thousands now fled. As historian Julian Jackson has astutely written, "This 'exodus' of the summer of 1940 seems like some hideously distorted mirror image of that no less famous exodus of the summer of 1936 when hundreds of thousands of workers departed on their first ever paid holidays."

Nice's guests from Britain and Belgium, of course, were gone. But they were in part supplanted by soldiers on leave; refugees from the north, their possessions reduced to diamonds sewn into the linings of their coats; and *nouveaux riches* bent on profiting from the black market. For a while, if perversely, cabarets, theaters, and movie houses thrived. During the winter of 1941, betting at Nice's racetrack beside the Var broke every record. The hotels—many larger ones now run on behalf of German or Italian interests—at first didn't do as well; one in six Nice unemployed at the end of the summer of 1940 was a hotel worker. By the following spring, however, with the reopening of the casinos, business was better. In June 1941, a regional committee for tourism was formed in Nice, replacing an earlier "festivals committee" that the Vichy regime deemed unduly frivolous.

Among those arriving in Nice, Cannes, and other Riviera towns during these first two years of the war were Jews from all over Europe. Jews had lived in Nice for centuries, had their own cemetery on the Château Hill, numbered perhaps a thousand. Now, though, many more came—from Paris and elsewhere in France; from Germany, Austria, Eastern Europe. By one account, they and other Northern refugees were "the ones dressed in black, the men and women whose clothes looked too big for them, cramming the sidewalk cafés, crowding the parks, spilling over onto the beach." Nice sheltered five thousand Jews on the eve of the war. Some carried Baedekers and Michelins as if they were on vacation. But they weren't on vacation. They were running for their lives.

Some of the well-off and well-known among them, including actors, writers, and musicians, took rooms in hotels on the Promenade des Anglais in Nice, or the Croisette in Cannes, *its* Promenade; one anti-Semitic screed took to calling it "Kahn." But, as one account recalls, most of the Jews "faced hardship and holed up in miserable hotels." The International Red Cross helped. So did Jewish self-help societies in Nice. The Hôtel Roosevelt became a center of Orthodox Jewry. "Here," it was said, "one could see rabbis in their traditional apparel walking through the streets, listen to Talmudic discussions and hear the old tunes of Hebrew prayer and Talmudic study."

We have at least one other slant on Nice's Jews from this period, thanks to a memo written by SS Hauptsturmführer Dannecker, chief of the Gestapo's Jewish office in France. Charged with ridding France of its Jews, Theodor Dannecker visited Nice in mid-July 1942. He reported that on the Promenade des Anglais there were "an enormous number of Jews"; that the Niçois avoided the Promenade because of them; that the Jews at one casino represented 60 percent of its visitors.

From the start, the anti-Semitic Vichy regime painted Jews as living extravagantly while real Frenchmen suffered; as criminals, speculators, and black-marketeers who sucked the lifeblood out of France. In Nice, the names of rue Rothschild and another street honoring a Jew had been changed. Jewish businesses had been shut down. *Affiches* went up saying "Down with the Jews."

Foreign Jews were the special target of these attacks. To most native French, even including some French Jews, the refugees from the North seemed alien. They looked different, spoke strangely. And they *weren't French*. So, after Dannecker's visit, as Vichy stepped up its anti-Semitic measures, it aimed them at the foreigners. On August 26, 1942, police rounded up six hundred of them in Nice and, five days later, shipped them to Drancy, the infamous camp outside Paris that served as waystation for Auschwitz. The police, wrote one Jewish survivor, "surrounded hotels, villas, whole blocks of houses and dragged out of their beds terrified Jews who had come to France after 1936. The shouts, the wailing and the groaning broke the stillness of the morning." These performances did not enjoy wide acclaim among the Niçois. "The methods employed," a subsequent report admitted, "are clearly unpopular."

In November 1942, Hitler ordered his armies into southern France—except, that is, for eight *départements* east of the Rhone; this pocket of France, which included Nice, was Italy's. But Fascist rule didn't make things worse for Nice's Jews, it made them better; ignoring protests from their German allies, the Italians scarcely laid a hand on them. German Foreign Minister Ribbentrop complained personally to Mussolini when he met with him in February 1943; oh, yes, certainly, the Italian dictator assured him, but he did nothing. An SS officer's report three months later lamented that the Italians had resolved the Jewish question "in a special manner—to use their expression, 'in the Latin way,' the antithesis of 'the German way'" prevalent elsewhere in France. In other words, they left the Jews alone, as they mostly did during the war. Even those holding plainly false papers, lamented this officer, enjoyed Italian protection.

By train and boat, Jews from the rest of France converged on this sun-blessed haven; thirty thousand of them crowded twenty miles of coast. The Italian *carabinieri* protected Nice's Jewish sites; when French anti-Semites marched on a Nice synagogue, the local commander ordered the arrest of anyone who threatened it. For almost a year, in the middle of the war, at the height of the Holocaust's frightful fury, the hotels, villas, boarding houses, and apartments of the Riviera represented life and hope to European Jews.

But in September 1943, following the Allied invasion of Sicily and southern Italy, the Italians capitulated. German armies rushed south to fill the Axis void, occupying Nice, which Italian forces were evacuating. Raoul Mille depicted the moment in a novel, *Les Amants du paradis:*

> From the west, where the sky glowed with a faint, milky light, rose the distant murmur of a panting beast. Its moan grew into a throbbing. The soil, the foundations, the walls, the beach itself shook in slow, heavy spasms. The day dawned, gray and pink, like the belly of a fish pulled from the sea. A mist blurred the horizon. It was against this surreal and quavering backdrop that the first tank appeared, then cars and trucks.

> The Germans were on the Promenade des Anglais.

Could any contrast be more grotesque? On the one hand, the gray-uniformed German troops, with all they conjured up of merciless severity. On the other, the wide, palm-crowned Promenade, with all *it* conjured up of abandon, of easy living, of a leisure that workers and worriers everywhere—all the world's hurried, nervous, and sick—craved.

And now it shook to the roar of German tanks.

The Germans tried to come across as benign. They sent out photographers to snap soldiers at tourist spots—gesturing meaningfully beside the Emperor Augustus's monument at La Turbie; or mingling with street urchins; or camera in hand, strolling along the Promenade, flanked by beach umbrellas and sidewalk merchants. If the Germans were just tourists, the photographs as much as said, why fear them?

For a while, cabarets filled with Wehrmacht officers and Gestapo men, and cash registers rang with purchases of perfume, furs, and wines for fräuleins back home. But as the war wore on, such extravagance dried up. Receipts from the *taxe de séjour* fell from 190,000 francs in December 1943, soon after the Italians left, to fourteen thousand the following May.

With its principal source of revenue gone and Germany siphoning its resources to the Fatherland, Nice had trouble even feeding itself. Staples became scarce. As malnutrition took its toll, teeth grew brittle, finger- and toenails tore loose. All anyone talked about, besides the war, was food.

As the Allied noose tightened, and after Field Marshal Erwin Rommel expressed displeasure with anti-invasion defenses he'd inspected along the south coast, the Germans began to disfigure the pretty tourist face of Nice. In October 1943, they banned bicycles from the Promenade. In December, cement barricades twelve feet high went up, blocking access to the Promenade save for a small pedestrian opening. In January, the Germans closed all of Nice's restaurants and cinemas and declared the Promenade off limits. Blockhouses were erected, machine-gun and anti-aircraft emplacements set up. Young, bare-chested soldiers, rifles stacked neatly beside them as they worked in the sun, dug trenches, laid barbed wire, mined the beach.

In April 1944, Elizabeth Foster, an elderly American unaccountably stuck in Nice for the duration of the war, recorded in her secret journal that the authorities had ordered every civilian to "produce a specified amount of copper," else draw a heavy fine; her quota was thirty pounds, which sent her rummaging among candlesticks and fireplace ornaments. The Germans demanded copper, among other metals; the previous month, they'd turned to that tourist shrine the Jetée-Promenade for a thousand tons of it.

Back in the thirties, Klaus Mann, son of German novelist Thomas Mann, had described the Jetée as an "enchanted Moorish palace" that was "frankly hideous, in abominable taste." And yet, he admitted in the same breath, when it sparkled in the night, glowing like "the sumptuous center of some enormous jewel," irony evaporated and the Jetée truly *was* an enchanted palace.

The Germans scavenged the Jetée's brass and bronze, its electric cable, its zinc counters, stripping it of finery that had delighted generations of visitors. A small army of workers dismantled the rest of the edifice. Soon its great cupola was just a filigree of bare ironwork. Finally, Nice's Eiffel Tower was reduced to stumpy pylons—in the right light, they looked like tombstones—washed by the sea.

∞

Soon after their arrival, the Germans moved key offices into Nice hotels. The German commander installed himself at the Atlantic, on boulevard Victor-Hugo. The navy took over the camouflaged Hôtel Suisse, built into the Château Hill. The Gestapo got the Hermitage. The Milice, the French Gestapo with whom the Germans collaborated, got the Concordia. As for the Jew-hunting operation that followed German armies across Europe, this, too, had its headquarters. Arriving in Nice on September 10, 1943, on the heels of the Wehrmacht, was SS Hauptsturmführer Alois Brunner, fresh from rounding up Jews in Austria and Greece. Brunner, a thirty-one-year-old Austrian, was charged with overseeing the final solution of the Jewish problem in the Alpes-Maritimes. He established his headquarters at the Hôtel Excelsior.

Originally known as the Saint-Ermin, the Excelsior—it had no connection to the old Excelsior Regina—had gone up around the turn of the century, and for years had served as one of Nice's many second-rank hotels. Today it remains a hotel, a handsome one, all arches and pediments and Belle Époque detailing. Its charming inner courtyard, dotted with blue umbrellas, is lush with flowers and bushes. The courtyard's whole interior façade is green with luxuriant ivy that hangs down from iron balconies. The desk clerk gives you a brochure that recounts the hotel's history and architectural features—florid stuff about harmonious proportions and restored ornamental plasterwork. The brochure does not, of course, mention 1943 and 1944, when its wide hallways bore the tread of Alois Brunner and his men, when Jews were stuffed into bedless rooms until they were ready to be marched up the street to the station and loaded onto rail cars.

Nice's Jews had been trapped by fast-changing events. Before the Italians surrendered, an influential Italian Jewish banker had worked out a way to get most of them across the border to Italy or North Africa. But all depended on word of the Armistice's being delayed for a few weeks. It wasn't; the announcement came on September 8. "By nightfall," according to one account, "Nice was one huge party," with women kissing Italian soldiers, accordions playing, couples dancing in the street. The jubilation, however, was short-lived. When Hitler sent his crack Panzer divisions into northern Italy and the Italian-occupied zone of France, panic seized Nice's Jews, now swollen to perhaps twenty thousand. Desperate to reach safe haven, a few would trek for days through the Alps. Most, though, stayed in the city and nervously waited. On September 9, the day after the announcement, German troops crossed the Var; two days later, they arrived in Nice.

Immediately, Brunner's men set to work. They picked up forty-five Jews as they tried to cross the Var, arrested a hundred more at the train station on September 13. Even from high up in her apartment over rue de Rivoli, Elizabeth Foster could see what was going on. "Poor souls," she wrote on September 21. "All Jews are arrested wherever found, their belongings confiscated."

In menacing black Citroëns, the Germans and their French henchmen hunted down Nice's Jews. They'd abruptly surround an intersection, a market, or a street and stop anyone they even remotely suspected. They'd subject the men to "medical examinations"; those circumcised, including some Christians and Muslims, were seized on the spot. Women were judged Jewish on the basis of facial features. A Catholic nurse was arrested because her name was Esther. Official papers meant nothing; they were assumed fake.

Brought by truck to the Excelsior—Brunner would watch them pull up from a second-story balcony overlooking rue Durante—the Jews were relieved of their possessions; their money and jewelry were supposed to reimburse the hotel for food and lodging during the days or weeks before they went to Drancy. Many were tortured for information about brothers, parents, and children not yet caught in the net. One begged an attending physician for a lethal injection; refused, he threw himself from a window. Some young Jewish women, it was rumored, were kept at the Excelsior, sterilized, then shipped out "for the pleasure of the soldiers on the eastern front."

Finally, in groups of sixty or so at a time, they'd be herded to the station, a few hundred shuffling paces up the street. "The road between the sinister hotel-prison 'Excelsior' and the station became," by one 1944 account, "a Calvary for the Jewish population of Nice. Two or three times a week the same heart-rending procession takes place, before a silent, tearful crowd held back by a large police contingent." Then it was onto the train. Some Jews, picked up on the beach, arrived at Drancy in shorts, shivering.

Many of the first seizures took place in hotels. The Germans would barricade the street, burst into the hotel, and haul off anyone suspected as Jewish. They picked up Joseph and Etka Dyzenchanz, Polish Jews in their sixties, who were staying at the Hotel P.L.M. ("Moderate prices, open all year" said the hotel's ad in a 1939 guidebook.) They picked up Abram Klajman, forty-two, and his family, at the Hôtel Busby. ("Every Modern Comfort.") One who survived the war, Léon Poliakov, then staying at Hôtel de Lausanne, on rue Rossini, noticed that the Germans hit ten of Nice's 170 or so hotels each night. Before going to bed, he'd reassure himself that there was only a one-in-seventeen chance they'd come for him.

Early on, the Gestapo stopped a married Jewish couple in the lobby of the Negresco.

"May I go upstairs to get my coat?" asked the wife.

"Yes, but if you try to get away, your husband will answer for it."

When she didn't come right back down, they went up to the room, only to find her dead; she had poisoned herself.

Soon the Jews abandoned the hotels that had given them such fleeting refuge. The Splendid, a hotel doing a particularly brisk business in refugee Jews, lost two-thirds of its trade within a month. A German dispatch exulted in late September:

> The city of Nice has lost its ghetto appearance. The Jews no longer circulate. The synagogues are closed. And the Promenade des Anglais offers to Aryan walkers numerous chairs which, up to now, were occupied by Jews.

Tourist Nice had become *judenrein*, free of Jews. The manhunt moved from hotels and other tourist haunts to hospitals, apartments, basements, and other refuges. In the end, the Germans in Nice wound up shipping off to Drancy about three thousand Jews, most of whom died at Auschwitz. After the initial easy harvest, the Germans had increasingly to rely on informers who—paid a hundred, a thousand, even five thousand francs per Jewish head—would come by the Excelsior to report, and collect.

On August 15, 1944, two months after D-Day in Normandy, the Allies landed across a forty-mile-wide front near Saint-Raphaël and quickly moved inland. Four days later, about a week before the city's liberation, Elizabeth Foster noted how few blows the Niçois were striking against the occupiers, even now, with the issue little in doubt and the Germans set to pull out. "If one lives on the Riviera it is very hard to believe in the Resurrection of France," she wrote. The rest of the country, she felt, had exhibited courage, patience, and now joy. But not, from all she could see, Nice. "I try not to forget that the Riviera is,

as someone said of Palm Beach, an atmosphere which 'melts the moral marrow.'"

Tourist towns, she was saying, did not make for men and women ardent of principle. As for Nice, whether because of its historically blurred national identity, or its sweet Italian streak, or tolerance born of welcoming visitors from everywhere, it couldn't be much bothered with choosing sides. Italians? French? Germans? Americans? Did it matter in the end? Not so long as visitors filled the hotels, crowded the clubs, and left fat tips.

The Niçois, it seemed to Foster, wanted nothing more than that the war end—*whoever* won.

∞

Some years before, during the winter of 1936, a group of young soldiers wearing berets at jaunty angles, cigarettes poking from the corners of their mouths, had posed for a picture on the Promenade des Anglais. The Mediterranean lay at their backs. They were bundled up against the chill, but looked happy and free. Later, they had the photo made into a picture postcard. On the back, one of them wrote in French: "Souvenir of first trip to Nice, January 12, 1936."

I have seen many picture postcards from Nice, in color and black and white, from before and after World War II. They show the Promenade des Anglais at night, all aglow; the great arc of the Baie des Anges; the Jetée-Promenade before the Germans got to it. The messages on the back never say much. They tell of hotels stayed at, sights seen. Or they report on the state of the sender's health. Or tell of the joys of the climate. Or complain when it falls short of expectations. They're almost never the small literary gems one might wish. *I am here,* they say, *I am thinking of you.* They are entirely innocuous, reflecting minds happily vacant.

Which is probably how most visitors have experienced Nice over the centuries. Their letters and journals, most of them, sputter about the blueness of the sea and the sky. Two days or two weeks of easy ambles along the seashore, of wandering though shops, of rich meals and mild entertainments, leave them with little on their minds and less to say.

World War II, on the contrary, left people with plenty to say. The workers liberated from their factories, the lovers arm in arm, were gone. In their stead were Nazi stormtroopers, Jews running for their lives, Resistance fighters, black-marketeers, most of them riven by urgency, worry, or fear; *these* were Nice's wartime visitors, and later they'd have no want of life-and-death drama with which to regale their grandchildren.

Here, then, is the perverse paradox of tourism: It is mostly banal, it is often artificial and contrived, it makes little claim on the intellect. And yet it stands high among the dividends of peace. For it supplies some of those rare moments of life at its sweetest—of repose, amusement, pleasure, and joy—for which the mass of men and women ache.

15 DIGGING OUT

TO VISITING AMERICAN GI'S, VETERANS OF FIGHTING THAT HAD reduced Europe to rubble, Nice in 1945 could seem a paradise untouched by war. By the standards of a coddled tourist, though, it was a shambles.

The Promenade des Anglais, one journal observed right after the city's liberation, was no longer a jewel admired by the world. "In a year, the German barbarians have managed to transform this magnificent vista into a twisted scrapheap of iron and stone." Eight months later, the fountains in the Public Garden were still dry, the oleander was tangled in barbed wire, the flower beds were arid mounds of earth lying atop bomb shelters.

In the Alpes-Maritimes generally, fourteen thousand buildings had been destroyed or damaged. One hundred thirty bridges were down, including one over the Var knocked out by Allied bombs. Thousands of German POWs were set to work rebuilding Nice; their job included disarming the forty-three thousand mines that their army had left behind—and which, just in the latter half of 1945, killed thirty-three people.

Men wielded shovels and picks. The city rebuilt. But scars persisted long into the postwar period. When English writer Charles Graves visited in 1947, the foundations of German blockhouses were still visible. So were "whole rows of dragon's teeth," an antitank defense. Meanwhile, war deaths and years of low birthrates had shaved Nice's population; it would not reach prewar levels again until 1954. Food shortages kept rationing in place until 1949. The black market flourished; a liter of olive oil went for eight hundred francs—a week's wages for some workers.

Yet, when, in September 1947, Henri Tschann, secretary general of Nice's *syndicat d'initiative*, reviewed the recent summer season, it was not the war that weighed on him. Rather, it was the seismic shift to the tourism industry evident in its wake. That past summer had "given the impression of being a good one," he led off, but it was "crucial to try to examine the facts a little more closely." And this, over ten single-spaced pages, he did, peering deep into the numbers for troubling truths.

With every festival or civic event, Nice railway officials would report how many passengers got off at the *gare*. The papers would bruit them about, make as if Nice had been restored to its prewar glory. But these numbers, Tschann felt, meant nothing, because they didn't show how long people stayed. That was best reckoned in a unit called the *nuitée*, one room occupied for one night; two rooms occupied for four nights represented eight *nuitées*. And this measure showed that the typical visitor stayed in Nice only a few days—five, on average. Postwar tourists, he concluded, "are interested *more in traveling than in staying*."

There was much more to Tschann's report. He looked at visitors by month of arrival, by the sorts of hotel they stayed at, by national origin. He pointed out that, for two-thirds of the year, most Nice hotels limped along one-quarter full. That Nice needed visitors all summer, not just in August. That many of those who ventured abroad—eight in ten among the British and the Belgians—were doing so for the first time. That Americans, as visitors, had been oversold; they'd never surpass the English, for example, since there weren't enough boats and planes to get them over. Not all Tschann said proved prescient. But, plainly, he had been thinking hard about tourism.

And it was about time, too. Nice tourism had suffered thirty years of turmoil, with scarcely a moment to catch its breath: The abrupt end of Belle Époque order, peace, and prosperity. The disappearance of Nice's aristocratic visitors. The coming of the automobile. The winter season's giving way to summer. Worldwide depression. *Congés payés* and the new class of visitor. Defeat and occupation. And now, afterward, a decaying tourism infrastructure; ruinous inflation; and the coming of age of air travel.

Already by 1946, the number of French men and women using cheap *congés-payés* tickets (suspended during the war) was up to that of 1937, about two million; want of travelers wasn't a problem. But Henri Tschann was saying that a bustling *gare* didn't mean a healthy hotel industry. And two months later, the head of the Riviera hotel association, Monsieur Lambert, praising Tschann's report as "eloquent," developed the point further.

"As many people as before the war!" Lambert has the man in the street, misled by upbeat press accounts, saying. "So you're happy. No? Ah, these *hôteliers*, never satisfied. What are they complaining about?" What they were complaining about, he said, was "the slow, painful death being inflicted upon them." And those short stays were the culprit.

Many tourists good, fewer tourists bad? It wasn't so simple. Fill a room for a week and you made money; expenses like laundry, fresh linen, and upkeep could be written off against that whole week of receipts. But fill it for a night here, a night there—*location de passage,* Lambert called it—and you chalked up most of the same costs, but not the revenue to balance them; you lost money. And with shorter stays, more and more rooms were losing money. *No wonder* Riviera hotelkeepers wrung their hands.

The whole business was unsettled, captive to new and wrenching paradoxes. There were plenty of tourists, yet hotel restaurants and bars were empty; only the souvenir merchants were happy. By 1952, almost three-quarters of Nice hotel guests stayed in the city's one- and two-stars, the bottom rungs. In a tourist economy traditionally fueled by the big-spenders at the Negrescos and Ruhls, that was unwelcome news enough. But many postwar visitors never checked into hotels at all. They stayed in furnished rooms or little studio apartments, or camped out with relatives. Or *literally* camped out—in 1953, at one of seven thousand Riviera campsites, most of them on the other side of the Var, where it was flat enough to pitch a tent.

Some of Nice's newest "visitors" *weren't* visitors at all, but retired businessmen, government officials, and military officers. In Nice, they sought for the rest of their lives what travelers had customarily hoped to find there for a few days or weeks at a time. And by fueling the demand for apartments (which sometimes *were* former hotels), they changed the face of the tourist's Nice.

In the two or three years right after the war, spurred by damage done during the occupation and the unsettled economy, fourteen more Nice hotels, with eight hundred rooms, shut down. "Will Nice," it was asked, "become a hotel cemetery?"

∞

The Splendid, a 120-room hotel on boulevard Victor-Hugo, was Henri Tschann's own. Built in 1880 as a sumptuous cocoon from which guests need scarcely stir, it was surrounded by fence and garden, boasted fine formal lobbies, a huge restaurant. Its lopsided distribution of rooms testified to its Belle Époque roots—vast suites to indulge wealthy guests for months at a time, tiny rooms for the maids and valets who served them. Like other Nice hotels, it had had its ups and downs. The twenties, profitable; losses during the Depression; a reprise thanks to the summer season. In 1947, the Splendid had been among the first in line for government funds to repair two million francs' worth of damage sustained during the war.

Through the fifties, the Splendid eked out a profit. But for how long? Tschann asked himself in the early 1960s. These days, many of his French customers were traveling abroad. As for foreign visitors, other regions and other countries beckoned. Taxes were high and bound higher. Meanwhile, the hotel's decaying physical plant cried out for repairs. The place was three-quarters of a century old. Since the war, they'd sunk 120 million francs into fixing it up. And *still* it looked decrepit.

What to do? Sink ever more money into the Nice landmark, and maybe never earn a franc? Or curtail investment, earn slim, short-term profits, and gradually run it into the ground?

Tschann did neither. The Splendid was just the sort of place, it seemed to him, bound to disappear anyway. What else to do with this dinosaur but tear it down? They'd sell off maybe three-fifths of the property on which the old hotel stood. On the rest they'd build a modern eight-story hotel, each of its rooms with private bath, balcony, and air-conditioning, designed for easy maintenance and to move short-staying guests in and out efficiently.

The Splendid came down. A new Splendid went up.

A few blocks away, at the Negresco, owner Paul Augier embraced different reasoning. Airplanes brought people in for ever-briefer stays; the sheer number of arrivals and departures, ten times what it had once been, demanded numerous employees simply to attend to them. Generally, business was down. The hotel's elite clientele were fewer. The Negresco presented a mournful sight.

But tear it down? *Impossible!* Augier decided instead to try to both hold the old clientele and go after a new.

Eight in ten Negresco guests were foreigners, typically charmed by all things French. So each room would be elaborately redecorated in classic French styles sure to appeal to them—an Empire room, a Louis XIII room, a Provençal room. Sure enough, delivered from the generic banality of the modern hotel, former guests returned. Some of them, Augier crowed, "perfectly happy with their own rooms, would ask to see others just out of curiosity, or for decorating tips for their own homes."

But the hotel also went after business travelers—regional sales representatives, members of professional associations, and the like, a new species of traveler escaping from home, but not from work. Business meetings required conference rooms, facilities for tape recording and simultaneous translation, meticulous organization. The Negresco created a special office to reserve meeting rooms and supply scheduling information. Business grew.

"The deluxe hotel remains viable," Augier concluded in the early sixties. "But the *hôtelier* can no longer remain shut off in his little retreat." Success depended on "his faculty of adaptation."

❧

Adaptation? During the forties and fifties, every sort of idea got a hearing in Nice.

One was for a jazz festival, inspired in part by the Cannes Film Festival, first held in 1946. Cannes wasn't yet the star-studded extravaganza of see-and-be-seen it became later. But Nice's Comité des Fêtes responded to the competition with the first Nice Jazz Festival, in February 1948.

Jazz went way back in Nice, to the Sammies, the American servicemen who visited after World War I. The festival did succeed in drawing Louis Armstrong and other American jazz legends. Shows in the Municipal Casino and the opera house, some broadcast over French radio, drew appreciative crowds. And on the final night, six hundred people paid five thousand francs each to see Armstrong receive a Sèvres vase in the great hall of the Negresco.

But the media impact was not all the Comité des Fêtes might have wished. Several journalists had been invited from Paris, put up at Nice hotels. You would expect from them, one press account had it later, "not an embellishment of the truth, certainly, but a true picture" of Nice's touristic pleasures. And what appeared in the weekly *Images du monde?* The story was headlined "CÔTE D'AZUR, LOST PARADISE" and began: "The Côte d'Azur is dead." Text and photo showed the Promenade des Anglais forlorn, the beach unappealing, the palaces deserted.

The following year, Nice had no jazz festival.

In 1953, a promoter decided that what the Côte d'Azur really needed was American-style motels, and wrote a five-page proposal outlining how that happy outcome might be achieved. Imagine in Nice, he said, "a hundred little *maisonnettes*, easily accessible and reasonably comfortable, grouped . . . in four or five Motels of 20 or 25 units each." Each would be constructed with walls, floor, and furniture requiring the least possible care, by specially trained teams of workers using standard techniques and materials.

And finished in four days flat.

The Côte d'Azur was changing, drawing those of "more diverse social origins"; low-cost motels would suit them. The trailer-park movement couldn't grow forever, not without destroying the aesthetics of La

Côte. The American Motel—it was still so novel an idea that he invariably capitalized the word, flanked it with quotation marks, or both—would solve the problem.

But he hadn't quite *got* it, it seemed to Henri Tschann, still head of Nice's *syndicat d'initiative*. An American motel room, otherwise needing few hotel services, did at least need its own carport, "to ease baggage handling, and that the car might serve almost as supplementary armoire." This feature the promoter had forgotten.

Tschann went on to argue that American-style motels would need to be tightly regulated, so "that our countryside is not disfigured by slipshod construction." Another asked to comment on the proposal pointed out that motels would undercut existing hotels. A third noted, "The situation in France cannot be compared to that of America, where tourists travel great distances without meeting a soul."

So this idea didn't get far; even today, the Riviera has few American-style motels. But others did. From the late forties on, in the press, from offices in Paris and Nice, reports, editorials, and studies spewed out suggestions, strategies, warnings, and ideas. On competition from the Italian side of the Riviera. On hotel and restaurant "supplements" reviled by foreign tourists. On currency fluctuations; extending the seasons; honeymoon business; a Nice conference center; a Nice airport . . .

From the bridging of the Var and the building of the *corniches* to the coming of the railroad, transportation advances had always helped drive Nice's growth as a travel destination. So it was after the war, with commercial air service and the airport. "The first Nice-Paris flight takes place June 12," *L'Espoir* advised its readers on June 9, 1945. "The trip takes five hours and costs 2200 francs," compared with twenty-two hours and thirteen hundred francs by train. The age-old obstacles to reaching Nice were mountain and sea; now you could just fly over them.

In 1935, Mayor Jean Médecin had declared a new airport among municipal improvements closest to his heart. The war intervened, but within months of the Liberation, the Allies took over the grass strip that had served until then and hard-paved a runway nearly a mile long; it was situated along a flat stretch beside the Var, tucked between the far western reaches of the Promenade des Anglais and the sea. At first, the airport was just one runway, an area to park planes, and a few scattered buildings. A villa across the road served as reception area to which passengers were driven by cab or in a little bus. Among the dozen or so planes lined up at the airport one August day in 1946 was an American DC-3, a German JU 52 dressed in Air France colors, and a few prewar biplanes. Passersby leaned against the fence by the side of the strip to watch planes take off and land.

Air travel was at first a luxury; you paid a premium for speed. An American on a budget seeking adventure in Europe after the war was as apt to take a tramp steamer as a plane. But prices dropped. Patronage shot up. In 1946, takeoffs and landings at Nice averaged just fourteen per day—about one per daylight hour; the airport handled thirty-four thousand passengers that year. But soon Nice had service to London, Marseilles, Madrid, Casablanca. . . . Planes grew bigger and faster. By 1950, the airport handled 225,000 passengers a year; by 1954, 450,000. Many names familiar today were already represented: Air France, KLM, Alitalia.

By 1957, Nice's airport *looked* like an airport—duly impressive façade, customs offices, parking lot, ten check-in counters, a couple of restaurants. In that year, the authorities estimated they would not have a million passengers a year until 1975; they had only to wait until 1962.

Easy air travel, though, wasn't an unmixed blessing; in some ways it added to the Riviera's postwar woes. Nice's airport became the second largest in France, after that of Paris. But if it was easy to get to Nice, it was easy to get *anywhere.* "You who love to travel comfortably and fast, take Air France," a 1955 ad advised; Nice was less than two hours from Paris, three from North Africa, twenty-four from Rio. But, then again, Rio was just twenty-four hours from Nice. The French represented 60 percent of La Côte's business. And now they could get their sun in Egypt, Hawaii, or the Caribbean.

It was no longer just Cannes or the Italian Riviera against which Nice competed. It was the whole world.

∞

Early in 1947, the Comité Régional du Tourisme established a Côte d'Azur welcome bureau, based in Nice, and directed by Madame Berthe Pourrière, a treasure of energy and initiative. Want to photograph the dogs of the Riviera? She or one of her aides would guide you through the streets and kennels of Nice. Want to learn to play a clarinet during your stay? She'd track down an instructor. You're a journalist from Brazil, where the casinos have been shut down? She'd show you those of La Côte. Everybody knew of the Riviera climate; her job was to sell foreign journalists, travel-agency directors, and celebrities on everything *else* about it, make sure they felt at home, and came away with pleasant memories, cheerful stories.

Madame Pourrière was a real pro. But to view tourism as a profession in the first place, an industry like any other, was still a new idea. When, in August 1948, word got out that Nice had dedicated three hundred thousand dollars to pulling in American visitors, *Nice-Matin* writer Pierre Rocher poked fun at those behind it.

> I hear that tourism is an industry. That it has technicians. There are those who make the beds. Those who salt the roast. Those who repaint storefronts. There are those who handle publicity, who coordinate bus and train schedules, who sell our sun on the Bourse, who transform palace hotels into furnished apartments, who bring comedy, ballet, opera to town. There are the animal trainers. There are also the magicians. Everyone counts.

Rocher left no doubt as to what he made of all this: Riviera tourism needed not arid technical skills but real imagination.

Still, in the postwar years, the trend was clear. The professionals were taking over. At a hotelkeepers' conference at Nice in November 1946, the idea for a France-wide tourism conference was born; the first was held, over six days in April 1948, at Biarritz. Tourism could no longer be dismissed as peripheral. It was serious business, ever more organized, replete with committees, associations, specialists. By the 1950s, a Nice school begun modestly in 1914 for the training of hotel workers was turning out *techniciens du tourisme* who learned art, foreign language, and history alongside accounting and travel-agency administration. "We are no longer in the time of the *diligences* and excursions by mule-back," wrote Robert Viers, director of the Nice-based Alpes-Maritimes hotel association, in a 1959 issue of its professional journal. Tourism was past its infancy.

Gone were the days of the *hivernants*, of the palaces, of a well-ordered society in which people knew their places. And this profound change was the work not of centuries but of just the four decades since World War I. There were men and women who had lived through it all—who had grown up with firm notions about who tourists were, why they traveled, and how they spent their time—and, within their lifetimes, seen these ideas overturned.

One of them, if more articulate than most, was André Siegfried. In a lecture he gave in 1954, the distinguished French economist and historian, a member of the Académie Française, pictured the leisurely travel with which he'd grown up menaced by the same machinelike forces he saw at work in modern life. Wistfully, he spoke of the *tables d'hôte* and magnificent reading rooms of the old palaces, of English lords and ladies who passed winter on the Riviera, of Russian princes dispensing princely sums. Seventy-nine now—he was twenty-five in 1900—he'd seen the old tourism swept away, replaced by "organized tourism, a mass-produced tourism which has become one of the most marked aspects of our century." Many travelers were still well off, of course. But somehow it was the Everyman "who sets the tone for vacations and travel." In leisure, as at work, the assembly line ruled. Travel became a product. "Individuality and fantasy give way to organization."

"Tourism's heroic age has now passed," he declared, plainly deploring the idea. Eminent names from the celebrated resorts of the past didn't count, only organization did.

> The stage we've reached is that of efficiency. Tourism is now constituted as a profession—and magnificently so, with its national and international agencies, its specialized personnel, its guidebook literature . . . its publicity, its credit networks.

As to who was responsible for all this, plainly it was the Americans. The English had had their day; now it was the Americans' turn. American informality. Brutal American-style factory organization that practically *demanded* regular vacations. And, of course, taking over Europe, the American hotel, "menaced by banality even in its perfection," with its telephones and radios, its two bathrooms, "one for Monsieur, the other for Madame."

Everywhere in the postwar world, it was the Americans who seemed to run everything, have all the money, do as they pleased.

16 ZOWIE!!

BACK TO THE SUMMER OF 1945. GERMANY HAD BEEN DEFEATED. refugees streamed along rutted roads, pushing carts and wheelbarrows. Robert Lasson, who'd served with the 101st Airborne Division in Germany, piled into a truck with a bunch of other GIs and went to Nice. There, at the entrance to the Promenade des Anglais, a sign was posted in English:

> You are entering
> NICE
> the EM's [Enlisted Men's] rest area
> One of the cities
> of the
> United States
> Riviera
> Recreational Area
> NICE
> Off limits
> to officers

Probably even before the invasion ships had left Africa, the Riviera Recreational Area had been divided up—Cannes to officers, Juan-les-Pins to Red Cross women and nurses, Nice to enlisted men; the Riviera Rest Command itself got the Negresco. For a week, Lasson enjoyed Nice with about ten thousand other GIs. He was assigned a room in the

HIGH SEASON IN NICE

Hôtel Regina, one of twenty-eight the Americans requisitioned. On August 9, 1945, he sat on the hotel steps, reading *Stars and Stripes*, scratching his head about just what an atom bomb might be.

The GIs had their own *Pocket Guide to the Cities of Southern France*, issued around 1944 and offering standard guidebook fare about the Paris showgirls of Nice's Carnaval and the six tons of roses needed to make a pint of rose oil in Grasse. Of course, Riviera towns had been bombed and shelled, and so might present quite a different face from that of before the war. And soldiers ought not patronize the black market or otherwise harm civilians. But, having issued these caveats, it advised, "So far as your military duties permit, see as much as you can. You've got a great chance to do now, major expenses paid, what would cost you a lot of your own money after the war. Take advantage of it."

And, oh, did they ever. "The local girls were gorgeous," remembers Lasson, "and hungry for male attention, although middle-class girls were careful not to get too involved with GIs. Like all French women, they seemed to have an innate chic." The GIs couldn't take women back to their hotels, so numerous "hot-pillow" joints cropped up. And Americans *did* fuel the black market. "The economy had been stripped bare." You could buy or sell anything, from candy bars and soap to shirts and parachute silk.

Each soldier got a booklet, *Don't Snafu Your Leave*, filled with dos and don'ts. Do obey the 2 A.M. curfew. Don't waste the water, or accept outdated French currency. Each directive was illustrated with a little cartoon. One showed a GI passed out in his room, liquor bottle by his side, hotel bed in splinters. "Don't destroy hotel property!"

But, sure enough, the GIs got in trouble. To hear the Niçois, the Americans were forever drinking and brawling and whoring, breaking windows, driving dangerously, pilfering from shop displays. Why, even the Germans had been better behaved; one barkeeper told Lasson of some who bolted during an attack by the Resistance, then returned the next day to settle their tab—"unlike the Yanks," Lasson adds, "who would have grabbed a few bottles and tried to screw the barmaid on the way out."

"The streets of Nice are not safe at night," howled the *Aurore* in

May 1945. Prostitutes from Marseilles and Toulouse, even Paris, blanketed the city; and the five or ten thousand francs they could make each night lured underage local girls desperate to cash in on the bonanza. *Please*, the Niçois begged American authorities, rein the boys in. Though "thankful to America for its help in liberating us," a local physician said at a municipal hearing called in protest, he and his confrères would not want their feelings for the Americans "tarnished by the thoughtless acts of a few isolated soldiers who forget that Nice for them is a place of repose, not an extension of the field of battle."

Still, soldiers dispensed "quite a tidy sum," as one account had it, no doubt nourishing visions, during these lean years, of better-behaved Americans to come. But their ranks were not at first replenished with civilians. "When the Americans were here there was a party every night," a Nice casino manager told American travel writer Horace Sutton in 1948; he meant the GIs, the last Americans he'd seen. Just then, even at the height of summer, American tourists in Nice numbered only a few hundred.

But France already had designs on what its high commissioner for tourism heard described as an "enormous 'reservoir' of [American] tourists and would-be tourists." After reminding the commissioner of the glories of French culture, the author of a 1948 report noted that Americans were put off by absurdly high prices, vexatious administrative formalities, and French xenophobia. These failings were "ably used against us by various countries jealous of our superiority in touristic resources." The problem could be addressed through publicity, advertising, and other means—he used the word *propagande*—that were "intense, sustained, and persevering."

The Americans did come back—to Europe, to France, to the Riviera, to Nice. In July 1951, Nice's twenty-seven thousand foreign tourists included almost four thousand Americans.

∞

Bob Allen saw Nice while serving in the navy. He was twenty-four years old in 1954, when he first arrived at Villefranche, the deep-water port just across the peninsula from Nice's Château Hill and about as close to it as Cimiez.

Son of a Newton, Massachusetts, physician, Allen had gotten out of Boston University two years earlier, signed up for Officer Candidate School, and shipped out aboard a communications ship, the *Northampton*, nerve center for a Sixth Fleet carrier task-force. Gibraltar was Allen's first port of call. Then came Algeciras, Spain—nothing much. Then Villefranche, from which he mailed a picture postcard to his parents in Massachusetts:

> Villefranche-sur-Mer is so unspoiled. . . . Gorgeous. The peo-
> ple so wonderful . . . I love the place and if I see nothing more
> I'm ecstatic. Scenery exquisite. 18 days on the Riviera. I'll work
> like a dog for *this*!!

The ship's boat had deposited him right on the waterfront: "Two steps and you're sitting in a sidewalk cafe," visible on the other side of the card—a black-and-white photo of the waterfront hand-tinted: Unnaturally blue water, steep hills rising up from the water's edge. Red-tiled roofs. Boats pulled up onto the shore. And, finally, the red-awninged Nautic, the sidewalk café where Lieutenant Allen found himself, tables spilled out onto the dock, brightly hued umbrellas. Even a sports car—top down, of course—parked out front.

Cool.

And it only got better. Europe, for this young high-spirited officer, was a blast. Leaves with his buddies to Geneva and Paris. Then back aboard ship, as communications officer, indulging in harmless hijinks. Like the time he made over the ship's newspaper into a faux–*Time* magazine, down to typefaces, departments, and a cover photo of the *Northampton*'s skipper. In the letters section, a reader faulted an article for its disregard of the "eye appeal" of European beaches. The letter was signed "Marcella Sartor, pretty girl," and came with a picture of her voluptuous bikinied body on the Nice beach. Allen ran it two columns wide and halfway down the page.

Allen loved the whole Riviera, but especially Nice and Villefranche, or "Ville," as the sailors called it, alive with home-grown girls and home-cooked meals. Its town square was the little stretch of waterfront beside the Hôtel Welcome, where street performers—once it was a bicyclist who rode no-hands while playing a fiddle—entertained knots of Sixth Fleet sailors and hotel guests.

Allen was no great ladies' man, yet now the dark-featured naval officer was befriending women all over the Riviera. Cathy, whose parents owned a hotel in Nice . . . Suzanne, budding movie starlet, who on one of his visits was in Cannes for the film festival . . . "You are right about girls in Europe being glad to be with an American," he wrote home in 1955, "especially in southern France where the war decimated the male population."

For him, the Riviera's radiance never faded. In July 1956, back in Nice after a cruise, he found "the hustle, bustle, lush green tree-awning over Victor Hugo Boulevard and Avenue Victoire" just as he remembered them. This was one of his "Allen-o-grams," the public missives, stocked with accounts of all he'd seen and done, with which he'd regale friends back home and fellow sailors:

> The put-put-put of the motor scooters. The hum of the little cars. The whirling, waving arms in white of the traffic policemen. And stunning and smart window displays have not changed a bit. . . . The band concerts in the park. Clean scrubbed children and parents with time to attend to them. Flowers at every turn with carnations in abundance. All that gave and gives Nice its charm are still there.

One postcard he mailed home showed a high-living partygoer of a cat, with green bow tie and Maurice Chevalier–style cane. In Nice, it said, "*la vie est belle.*" On the back, Allen wrote:

> I'm in 7th Heaven a million times over. The place is lousy with tourists, but our fare was very reasonable and we have 1300 liberty every day.
>
> Oh, I'm so so very happy I could scream. It's too much! It

couldn't really be me!! Nice . . . *un nuit de Nice après un jour à mer.* ZOWIE!!!

⌘

In 1946, a quirky postwar *affiche* showed an anti-aircraft gun mutated into a movie camera, its ammunition belt spewing national flags, the gunner's head a globe of the world. Thus was heralded the first Cannes International Film Festival, which by the 1950s had become a two-week extravaganza of movie screenings and staged publicity events thronged with film stars, directors, moguls, journalists, photographers, and assorted hangers-on.

A young Irish photographer named Edward Quinn hung out his shingle in Nice after the war and soon his pictures, fed to *Life, Paris Match,* and other glossies, were recording the Riviera celebrity culture of the fifties: Charlie Chaplin's kids getting off the plane at the Nice airport; a turbaned Elizabeth Taylor, regal with furs and poodles, husband and sons in tow, arriving at the *gare* in Nice; Brigitte Bardot, in a car outside the Negresco, on the brink of fame in Roger Vadim's *And God Created Woman.*

Vadim's film celebrated not only his sex kitten of a wife but the village of Saint-Tropez, down the coast beyond Cannes and Saint-Raphaël and until then mostly unspoiled. Its streets, one 1949 account had it, "are narrow, medieval and Spanish-looking with high tenements with green shutters and old white-haired women in black sitting mending fishermen's nets." Rubble left from the Allied invasion in 1944 could still be seen.

But, almost overnight, S'Trop was anointed the Riviera's in-est of in places, its Tahiti Beach a proving ground for bikinis that shrank each season. "The sheen of sun oil on brown girlish periphery was blinding," wrote David Dodge in *The Rich Man's Guide to the Riviera* in 1962. Brigitte appeared one summer in a suit consisting of "three butterflies of pink-and-white checked gingham. . . . By August you could not tell where the tablecloths of the Saint-Tropez waterfront cafes ended and the beach began, except that the beach had navels." If, during the fifties and sixties, the Riviera was the place to be seen, the place to be seen *on* the Riviera was Saint-Tropez, or maybe Cannes, not Nice.

∞

And yet, just as in the twenties, when it had first fallen out of fashion, Nice was as crowded as ever. Indeed, *more* of it was crowded. Bob Allen still has a souvenir from Da Bouttau, a Nice landmark where they'd write your dinner order on a flier you could keep, in crude hieroglyphic squiggles that stood for the various dishes. The old family restaurant was located on Place Halle-aux-Herbes, in Nice's *vieille ville*, a dark warren of streets that had, over the centuries, mostly impressed its occasional visitors with its dirt, stink, and decay. But now, after almost two centuries of tourism anchored on the Croix-de-Marbre side of the Paillon, the old town was being rediscovered, becoming almost a new *kind* of tourist attraction.

Back in the 1870s, Marie Bashkirtseff had been among the few to see the old town sympathetically, sampling its streets and shops, writing of it in her journal. One time, she and some cousins stopped at a grocer's, bought a chunk of cheese, and stood on the street, eating it right there with their fingers—"to the stupefied eyes of the Niçois out in their Sunday best." Robert de Souza likewise looked warmly upon the old town, which some were suggesting be torn down altogether. No, he wrote in 1912, the *vieille ville* offered a "seduction of the eyes." Against the merciless Mediterranean sun, its dark streets could feel sheltered, shadowy, and cool.

After World War II, the American authorities pictured the old town as a den of vice. Their little dos-and-don'ts book showed a sinister streetscape labeled "Old Nice," a GI scared witless by a scraggly cat's meow, and the caption: "Old town is strictly off limits!" But during the fifties, the city flirted with slum clearance. The Château Hill rising above the old town was fitted with an elevator the better to suit auto-borne tourists, their muscles withered by disuse; its grounds were prettied up, with supporting walls for the ancient ruins, and paths, plantings, and stairways leading back down to the old town.

Pierre-Hugues Palacci

Fortunately, the *vieille ville* itself survived intact—just in time to be re-discovered as chicly offbeat. The guidebooks had first begun to notice it before the war; now, sills dripping with flowers, drying laundry set against walls of mustard and ocher, it seemed exotic and bohemian.

In 1953, Robert Daley, an American Korean War veteran, was determined to write novels, fall in love, and discover France and the French—the real French of Nice. "The young man strolled through the old town," he wrote of himself in the third person. "There were no sidewalks. Women with string bags shopped for dinner. He inhaled the pungent odors that rushed out of doors at him and made him hungry: bread hot from the ovens, coffee, spilled wine."

Prostitutes beckoned.

> *Tu viens, chéri?*
> They seemed to patrol several meters of sidewalk each. Some walked along swinging handbags. Some stood beside or were led along by lapdogs on the leash. All looked to him expensively dressed. Some were young and pretty. It was broad daylight and he didn't even realize they were whores at first. He had never seen whores on sidewalks before.

It was Daley's first day in Nice and, as much as any duke's son on the Grand Tour, he was embarked on a voyage of discovery. To Americans in those years, flush with prosperity, all Europe seemed ripe for footloose adventures of mind and spirit.

"Type this up for me, will you?" Earle Taylor's boss barked at him one day in May 1958. "I need it right away." *Everybody*, it seemed to Taylor, needed it right away. He was thirty-three, single, and fed up. So, after six years as a stenographer for an oil company, he chucked it all and quit. He cashed in his savings and his pension plan, booked passage to Europe, packed up an army duffel, and boarded a plane, his first, for New York. A few days later, he was in a third-class cabin with three other men on a floating skyscraper of a ship, the *Île de France*, bound for England, eating better than he ever had in his life.

After a week in London and two in Paris, he took a bus through the wine country to Nice. He'd studied French in college, but couldn't speak it. And there, in Nice, the sheer relentless *pressure* of the language, of all things French, got to him. He felt homesick, missed America, obsessed about American home cooking. "My ears were filled with this alien language," he wrote later. "I looked sadly for Americans in Nice."

Finally, he spotted a restaurant that bore a Star of David. Taylor wasn't Jewish but, through a bout of inspired reasoning, concluded that, hmm, maybe a Jewish restaurant would attract American Jews. And American Jews were, after all, Americans. And that's what happened. "They welcomed me with open arms," he wrote later. They invited him to their table, asked where he was from, clamored to know all about him.

Old Home Week, Nice, 1958.

"From there I went to Monte Carlo and tried to pretend I was Humphrey Bogart."

∞

In Nice around this time, too, was Mary Burr Hulsizer, who one day got to talking with another American traveler. "Except for Copenhagen," she recounted in her journal later, "he'd not seen anything that interested him!!" This astonished her. She was sixty-eight, but brought to her travels the wonder and enthusiasm of a teenager. She was interested in everything. She consumed books voraciously—here a novel, there a life of Gauguin. She went everywhere, talked to everyone. When a Niçois merchant bitched to her about some untrusting American women who'd accused him of cheating, she speculated in her journal: They "went to church too much." One day, Hulsizer took a day trip to Grasse. She wrote of passing "olive groves, citrus fruit trees, gardens of violets and other flowers grown for the market—over hills with many strange, very old lava flows; through deep gorges on narrow winding roads." That evening, back in Nice, she looked up into the darkening sky—it was just three weeks since the stunning news from Russia—and saw the faint, slow-moving spot of light that was Sputnik.

This happened in October 1957. Six months earlier, Hulsizer had retired from the Newark public schools, where for twenty-seven years she'd been a nursing supervisor. Boarding the *Liberté* in New York, she'd embarked on an eleven-country tour of Europe. On arriving in Nice, she'd checked into a hotel. The hotel was the Westminster, on the Promenade des Anglais, a four-star. In this respect, if not in some others, Mary Burr Hulsizer was an entirely typical American.

A 1960 study for the Comité Régional du Tourisme found that American visitors generally didn't stay on the Riviera as long as the British, or the French, or for that matter anyone else—only about three days on average. But during their short stays, they spent and spent and spent—thirteen hundred francs on average, more than twice as much as the British or French. Among campers, those low-end Riviera visitors, there weren't enough Americans to count. But of foreign guests patronizing the top hotels, they represented more than four in ten—triple their proportion among foreigners generally.

Riviera officials could hardly be oblivious to their spending power. Or, increasingly, their numbers. In 1964, fifty-two thousand Americans registered at Nice hotels. That was more than the Italians, the Germans, or the Belgians, and twice as many as the British. More, in fact, than anyone else but the French themselves. It was fitting, then, that in April 1966, when Côte d'Azur tourism officials based abroad met in Nice, every country had one representative, save the United States, which had three.

René Bardy, the New York rep, reported that over the past ten years the number of Americans earning more than ten thousand dollars a year—the threshold, more or less, for European travel, and worth about fifty thousand today—had more than doubled, to almost fifty million.

About a third of American visitors to the Côte d'Azur, typically novice travelers, came on organized tours. Others came for a particular festival or conference. Or they traveled on their own by automobile. Or they lingered for a while, like old-style tourists. "Our advertising," said Bardy, "must adapt to each of these clienteles."

Before detailing publicity efforts over the previous year—so much spent on print ads, so much on TV commercials, public relations, and hotel lists, so many information requests handled—Bardy tried to picture just how Americans thought about La Côte. First, they didn't *call* it "the Côte d'Azur," but "the Riviera," which for many of them meant a place not French but international. Emphasizing its Frenchness would not, at this particular time of shaky Franco-American relations, work to its advantage; Americans judged the French haughty, Riviera folk friendly.

Bardy's west-coast counterpart pointed out that, although English was widely spoken on the Riviera, hotel personnel who dealt with Americans needed to know it still better. The language barrier caused much mistrust. "Americans who speak a little French," he added, "are more numerous than you might think. But they are exasperated when, trying to demonstrate their talents, our compatriots make out as if they don't understand them."

To entice more Americans, René Bardy had no want of ideas. More direct flights from the States. Conventions offering special travel kits. Beefed-up advertising. Maybe something like Riviera equivalents of the "April in Paris" shows popular in America just then. Air-conditioning in the hotels. American-style gambling in the casinos.

As the great sixties boom continued, wealth piled up, and more and more Americans could afford to go to Europe, most of them by plane. Back in 1953, when six hundred thousand North Americans visited Europe, three in five got there by boat. By 1970, four million did so, 97 percent by plane.

Meanwhile, ad copywriters maintained the pressure:

Nestled on the sun-drenched strip of the most famous coast in the world, Nice lives up to its reputation by blending nonstop energy and international glamour with the picturesque enchantment of old-world charm.

This ad, issued by Nice's New York office and garnished by a classic shot of the city from a neighboring hill, appeared in *Town and Country* in 1977.

Painted in the vivid colors of the imagination, Nice beckons travelers with its splendid visual panorama. Sunswept skies . . . carpets of rare, brightly-colored flowers . . . rippling hills dotted with villas . . . all framing the sparkling Mediterranean bay . . .

Ads like this, of course, were the work of men and women whose jobs were to bring ever more tourists to the Riviera. It was their business, their *métier.* They took pride in it.

During the 1960s, two photos splashed across a Belgian newspaper showed fierce winds hammering the streets of Ostende, women bundled up in winter coats hunched over against the wind, walking arm in arm to stay upright. "Bow down before Her Majesty the Wind," the headline said. A third photo, at the bottom of the page, showed swimsuited bodies basking in the Nice sun. *Its* headline read: "At the same time on the Mediterranean . . ." The photos, and their inspired pairing, were the work of French tourism officials in Brussels. Filing away this sample of their handiwork, one of them wrote, "Could anyone dream of more beautiful publicity!!"

Since back almost to Tobias Smollett, bridges, roads, trains, planes, guidebooks, ads, posters, and human imagination had helped bring visitors to Nice. In recent years, paid vacations helped. Postwar prosperity helped. Jets helped. To sustain the flow of tourists was ingrained in Nice's collective mind. To suggest the contrary—that visitors be *discouraged*—would have struck any self-respecting Niçois, any Riviera tourism official, anyone who recalled the Depression, or the war, or the bleak days right after it, as criminal, mad, or both.

Tourists were good. Could you ever have too much of a good thing?

17 THE TRAGEDY OF THE COMMONS

YOU COULD VERY WELL HAVE TOO MUCH OF A GOOD THING, SAID American biologist Garrett Hardin in a wide-ranging essay, "The Tragedy of the Commons," that appeared in the journal *Science* in 1968.

Hardin's hypothetical "commons" was pastureland held in common. A herdsman, acting in his own interests, adds cattle to his herd; more cattle, more income. But *each* herdsman, moved by the same implacable logic, does likewise. In Hardin's language, the commons suffers from "overgrazing," ultimately reaching its "carrying capacity," and starts to decline.

More cattle, *less* income.

Hardin applied the idea to pollution, national parks, and, especially, population. In each case, people pursuing their own interests undermine them. "Freedom in a commons," writes Hardin, "brings ruin to all." A stream becomes polluted. A region grows overpopulated.

A Mediterranean paradise is laid waste.

Back in 1884, J. C. Harris worried about Nice's fevered development in the wake of the railroad. Later, Robert de Souza argued that Nice, wracked by the architectural and land-use horrors visited on it by individuals pursuing their own interests, needed "rational civic discipline"; even those shackled by restrictions would, in the end, be better off. Public and private good were intertwined.

> The general prosperity is the work of the thousand and one personal fortunes that freely constitute it. But the simple principle

of "enrich yourself" can become, at certain times in the life of a community or nation, a danger to the community or nation— times, that is, when higher leadership fails to maintain an equilibrium between the interests of each and the interests of all.

His "danger to the community," of course, was something like Hardin's "tragedy of the commons."

As usual, de Souza was ahead of his time. Even in the late 1960s, when Garrett Hardin's essay appeared, environmental sensibilities were only just taking hold. Europe was crowded with Americans. *If It's Tuesday, This Must Be Belgium* played in American movie theaters. The Boeing 747 jumbo jet was set to make its first transatlantic flight. Françoise Cribier's monumental *La Grande Migration d'été des citadins en France* was documenting the hold summer vacations exerted on French national life. It was perhaps the last time you could draw unmixed pleasure from luring yet another tourist to the Riviera.

∞

In 1981, sixty-year-old Anna Wolisin (not her real name) saw an ad in a university magazine for an eighteen-day art tour of Portugal, Spain, and southern France, including the Riviera.

> How about Lisbon,
> Madrid, Barcelona,
> Carcassonne, Arles,
> Nice? NICE!

It was actually Carcassonne, the thirteenth-century city of turrets and towers, that sold her. Back in Brooklyn, around 1932, Anna's sixth-grade World Cultures classroom sat at the end of a corridor in which hung a large framed poster of Carcassonne. All warm reds and browns, exuding the Middle Ages, it was breathlessly romantic to an eleven-year-old who'd barely set foot out of Brooklyn.

Six months after spotting the ad, Anna and her husband were in

Carcassonne. "We walked through the cobbled streets," she wrote in her journal, "and I felt very close, indeed, to Heaven."

From there, the tour proceeded to the Riviera, which left her more ambivalent. Much of the bus trip from Aix-en-Provence to Cannes stuck them in a godawful traffic jam. As for Cannes itself, "the place is one vast condominium." In Nice, they enjoyed a pleasant evening at their hotel on the Promenade des Anglais. They took in Èze, where they toured a perfume factory, and Monte Carlo. The next day, their last on the Riviera, they visited the Picasso Museum in Antibes, viewed paintings, sculptures, and wall hangings at the Léger Museum in Biot. What they didn't visit, a few towns over, was Vence.

Vence was a walled town about fifteen miles back into the hills that looked as if it had stepped out of the Middle Ages, which it had. In 1945, someone had loaned Anna a little book about it, *Immortal Village*, by Donald Culross Peattie; we met the author and his wife earlier, back in the twenties, eager to be out of Nice. In Vence, they found a low, white-walled house with red-tiled roof where they lived for three years; the book was his loving tribute to the town. And just as Anna, as a girl, had fallen for Carcassonne, so had she, as a young woman, for Vence.

In 1982, she was as close as she'd ever be to seeing it. Would they be going there? she asked Maria, their guide, as they made plans for their excursion the next day from Nice. Anna told her about Peattie, and *Immortal Village*, and how much it meant to her. Could they visit Vence?

Well, you know, Maria told her gently, Vence wasn't the same anymore. It was just another tourist town, with the same crowds, the same souvenir stands, the same wretched tourist ticky-tack as anyplace else. "Do yourself a favor," she said. "If that book meant so much to you, don't go to Vence. Don't spoil your memories."

In fact, even by Peattie's time Vence was no longer unsullied. Nineteenth-century guidebooks mentioned it. A railroad *affiche* in 1910 touted it as a "summer and winter resort." When Matisse decorated Vence's Chapel of the Rosary in the early 1950s, *Life* was there. When Robert Daley and his new French girlfriend toured the Riviera, they visited it. By the late seventies, just before Anna's trip, Michelin was giving it two and a half pages, colored maps and all.

Though Vence's transformation came later, and was squeezed into fewer years, it closely tracked that of Nice. Just as Nice would never again be that vision of freshness it had been in the early 1800s, neither would Vence. Rather, it was following the familiar pattern: a charming town becomes popular, suffers popularity's price, and has its place in the tourist's pantheon usurped by some other town, which in turn re-enacts the cycle.

∞

In the 1970s, scholars began to *study* this characteristic cycle of growth, stagnation, and decline.

After World War II, as travel to distant places became possible for more people and tourism came to be seen as vital to modern economies, scholars in numerous disciplines—history, geography, anthropology, sociology, economics, literature—began studying it seriously.

They broke up tourism into types—cultural, historical, recreational . . . ; tourists into types—drifters, explorers, mass tourists . . . ; hotel chains into types. . . .

They splayed open for view the border region between travel and tourism.

They totted up tourism's economic impact.

They cited the number of tons of garbage left by visitors to the Austrian Alps.

They fretted over the unreliability of tourism statistics.

They pointed up the "staged authenticity" of folk dances and other commercialized, bastardized forms of native culture put on for visitors.

They depicted tourism as a sacred journey.

They pictured it as a form of imperialism.

They debated whether, to borrow one book's subtitle, it was "blessing or blight."

Scholarly journals sprang up with titles like *Annals of Tourism Research*.

At Mexico City in 1974, the American Anthropological Association met with "the goal of legitimizing," as one participant described it later, "the study of tourism as an academic subdiscipline."

Some scholars focused on specific tourist destinations. One picked Atlantic City, New Jersey; another, nineteenth-century New England; a third, the American West. Early on, Nice swung under the scholarly magnifying glass. Charles Haug focused on the nineteenth century, Robert Rudney on the period between the wars. In a 1993 book, *Fashionable Resort Regions,* English geographer John V. N. Soane included Nice in a broad comparative study with Los Angeles; Bournemouth, England; and Wiesbaden, Germany.

Other scholars sought patterns in tourist-resort development. In a paper before the Travel Research Association in 1972, S. C. Plog pictured the typical resort moving inexorably "toward its own demise. Destination areas carry with them the potential seeds of their own destruction, as they allow themselves to become more commercialized and lose the qualities which originally attracted tourists."

Another scholar, R. W. Butler, a Canadian at the University of Western Ontario, left room for variant outcomes. Basing his model on industrial-product cycles and representing it in a hypothetical graph, he outlined in a 1980 paper what he called "The Concept of a Tourist Area Cycle of Evolution."

At first, a few hardy newcomers explore the new site, which scarcely boasts an inn or a restaurant worthy of the name. This was Nice around Smollett's time. Butler called it the exploration stage.

In the involvement stage, local residents begin catering to the visitors, provide facilities, maybe advertise a little; visitors come in greater numbers. This was Nice immediately before the French Revolution, and in the years after Waterloo.

Outside financing pours in. More and bigger hotels go up. The townscape changes radically, but not always for the better. This was Butler's development stage, and describes Nice during the frenetic years after the coming of the railroad.

A consolidation stage follows in which the number of visitors continues to grow, but more slowly. By now, the area's economy is irreparably tied to tourism, sometimes rousing second thoughts among the locals. A well-defined recreational-business district exists, some of it now "regarded as second rate and far from desirable." This is Nice around the time Robert de Souza turned his lens on it in 1913.

Later in Butler's taxonomy, as we'll see, comes a stagnation stage, in which no more visitors can be comfortably absorbed. And, sometimes, one of outright decline. But whatever the details, his overarching message was clear: "Tourist attractions are not infinite and timeless but should be viewed and treated as finite and possibly non-renewable resources." Butler wrote of "capacity limits," of "severe environmental damage" should they be breached; his were environmental sensibilities at work.

Back in 1966, at the Nice meeting of Côte d'Azur tourism representatives abroad, such thinking was not yet well established. But the problems themselves were unmistakable. And together they warned of a finite resource—the Riviera itself—that had become, in the words of New York representative René Bardy, "more and more difficult to maintain [as] an ideal setting for tourism." What he classed as the Riviera's *équipement collectif,* its public facilities, were being devastated. He could have been talking of Hardin's commons.

If during the Belle Époque the Côte d'Azur was enjoyed by too few, maybe now it was being enjoyed by too many.

∞

When the French economy took off around 1950, eight million French city-dwellers took vacations; by 1966, twenty million did. By the early seventies, the paid vacation hallowed by the Popular Front in 1936 had become part of French life, altering the very rhythms of the French calendar, fueling French industry. Camping-equipment suppliers profited. So did the banks that financed second homes. So did carmakers, who supplied Frenchmen their prime means of reaching mountain or shore. So did television and newspapers, through advertising; and travel agencies; and commercial tourist organizations like Club Méditerranée. In 1968, a reporter for *Le Monde* pictured vacations as merchandise; his article was headlined "An industry of the same importance as that of the automobile or chemicals." Born of thirties idealism, its economic

punch felt far beyond hotels and restaurants, the French vacation now enjoyed almost universal support; there was almost something *wrong* with you if you didn't take one.

More even than the rest of Europe, the French skewed their vacations to a slim segment of the year—not just a vague, indefinite "summer," but July and, more particularly, August. Paris in August became a ghost town, its population halved, its offices and factories largely shut down, its Métro bearing many fewer passengers. "The capital is so different from the rest of the year," Françoise Cribier wrote in 1969, "that the Parisian discovers another city, one not lacking in charm."

And where were they, those millions of Parisians, and others among their fellow Frenchmen? A lot of them were on the Côte d'Azur, where the season was now summer, wholly and irreversibly. There—along with Americans coming over on 747s, faithful English on low-cost charters, and half the rest of Europe—they fueled its environmental despoilment as well as its prosperity.

To scholars studying their impact on the places they visited, tourists bore a heavy burden. They depleted water supplies. They damaged riverbanks. They disrupted the breeding habits of wildlife, trampled vegetation, littered the countryside. Their numbers encouraged alien, ill-scaled architectural styles. They overloaded the electricity grid. They invited prostitution. They undermined traditional agriculture. A litany of their affronts to the natural, built, and cultural environments could go on for pages, and in scholarly journals did.

Figuring big in tourism's toll on the Riviera, of course, was the automobile. It was the Renault 4CV that did it; this French species of Model T or VW Beetle was simple and cheap enough to make travel possible for millions, and helped supplant the train as chief means of reaching La Côte. In mid-August 1953, twenty-six thousand vehicles were each day crossing the Var at Saint-Laurent, near where human shoulders bore travelers across in the 1770s. Once they were in Nice, traffic jams—in French, the word is *embouteillage* or *bouchon,* both suggesting the cork-stuffed neck of a wine bottle—were so frequent that just getting from one end of town to the other could represent a feat.

Riviera vacationers gagged on the smoke coughing up from their cars. They lay on befouled beaches, sewage pouring into the sea from water-treatment systems overloaded in summer. They saw a *mur de béton*, or concrete wall, of apartment buildings and hotels that rose up along much of the seafront from Menton to Cannes. And crowded marinas—forty-three of them between Menton and Sainte-Maxime by 1980. "If the phenomenon continues as it is," someone lamented, "where will it end? Where will we still see nature, the sea?"

The environmental price was worse for being channeled into such a narrow seafront belt. You'd go out for a walk on the Promenade des Anglais and have every peaceful, private thought drowned out by the incessant rumble of the traffic.

Or go down to the beach and, as one visitor described in a Nice newspaper, come almost to blows with some jerk ordering you off "his" beach. Legally, the beach was public to the high-water line, but with so little coastline and so many coveting it, conflict was inevitable.

You'd go for a swim in an idyllic, out-of-the-way cove only to feel a slick, slimy something creeping up your thigh—not a jellyfish, but a shopping bag.

Or spend the day fishing, in what was supposed to be a nature preserve near the mouth of the Var—complete with pretty information panels describing its hundreds of bird species—only to face mounds of trash piled up on the *galets*, wine bottles bobbing up in the marsh grass along the riverbank.

In the early days, especially, solutions to problems posed by ever-growing numbers took predictable form. The old local roads that brought cars to La Côte were too crowded? Well, build more highways and bridges. By 1961, the A8 autoroute, a divided superhighway, was bringing tourists over the Esterels to the Riviera. Until 1979, it stopped at the Var. But in that year, it got its own bridge across, turned north up the east bank, and then, through a series of costly tunnels around Nice, was linked up to Italy. Now you could drive from Paris to Palermo, Sicily, without leaving the autoroute; Nice was on the main line. The airport, too, was forever being enlarged, with new runways and new terminals; eighteen million cubic meters of sand and gravel were dumped into coastal landfill to make room for them.

Solutions like these, of course, were not solutions. They brought more crowds, compounded problems they were supposed to relieve; the Riviera "commons" was still being "overgrazed." The air could soak up only so much pollution, people only so much noise. In the 1990s, plans were announced for another autoroute that would fork off the tourist-clogged A8 at Mandelieu, veer north into the *arrière-pays* near Grasse, and parallel the coast for fifty kilometers. This time, though, civic groups from Saint-Paul-de-Vence, Tourrettes-sur-Loup, and other towns in the Nice hinterlands fought it. "When it comes to tourism, we remain cautious, and reject every major building program," declared the mayor of Tourrettes. "We will not let down those who have chosen to live here."

Tourism was not, at last, the *only* value on the Riviera.

Today the watchwords are "sustainable" tourism, "green" tourism, and other variations on the theme that air, water, and space are finite, and precious. Riviera authorities trumpet improvements—a new water-treatment plant here, protection of endangered species there. Scholars speak routinely of a region's "tourist-carrying capacity." Third World tourist destinations, still early in their cycles of development, are sure to benefit.

But for Nice, it is too late. It's a big city now, France's fifth largest, its population close to half a million. It has gardens, flowers, palm trees, and sun—but it's no paradise. In absorbing visitors and their cars, it runs hard up against its limits. Never again will it be lusted after solely for its beauty.

The same goes for the rest of the Côte d'Azur. Less and less does it resemble the exotic island paradise or perfect little backcountry retreat many sophisticated travelers seek. It has fallen off their mental maps. You'll see there all the flabby unfashionables you'd as soon not see, any environmental insult you care to imagine, every cheap souvenir stand of your worst nightmare.

For Nice, the seventies, during the reign of Jacques Médecin, its corrupt yet popular mayor, were the low point, both morally and ecologically. *J'Accuse: The Dark Side of Nice* is how British author Graham Greene titled one bleak account. René Louis Maurice and Ken Follett, authors of *The Gentlemen of 16 July,* the story of a Nice bank heist, pic-

tured the city as "unpleasantly reminiscent of the Chicago of the thirties," rife with depravity and crime, dominated by a Mafia-like *milieu*.
"On the Promenade des Anglais you could buy anything from a couple
of hits of cocaine to a male prostitute. People said it was the most corrupt town in France."

One American recalled how Nice Gypsies, the aggressive beggars
among them, "came at you like a plague of locusts. Oh, you should
have seen me warding them off, flailing my arms!" Another told of
hitchhiking to Nice as a twenty-one-year-old, anticipating something
out of a James Baldwin novel, only to find it instead "utterly strange to
me, with its big apartment houses, big hotels, and old people." Miami
Beach with a French accent.

Of course, Nice and the Riviera had been getting bad press for at
least a century; remember Adelaide Hall? But a nadir of sorts was
reached in an idiosyncratic, charmingly hostile travel guide, *French Leave
Encore*, by Richard Binns, published in England in 1992. To Binns, Nice
was the pits, and so was most of the rest of the Côte d'Azur.

> Much of the coastal strip is appalling: concrete mutations
> litter the landscape, a grim memorial to the planners (aided by
> backhanders [bribes]) who conceived and continue to extend
> this 20th-century nightmare; pollution in both sea and atmos-
> phere is rampant; the sound of traffic is deafening.

No, Binns would not misdirect his faithful readers to Nice, Monte
Carlo, Cannes, and the other ruined Riviera showpieces. He would con-
centrate instead on *l'arrière-pays*, the once-impoverished backcountry.
Winter sports had long before made places like Peira-Cava and Saint-
Martin-Vésubie, way up in the Alps, real resorts. But to Binns, the *arrière-
pays* at its best was represented by a little town named Peillon, "an oasis
of calm perched atop huge vertical slabs of rock. The village is minutes
from the coast yet remains hidden from the ever-creeping, ever-nearing
tentacles of Nice's ghastly suburbs."

Of course, he admitted, "the coastal 'menace' has crept close to

Peillon." Mougins had been engulfed. "Grasse and Vence are close to the same fate. . . ."

Nice.

Vence.

Peillon?

Was Riviera tourism doomed to a bleak, down-spinning spiral of moral and environmental decline?

∞

A couple of years after Richard Binns issued his indictment of the Riviera, Abby Green, a nineteen-year-old college student, came there to learn French.

It was April 1994, and Abby had enrolled in a seven-week language-immersion school. From the Nice *gare*, it was just a few minutes through the Mont Alban tunnel to Villefranche, where the school was. Soon she was installed at Chez Betty, a little hotel with rooms on the second floor, restaurant, pool tables, and juke box on the first. The next morning, she got up early to explore the town. She wandered through narrow winding streets. She climbed steep stone stairways. Sometimes, she wrote in her journal, she was "blinded by the bright sunlight reflecting off the sparkling bay, dotted with yachts."

The next weeks were a succession of classes, new faces, and excursions. She was forever hopping on the bus or taking a cab to Nice. Buying a jacket to keep warm against the unexpected April chill. Eating *salade niçoise* and *tagliatelle au saumon* in an outdoor restaurant. Visiting the Chagall Museum. Shopping in the *vieille ville*. One time in Monaco, "we walked through the streets gazing into the windows of Chanel, Dior, etc., laughing at the ridiculous clothes and prices!"

Abby was young, pretty, and intelligent, but had the usual run of teenage insecurities, and her boyfriend was far away, back home in the States. The people she met were from everywhere, most of them older and worldlier than she—Danes, Dutch, Brits, Swiss. In jeans and flannel shirt, wearing no jewelry and little makeup, she felt shabby beside the chic Europeans. Sometimes, she felt "lonely, immature, out of place. . . . Here I am in this stunningly beautiful place in France, and I am still not very happy. What the hell's wrong with me?!"

Things first went better in an *exposé*, or informal talk, she had to give in French. She told of her disillusionment with college, about apathy among her peers, about what it was like being a Generation X–er. Her classmates "jumped in to reassure me." They told her their own stories, gave her bits of advice. "I'm beginning to feel more comfortable and more like myself in the class. I even joke around a little now."

Gradually, she felt more at home. She heard dirty jokes told in French—and started to get them.

She learned French terms of endearment—not just the ubiquitous *mon petit chou*, darling, but also "'*mon petit crotte*,' which means—I am not making this up—MY LITTLE PILE OF DOG CRAP!!! What the hell?! It really *is* a different culture here!"

On the beach, she at first couldn't bring herself to take off her top, as most women did. Later, she did. "It wasn't so embarrassing after all, and actually quite a liberating feeling."

She grew up fast. She learned of a classmate having an affair with her teacher, down to intimate conversations in the language lab, over the headphones, when the teacher was supposed to be correcting her pronunciation. "It sounds so risqué and exciting!"

She tried on European ways. "I'm actually starting to like wine with dinner!" she wrote. "What a shock it's going to be to go back to the stupid laws at home."

Then a week later: "This has been the best weekend! It's made me one hundred per cent glad that I came here." The time was Friday evening; the place, the apartment of a classmate's parents; the occasion, a dinner party.' "It was incredible! It's on the top floor, with balconies all around and spectacular views of Nice, the sea, the hills, everything. Wow!" All evening she talked with people in the film business, heard juicy gossip about supermodels and face lifts, joked about her teachers. She didn't get home till two.

Abby saw the same Côte d'Azur that Richard Binns had seen, mostly the very parts of it he could least abide. And she found plenty to complain about—imperious waiters, snotty doormen, rude sales-clerks, and overpriced drinks. "All the restaurants now are starting to have shitty service and smaller portions," she wrote in early May, "be-cause the tourists are starting to come." But her seventy-five-page Riv-iera journal scarcely mentioned traffic jams, dirty water, dirty air, or too many tourists.

Just before she left, she began to see the Riviera with new eyes.

Right now there are millions of flowers blooming everywhere, roses and poppies, and this purple stuff that climbs up walls. There are also birds of paradise, daisies, and these huge aloe vera–type plants and cacti. It's really quite a wide spectrum of vegetation. It's like nothing I've seen before, though. I'm taking the day off tomorrow to better enjoy all this nature while I can. Now I'm starting to panic because there are so many things I still want to do, things I wanted to see and visit. . . . But there's just so much you can do in six weeks. I guess I should be satis-fied that I've seen quite a bit and had a good time.

Periodically, she'd despaired of what felt like her slow progress in French, but sometimes she'd take heart. Once, she and some classmates went out to dinner at a *cave* in Nice. Midst much joking and laughing, she quaffed a couple of glasses of champagne and figured that, back in Villefranche, she'd head right to sleep. Instead, she was dragged to an-other local hangout, got to talking with "this French guy James knew," and everything clicked. "We were really having a conversation and un-derstanding each other and I wasn't messing up at all!"

Back in 1966, at the same meeting of French tourism officials at which René Bardy had described mass tourism's environmental and aesthetic toll on La Côte, Georges Sauvayre had observed the same landscape through quite a different lens. "The broad democratization of tourism over the last few years," wrote Sauvayre, the Commissariat du Tourisme's

Midwestern representative, based in Chicago, "has opened the doors of the Riviera to practically every level of society and . . . every purse." American Midwesterners battered by cruel heartland winters struck him as particularly susceptible to seductions of sea and sun. Among them he detected "a real thirst to know the 'Far Away Places'"—this in English—"that they hear about everywhere and see in the movies and on television: Paris, the Côte d'Azur, Nice, Cannes."

Sauvayre was a tourism professional, analyzing a market, thinking hard about how best to detach tourists from their dollars. But his vision of Far Away Places paid tribute to an ordinary human hunger—the longing to go to a distant place and throw off the chains of the everyday, to savor beauty and pleasure, to partake of personal enrichment and renewal. Growing environmental awareness since the 1970s has made it impossible to blithely ignore tourism's dark side. And yet to deplore too primly the noisy, crowded Rivieras of the world risks overlooking the real human needs they satisfy.

A map in Nice's archeology museum shows that the region around today's Cimiez was once inhabited by an early Ligurian tribe called Vediantii, most of whom doubtless remained among their own Alpine crags and swollen streams all their lives; no tourism industry, trading on their discontents, urged them toward places more exotic and more wonderful than their own. But if tribesmen in ages past mostly clung close to home, kings, crusaders, princes, and popes *did* travel. And today many more can do as they did. Many more can, like Abby Green, indulge their capacity for wonder.

A veteran Côte d'Azur guide, Ursula, was recalling visitors whom, over a span of thirty years, she had shepherded through the region by bus, from San Remo to Saint-Tropez—Russians, Israelis, Sicilians. . . . Among the French, the ones she remembered best were farmers, from places like Brittany or Normandy, who'd never been away from home, had saved a lifetime for the trip. "They get to the Côte for the first time and it's, 'This is ours, our country! This is France, too!'" They look around them, says Ursula, "and they just about burst open with pride."

Historian Eugen Weber has written how, in late-nineteenth-century France, more people traveled "out of idleness, curiosity, or, simply, for the pleasure of travel"—but also "for the pleasure of saying they had traveled." Fueling travel's spread was

> a longing to imitate lifestyles once reserved for those privileged (usually noble) classes that owned country estates and lived on them part of the year, mimicry that drove those who could afford it to acquire a country residence or at least to spend weekends in the country.

Marc Boyer, a French scholar of tourism, likewise pointed to mimicry at work. Until about 1930, he wrote, sea and mountain resorts drew mostly from the leisured, landowning class; here was "society," a French upper crust "admired and imitated" by everyone else. Today, he went on, the ways of the elite continue to filter down, penetrating "to other social levels by capillary action. The travels of the rich are first envied, then copied. . . . Newlyweds honeymoon in Nice." Vacations diffuse among the wider public, who "imitate the fashionable aristocracy" (who, in turn, find new places to make fashionable).

Perhaps the nuance in French differs, but in English to "imitate," "copy," and "mimic" all bear wisps of derision; whatever is done by the imitator, copier, or mimic differs profoundly from that of the originator—is second-rate, derivative, or otherwise inferior. This language of imitation suggests that places like Nice were once appreciated for all the right reasons, enjoyed at their fullest and best; but that then came the brutish copycat hordes, their motives impure and inauthentic, who brought them low. No self-respecting scholar would put it quite this way. Yet some flavor of the idea taints today's tourists.

Today's tourists, it bears saying, have no corner on being led by the nose of conformity and convention. The Countess of Blessington, the Englishwoman we met earlier, wrote of fashion's tyranny in the Nice of 1823, when trips into the country to visit grottoes and other stirring geological formations were all the rage. On one such trip, she had to climb rickety ladders down the side of a mountain. The next day, she and her friends compared notes, several admitting they'd "felt little interested by what they had taken so much trouble to see."

"Why go?" asked their host, a Comte Andriani.

"Oh, because Monsieur B., or Madame C., was always talking about it."

That was a good reason *not* to go, replied the count.

It was remarkable, wrote the countess later,

> how many persons submit to trouble and danger to witness sights for which they have not taste . . . in order that they may acquire the power of saying they saw as much as, or better still, more than, certain individuals of their acquaintance.

"Heaven defend me," she wrote a few days later, after an expedition in which they had to slither like snakes through the mouth of a cave, "from seeing any more grottoes."

For the Countess of Blessington and her friends, it was grottoes. In the twenties, it was beach pajamas. For our times, it might be parasailing, or Chagalls, or shopping for just the right villa on the Internet. Same thing. The tug of fashion. By this light, then, not so terribly much separates today's travelers from the Countesses of Blessington and Tobias Smolletts of times past. Imitating their betters? Maybe not.

Nice's earlier visitors were sick; they came to get well. They were tired, and came to rest. They were tense, and came to unwind. They were bored, and came to amuse themselves. They'd had their fill of the gray and the cold; they came for the sun and the warmth. So do millions of travelers today, from up and down the social ladder, and across the world.

Together, they constitute an environmental problem. Individually, they brighten and enrich their lives.

8 WWW.NICE.COM

EVERY TOURIST DESTINATION ULTIMATELY REACHES A STAGNATION point, where it enjoys an established image yet is no longer fashionable. This was Nice after World War I.

But what happens next? The development model offered by R. W. Butler in 1980 gets complicated here, forking every which way, each a possible path to the future. A mature resort like Nice might face decline. Or, worse, *immediate* decline—a kind of free fall to ruin. Or stabilization. Or reduced growth. Or rejuvenation. At times since World War I, Nice has seemed bound for each of these outcomes.

This much is clear: Nice no longer follows the old script. It is no longer City of the Season. Much of its natural charm, as we've seen, has faded, or lies buried under concrete. Likewise the Riviera as a whole.

And yet 97 percent of Riviera visitors go home satisfied; this, anyway, is the figure, however suspect, that the regional tourist bureau bruited about a few years back. Certainly, the Riviera keeps pulling in visitors—eight and a half million each year, almost half of them foreigners; a third stay in Nice itself. They spend five billion dollars. Despite its ills, the Riviera is no stretcher case. Nor is Nice itself. It has adapted, become a place that, in his 1998 novel, *Chasing Cézanne*, Peter Mayle's character could describe as "awake all through the year. Restaurants stay open, markets continue, the streets are busy, the Promenade des Anglais is a-bob with joggers who like their exercise with a sea view, the traffic spits and snarls, the town breathes and sweats and lives."

Invoked today to represent Nice's possible future are often Ameri-

NICE

BILLETS
à prix réduits

can models. It could turn ever more into a Miami Beach, retirement community in the sun, with thousands of *résidences secondaires.* Or a sprawling Los Angeles—*keep building and screw the environment.* Or a Silicon Valley, in the style of Sophia-Antipolis, the wooded, sculpture-dotted, six-thousand-acre science-and-industrial park just across the Var that feeds Nice scientific conferences and employs thousands.

Tourist guidebooks almost never treat Nice by itself anymore, but as part of the Côte d'Azur, or the Riviera, or the Alpes-Maritimes. Likewise, few tourists resolve to visit Nice while avoiding Antibes, Menton, or Beaulieu; it's the same air and sun. Still, Nice is *not* those other places. When it comes to courting tourists, it both competes with them and cooperates.

∞

From her spacious office facing a garden court within the Acropolis, the city's state-of-the-art conference center, Sylvie Grosgogeat, director of communication of Nice's Office du Tourisme et des Congrès, its convention-and-visitors bureau, helps keep visitors coming to Nice. Her fifty-person staff runs welcome bureaus at the *gare,* at the airport, and on the Promenade des Anglais; spews out press kits and calendars, publicity materials ranging from T-shirts to decorative mobiles; pushes Nice's cruise-ship business one month, its museums the next.

One campaign, Un Été en Or, A Golden Summer, was built on gorgeous photographic collages in postcards, posters, and brochures. Nice architecture, cuisine, summer festivals, and beachside pleasures each got the treatment, each in tones and tints of gold: a little girl's blond tresses, the mustard yellows of the old town, fireworks ablaze in the night sky, a golden sunset. For winter, as Hiver en Bleu, the campaign color scheme shifted to blue.

One April day, Grosgogeat's office received an information request from America. Two days later, a thick shrink-wrapped packet went out, bearing almost ten dollars' worth of postage, full of guides, maps, listings, and brochures. Again, the blue of sea and sky. Again, the golden sun. Again, common design elements. Typeface, fresh and playful—letters of almost random size broken away from the line, as if a child had snipped them from the newspaper and glued them down. Photos made to blur and fade at the edges, like old Victorian portraits. Old-town spires, pretty women, and a church's resplendent baroque ceiling made into a lush, dazzling dream.

Included in the packet was a teal-blue card:

NICE

WE ARE ON THE NET!

Come and Visit Nice

at our web address:

http://www.nice-coteazur.org

At the other end of town, its offices in a villa on the Promenade des Anglais, the Comité Régional du Tourisme maintained its own publicity apparatus, this time for the Côte d'Azur as a whole. *Its* Web site, hotel guides, and the like didn't stop with Nice, but included Cannes and Antibes, Peillon and Vence, Beausoleil and La Turbie. In many ways, of course, it was more of the same—more great photography, more blues and golds. A *comité* fact sheet recorded the number of restaurants on the Côte d'Azur (3,500), of *offices du tourisme* (48), of meeting halls in Cannes's Palais des Festivals (17). It listed the average price of a three-star hotel (414 francs, about $70). It noted that, on an average day in high season, the Riviera hosted 700,000 visitors.

It also recorded the number of visitors to particular Riviera attractions. One of them, drawing more than half a million people each year, was the Verrerie de Biot.

∞

Three or four deep, they stand against the steel railing that surrounds the *verrerie*, or glassworks, watching with devoted interest the men working within. No talking to the workers, they're advised; but attractive signs, hand-painted on wood panels, explain what's going on.

Red-hot glass is the medium of these workers, who mostly wear sandals, shorts, and T-shirts, to keep cool midst the heat of the furnaces and of summer. Into the furnace they insinuate long hollow steel tubes whose tips come out seconds later engulfed in globs of glowing molten glass. In later steps, they roll the glass on iron tables, shape it, pinch it, blow into it. The result is blown-glass goblets and vases, bottles and bowls, in a variety of colors, all with the telltale bubbles that are the *verrerie*'s trademark.

Some days, the men work through twelve hundred pounds of glass, most of it winding up in the adjoining retail showroom, its aisles of shelves heaped with glassware, in lavish profusion, glittering and gleaming. A sign near the exit asks, "Have you really seen all of the Verrerie de Biot?," then reminds you of galleries and boutiques you may have missed. *"Il serait dommage de partir déjà"*—such a shame to leave so soon.

Set a few miles back from the sea between Nice and Cannes, Biot goes back to the days of the Romans, but tourists began visiting only after World War II; today it's got half a dozen hotels, almost twenty restaurants. One big draw is the Fernand Léger Museum at the edge of town. The other is the *verrerie.* Along with the likes of the Grasse perfume works, and Villefranche's Citadel, the Verrerie de Biot stands squarely in the second rank of Côte d'Azur destinations. It has its own restaurant, a big parking lot, a place for tour buses to pull in; you can spend ten francs for a piece of glass, or three hundred thousand. More people come here each year than to either the Picasso Museum in Antibes or the Russian Cathedral in Nice.

It was pottery, not glass, for which Biot was known through the ages, but in 1956, a ceramicist and engineer, Éloi Monod, started up the *verrerie.* "A rough start!" the works' own capsule history recalls. The first glassware cracked. Customers were rare. Monod, a rough-edged man of communist sympathies, was no promoter.

Eighteen years later, Jean and Danielle Lechaczynski bought it. Until then, grown daughter Anne explains today, some looked at the bubbles in the hand-formed glass as defects. But her parents pitched them, along with Biot glass's distinctive colors, as desirable. "For every bubble," a publicity brochure says today, "a secret, a whisper, a tradition . . ." Trading on the luster of La Côte, they emphasized blue, redolent of the Mediterranean, instead of Provençal brown. They put fliers on the beach, in the hotels. Today Anne is forever on the phone with journalists, or pestering the regional tourist office (which she deems too linked to Marseilles, not enough to Nice) for more aggressive promotion.

Some years back, Jackie Onassis took a liking to the *verrerie*'s "Persian-blue" color and got exclusive rights to it for a while. Salespeople, says Lechaczynski, are specifically taught how to deal with celebrities: don't ignore them, but don't make a big fuss, either; they, like anyone else, come to relax and enjoy.

Monod and the others who started the *verrerie* kept it open to the public to show off its presumably superior working conditions. The Lechaczynskis continued the practice, but for different reasons. "People love to see the fire," she says. "It's magic, very visual." There's no admission fee, of course, but you can never miss that sign: *Have you really seen it all?*

❧

The Riviera is no longer the only riviera. Which is a seemingly nonsensical way of saying that, beginning in the 1960s, it became French national policy to relieve pressure on La Côte by channeling sun-starved vacationers to elsewhere on the Mediterranean coast. Paris looked to the map and saw Languedoc-Roussillon, on the *other* side of Marseilles. Its hundred miles of coastline were largely undeveloped, full of malarial lagoons. So upward of six billion francs went toward mosquito control, dredging, filling, highway and harbor building, reforestation, and otherwise suiting the region to visitors. By 1974, a decade after its inception, with grandiose, pyramid-style resort complexes dotting the coast, almost a million and a half people were visiting each year; by 1990, twice that many.

Aesthetically speaking, these first efforts were not universally admired. But for many a Frenchman, they weakened that old habit of thought that reflexively linked the sun and warm sea breezes only with the Côte d'Azur.

❧

In 1995, sixty thousand members of Rotary, the international service organization, converged on Nice from more than a hundred countries. It was the largest conference ever held there.

Delegates picked up badges, program brooks, and tickets at the bustling Acropolis convention center, also the site of luncheons, meetings, and fashion shows. Up the street at the Palais des Expositions, they enjoyed a performance of Niçois folk dancers, and a skirt-tossing can-can. Later, they heard from Suzanne Mubarak, wife of the Egyptian president; plenary sessions were translated into English, French, Italian, Japanese, Korean, and Spanish. A Rotary Village was set up in Nice's large Public Garden, featuring an outdoor café and service-project displays. Around Nice, Rotary's gear-wheel emblem was everywhere. A fleet of two hundred buses shuttled delegates among more than 150 hotels and convention sites. It was a monstrous event, years in the planning, a logistical nightmare. And it was by every yardstick a coup.

By every yardstick *including*, in a sense, environmental. For Rotary came in early June—eight weeks before the clogged and frenetic days of August. And *that*, of course, to city officials, was just the idea. Visitors arriving outside high season didn't push so hard against Nice's limits of air, water, and space—didn't "overgraze" it. Hotels, restaurants, and roads were already there.

Back in 1948, Robert Viers, head of the regional tourist commission, spoke of Zurich, Switzerland, which had built a big conference center, or *palais des congrès*, to lure professional conferences and international meetings; Nice, he said, should do the same, for the sake of the off-season. It would attract both national and international conferences. It could be installed in one of the city's old hotels.

In the fifties, Nice got something much grander, its Palais des Expositions, a great arched-roof affair, set atop vaulted conduits over the bed of the Paillon, which could accommodate an industrial fair, a horse contest, an automobile show, or a Rotary convention, and over the years did. By 1982, Nice was hosting three hundred conferences a year, which pumped a hundred million francs into the local economy. A few years later, Nice got the Acropolis, a warren of seminar rooms, exhibition areas, bars, lounges, and banquet halls, aimed especially at mid-sized scientific conferences.

No *hôtelier* who'd stared at blank room-registers for nine months of the year needed a finely honed environmental sense to understand that to have *congressistes,* or conference-goers, come in January or June was a good thing. In the years since World War II, business travelers, or *touristes d'affaires,* became a coveted catch for Nice's tourist industry, as every other's. They spent twice as much as other tourists. They remained for days at a time. And they normally stayed at hotels—not at campsites, or with relatives.

They helped Nice escape the ancient tyranny of the Season.

☙❧

One brochure going out from Madame Grosgogeat's office was called *Discover the Nice of the Natives.* Of its dozens of images, one was of a toddler sitting by the seashore, bare back to the camera, head a mop of brown ringlets, framed by the smooth white stones of the beach and the blue luminescence of the sea. The photo was the work of Pierre-Hugues Polacci, whose avant-garde photography made him a well-established figure in the Riviera arts community—and whose picture postcards for the tourist trade were among the sixteen thousand mailed out from Nice each summer day.

A native Niçois who occupied studio and living quarters in a high-windowed fourth-floor apartment crowded with posters and memorabilia in Nice's old town, Polacci had been taking pictures for about ten years when a friend suggested some of them might make great picture postcards; they were lush with color, redolent of Nice, showed laundry hanging from flowered balconies, priests trudging through the old town.

But Polacci's first cards got a cool reception, because they were so different from everyone else's. Different, certainly, because he had an eye for common objects seen in stark new ways. But that's not why his business took three years to develop. Different, rather, because his cards were the *wrong size.* Polacci's modest contribution to the Nice tourist industry was to help make them the right size.

Go some Sunday morning to the old-town plaza where the antique-postcard vendors meet and you'll find tables heaped with boxes of cards, classed by subject, some still bearing penned messages from a hundred years ago. Most are ten centimeters by fifteen, about the size of an American four-by-six index card—a standard so entrenched that if you buy some from thirty years ago and mix them with some of today's they'll stack so neatly you could shuffle them like a deck of playing cards.

Well, in the early 1980s, Polacci's cards *weren't* ten by fifteen. His, he felt, were art, and he wanted them to stand out. So he made them twelve by seventeen. But that meant they didn't fit the *tourniquet*, the standard revolving rack, which were all made for ten-by-fifteens; the whole *world* was set up for ten-by-fifteens. So at shop after shop, Polacci heard the same thing: *Pretty picture, but sorry . . .*

He tried to get someone to make an oversized *tourniquet*, but at first no one would make just one—ten or nothing. Soon, though, he was back on the street, with cards and custom-made *tourniquet*. A little camera shop in the old town, La Stenope, became his first customer.

Today you find Polacci's art cards in racks along rue de France, in the *vieille ville*, and a dozen shops around town; he drops by each to take orders, looseleaf book in hand, plastic-sleeved pages each bearing cards identified by number. At retail, they sell for about five francs, double the price of smaller ones.

By now, of course, other photographers have taken up the large format, too.

⚬⚭

A glassworks becomes a tourist attraction.

The Riviera is joined by another riviera.

Conventions make the off-season a little less *off.*

Picture postcards grow larger.

In ways both trifling and consequential, the old certitudes have broken down. Nothing is quite as it was. Compared with, say, a hundred years ago, there's less to Nice and the Riviera, and more. Like an aging *grande dame* made more alluring by the sheer weight of her life experience, the Riviera has become a more versatile and many-layered temptress.

In 1959, Richard Hauer Costa and his wife signed up for a four-week, five-hundred-dollar Experiment in International Living package that got them a tedious five-day course on cathedrals, a week with a French family near Paris, and then, after a rickety charter-bus trip south, what felt like an army barracks in a small coastal town. "First thing in the morning we'll get away from this hole," Costa told his wife, who was still nauseous after all those twisting mountain roads. "We'll go straight to Nice and maybe hire a car and drive down into Italy."

But they never reached Italy.

It seems that Costa, an upstate New York newspaperman in his forties, loved the work of W. Somerset Maugham, who wrote *Of Human Bondage* among many other novels and short stories; to Costa, Maugham was not just another famous author, but "the man whose books have given me more pleasure than any other's." Maugham, then in his eighties, had a villa on Cap Ferrat he'd first bought in 1926 as a kind of winter retreat. Costa, while still back in the States, had written him, wondering if he might stop by to pay his respects. He could make no promises, Maugham replied, but once in the area, Costa might certainly call.

Now Costa was back in Nice, which he'd enjoyed in 1945 along with thousands of other GIs. He and his wife ambled along the Promenade des Anglais, went for a swim. Then, finally, leaving her on the beach, he walked to the Negresco, summoned up his nerve, and called Maugham's villa from the lobby phone. *Demain,* call tomorrow, a spatter of French over the phone told him.

The next day, he did. This time, Maugham's English secretary told him to call at ten the next morning.

Costa did, *this* time being told to come by later that day.

"Our cab," wrote Costa later, "proceeded among olive groves, the sea shimmering in the sun on both sides of us." Soon they were at Villa Mauresque, passing through its gate, then along a path flanked by tropical flowers and cacti. Finally, they were in the great man's presence.

It little matters to us now just what that next hour was like, or what

Costa said to Maugham, or how Maugham replied; suffice it to say that Costa later called it the best day of his life. What does matter is that, whereas Maugham had first come to the Riviera for its climate and beauty, now *he* had become a Riviera attraction.

"Nowadays," Robert Daley wrote in his 1991 book *Portraits of France*,

> the Riviera is dotted with small museums devoted exclusively, or almost exclusively, to single painters. There are Picasso museums in Antibes and Vallauris, a Fernand Léger museum in Biot, a Renoir museum in Cagnes, and Matisse, Chagall, and Dufy museums in Nice. But at that time none of these places existed.

"That time" was just forty years earlier, in the 1950s, when, as a destination for art lovers, the Riviera was still unimportant. "The reader must bear in mind," a guidebook author had written in 1899, "that none of these [Riviera] towns have anything in the way of art or of antiquity to delay the visitor."

But in time, as we've seen, many of them became places for *making* art. By 1966, the Comité Régional du Tourisme could note that the Côte d'Azur had become "the place of choice for most of the great masters of modern painting," going on to cite Matisse, Dufy, and the others by name. "Here, more than elsewhere," it went on, "art is linked to tourism in an intimate, practically indissoluble, union. Museums are not cold structures to which one escapes on a rainy day, but stages in the exploration of magnificent settings, communions of art and nature."

The aura of that whole pantheon of modern art settled on the Riviera. Picasso, Matisse, Man Ray, Cocteau, and Marc Chagall, among others, were all recruited for posters. One, in 1962, by Chagall, showed a luxuriantly red-haired mermaid, suspended high over the distinctive arc of the Baie des Anges, embracing a bouquet. It needed few words: "NICE . . . Soleil . . . Fleurs . . . Marc Chagall."

At first, museums in Nice and the other towns were few and small; guidebooks could still write them off with barely a nod. But, gradually, things changed. The Matisse museum opened in 1963, at first sharing a large sienna-colored villa with the archeology museum—then getting it, and a 1993 addition, all to itself. The Chagall opened in 1970. The Anatole Jakovsky International Museum of Naïve Art, housed in the villa of perfumer François Coty, in the early 1970s. A large marble-clad modern art museum—this, too, situated over the Paillon—in 1990. That was just in Nice. In Biot, as we've seen, there was Léger. In Antibes, Picasso. In Villefranche, Cocteau . . .

When, in 1972, a sixteen-year-old American girl, Helen Glazer, visited the Riviera with her family, galleries and museums had shaped their itinerary. She filled her journal with drawings and descriptions of art. At a one-man show for Nicolas de Stael, the French abstract painter, she wrote of

> a garden of sculptures with Giacomettis spaced in the sun, crickets whirring. Inside N. de Stael. What beautiful structure. Outside again, a Miró mural and sculptures. A huge cement arch. An imposing structure. A giant Miró Easter egg in a clean pool of water.

In 1977, Nice Mayor Jacques Médecin, also then French minister of tourism, organized with Cannes and Monaco a traveling exhibition to Japan to promote the region. With them on their chartered jet, along with local wine and olive oil, were art treasures from local museums: paintings by Chagall, Matisse, Léger, and Fragonard; sculptures by Giacometti; even some Biot glass.

"Nice must become a city of art," Robert de Souza had written in 1913. And it did, as did the Riviera generally. In the summer of 1997, twenty-eight museums and galleries, eleven of them in Nice, joined in a Riviera-wide paean to the region's role in nurturing *modernité*. Exhibits were devoted to photography, fashion, and ceramics as well as painting and sculpture. Compared with, say, fifty years before, there was now one more compelling reason to visit La Côte.

But the appeal was not just the art itself. In her 1998 book, *Artists and Their Museums on the Riviera*, Barbara Freed wrote that the importance of

some of the sites she'd chosen "derives, in part, from the rare opportunity to view these objects in the actual environments in which they were created, and to reflect upon the spontaneous interaction of individual genius and local inspiration." In other words, the dead artists themselves—their very presence on La Côte—were part of the appeal. Guidebook in hand, the reader could walk in the footsteps of the masters, see what they had seen, imagine the making of what they had made.

This was not, of course, a new story, but a variation on an old one; the Napoleons of the world had long conferred luster upon battlefields and other historical sites. Now, though, it was not just warriors, kings, and popes. Now it was those who'd come, in the first place, as something like ordinary tourists but who had stamped the Riviera with a little of their stature and brilliance.

Berlioz and Paganini and Smollett came; streets in Nice today bear their names.

Matisse and Chagall came; museums attest to it.

Legendary jazz greats performed in Nice; their busts adorn an olive garden on the heights of Cimiez.

Lenin stayed at Nice's Hôtel Oasis in 1911, and Chekhov worked on *The Three Sisters* there; the hotel's brochure tells you so, as do plaques upon its walls.

In *The Innocents Abroad*, Mark Twain made light of how every church in the Holy Land claimed its piece of the one true cross. An easy target, certainly—yet testament to that part of us that seeks to touch, or gaze upon, places or artifacts that feel to us somehow sacred. In this sense, then, some Riviera visitors drawn to cultural or historical sites—like Maugham's visitor, Richard Costa—make of themselves pilgrims and the Riviera itself a shrine.

In 1998, food writer Cara de Silva wrote in the *New York Times* about scouring old Nice for the local snack food, *socca*, a crusty crêpe made of chickpea flour. Her piece was called "The Chickpea's Shining Moment," and it shook with paroxysms of nostalgia for

> an older, perhaps less dazzling, but more romantic Nice—that of Queen Victoria, Matisse, the czars, the early days of the Promenade des Anglais, summering English aristocrats, the Belle Époque and the distinctive Niçois when they were still Italian speakers.

Thus, even here, tendrils of Nice's past reached into the present, beguiling would-be visitors.

Nice today trades on its past, just as any other self-respecting pilgrimage site does. One 1985 brochure touted Nice as "The Rendezvous of Famous Names," its praises

> sung by poets from Banville to Lamartine. Its very special light has inspired painters, film producers, photographers, and the most famous names in the world of the arts have chosen it as a

secret haven. Nice, a place where famous names vibrate like a lyre.

Nice, then, seduces not alone on the strength of its climate, or its beauty, or even its arts and amusements, but on that of earlier visitors whose lives and works haunt the imaginations of new generations today.

We tourists go back home a little more deeply connected to a time, place, or person, perhaps just the least bit better for it. And is that so very different—if now for a vastly broader range of visitors—from what English aristocrats on the Grand Tour were expected to derive from *their* travels?

Back in 1813, Michael Faraday, the blacksmith's son who had never strayed more than three miles from London and never seen the sea, wrote of "ideas . . . forced on my mind" by his early travels. Almost two centuries later, the richest and most fashionable have elsewhere to go besides Nice. But as we've seen throughout this book, many others visiting it, who might occupy no place in the society pages of our time or the history books of tomorrow, likewise have ideas, insights, and impressions forced upon their minds.

Many an account of the Riviera directs its readers to the great days of the Belle Époque, establishing that era as touchstone or paradigm, perhaps giving a nod as well to the 1920s. Typically, it celebrates the celebrated—those fortunate few who were not mere tourists, of course, but *real* travelers, or adventurers, or proto-tourists, or *hivernants*, or, in any event, some other breed distinct from today's lowly mass tourist— who, after all, merely apes the ways of his betters.

My instinct, it will be clear by now, is quite otherwise—to see, despite the differences between them, a sharp line of continuity between Nice's earlier visitors and those of today. The much that links them overshadows whatever divides them. Differences of class and historical circumstance count for little beside all that binds the whole stream of travelers and tourists, over all the years, into one great human family, with similar needs and hopes.

Implicit in this is that to satisfy these needs and hopes is, on the whole, good. If Nice gave Smollett something, and Marie Bashkirtseff, and Queen Victoria, it might also me, and my family, and two hundred other tourists crowded aboard an Airbus. While this multiplication of opportunity takes a toll, not least an environmental one, it also confers a profound blessing.

Back in 1868, in the wake of the railroad, at just that moment in its history when Nice had irretrievably thrown in its lot with tourism, that ever-insightful observer Madame Rattazzi noted that Nice by then had a perfectly defined role:

> To protect the leisure of its guests, to hasten convalescence, to strengthen tubercular lungs, to revitalize anemics. What else? To put the rose on the face of woman, to lend a spark to tired eyes and ideas to exhausted minds, to wrap in the same veil the budding loves of yesterday and the buried regrets of tomorrow.

Need Madame Rattazzi's eloquence apply any less to accountants than to queens?

EPILOGUE

ON THE SEAWARD SIDE OF THE PROMENADE, A WOMAN IN HER forties with frosted blond hair, a floral scarf draped round her swimsuit, steps onto the pebbly beach and stakes out a spot for her rattan mat. She shakes off her shoes, slips off her wrap, and sits serenely looking out to sea.

On the other side of a low white fence from her, on a stretch of private beach belonging to one of the big hotels, a young bronzed god of a man, flawless of skin, ripe of muscle, sets up the beach furniture. He opens up wooden deck chairs, lays out striped blue-and-white mattresses.

It is early one summer morning in Nice near the end of the twentieth century.

Later, the sun is stronger, the beach busier, full of bodies pink, pallid, brown, flabby, feeble, and firm, in every permutation, lying atop air mattresses, towels, and mats, or on the bare stones. Out in the water, putting on a show for beachside viewers, a speedboat tows a woman into the air. For two hundred francs, thirty-five dollars, she's fitted with flotation vest, harness, and parachute, and tethered to a boat. The boat roars off, air fills the 'chute and, to squeals of delight, lifts her skyward. Periodically, the boat sputters slower, enough to dip her into the sea with a splash, then streaks ahead again just before the parachute can deflate.

Up on the Promenade, half a dozen American girls, with names like Casey and Bridget, sit out on Nice's ubiquitous blue armchairs, in a semicircle facing the sea, eating ice cream. They wear sunglasses. They are slim, browned, and unblemished. Their hair is straight and long. They are clones. "I think," declares one, with firm purpose, "that I'm going to stop shaving my armpits."

In an area beside the Promenade designated for *pétanque*, the local variation on the lawn bowling game known elsewhere as *boules* or *bocce*, a graying geezer in white sandals and T-shirt cut off at the shoulders, prepares for his underhand toss. He stands, feet together, facing the length of hard-packed dirt, the other players looking on, along with hundreds of beach denizens, the steel balls click-clacking in his hands. Finally, all concentration, he lets fly. . . .

Back from the beach in the *vieille ville*, at a checked-tablecloth brasserie at the far end of the Cours Saleya, a young woman with long black braided hair sings for the lunchtime crowd. She wears what is supposed to be traditional costume—flower-studded white dress, bright-hewed scarf, peasant bonnet. A basket of flowers hangs from her arm. When she's done, she wanders easily among the tables, harvesting her tips.

Over the heights of Cimiez waft sounds of jazz. It is the fiftieth anniversary of the original Nice Jazz Festival, now held, as it has been for some years, at Les Arènes, the old Roman arena, and in the adjoining olive gardens.

Late this summer evening, on a garishly lit stage at the south end of the arena, the Super Swing Machine backs up showman and crooner Michel Beel. "Fly me to the moon . . . ," sings Beel, in gray sharkskin suit, doing his Frank Sinatra best. The stone tiers of the original arena brim over with people. So does the central ellipse, where once gladiators fought, today a grid of plastic seating; the level plane of the audience's heads, woolly halos in the reflected stage lighting, looks like lustrous carpet.

In the olive garden, between the two main stages, a lull from one stage accentuates the thumping beat from the other. Strings of lights have been suspended between the olive trees, with their knotty, insouciantly irregular dark trunks. In the mottled shadows among them, on the ground, sit American jazz aficionados brought here by a San Diego travel agency; day trippers ferried up the hill on the shuttle bus from Place Masséna; a Michigan family renting an apartment at the Regina across the street; international students from a Nice language school; Italian under one tree, British accents under the next. Food stands sell Häagen-Dazs, beer, *socca* and *pissaladière,* candy apples and cotton candy.

A global country fair, Nice-style.

❧

The Russians, seventy thousand of them, are the talk of the Riviera this summer; maybe soon, the Russian consul general has said, they'll have to reinstate the train that once bore grand dukes from Saint Petersburg. A lot of the Russians, you hear it said, are suspiciously rich, buying up yachts and helicopters, renting limousines. You spot them the moment they walk in, says a twenty-something saleswoman in an upscale men's shop off rue Masséna, where a Portegiani T-shirt runs eight hundred francs. A sign on the door bids welcome in Cyrillic. These new-money Russians? Russian mafia, she says, getting rich off money laundering. They're good for business, but you should see them pull down from the rack three or four suits at a time. She acts it out, putting her whole body into it, *clutching* the overpriced clothes, contempt written across her face.

❧

On the busy pedestrian mall that backs up to Place Masséna, passersby gawk at two white-robed figures, human statues positioned atop pedestals. With infinite grace and slowness, they move to a hidden tape's haunting melody. A pot set in front, also sheathed in white, has been primed with coins and currency.

Artists, performers, and vendors line the street. One blanket is crowded with great-bellied African figurines; another with paintings, all breasts and luminous color, set out on acrylic stands.

From behind a velvet cloth thrown across a cardboard box, Elena and Martin run a brisk business. Elena, an Italian who looks as if she's stepped from a Renaissance painting, wraps colored glass in artful turns of aluminum wire. With a few deft twists and snips of her wire cutters, she fashions them into bracelets and necklaces—one for thirty francs, two for fifty. Martin, a bearded middle-aged New Yorker in shlumpy shorts and running shoes, fancies himself the P. T. Barnum of the two, pulling in customers with loud, caustic wisecracks. But Elena is at least as canny. When an Asian woman proffers a two-hundred-franc bill, she fusses, seemingly unable to muster up the change. Finally, she looks up at her waiting customer and, with big eyes and bigger smile, sweetly implores her: "Buy more."

∞

The three white cars of the *train touristique* gradually fill with passengers. Parked in front of the Public Garden, beside the seafront, the miniature rubber-tired train draws from tourists along the Promenade and the Quai des États-Unis. Six or seven times a day, it ferries a load of them through Nice's old town and up the Château Hill. It's supposed to leave every half-hour, but never pulls out before Sylvie pronounces it *rempli*, full. Sylvie, in her thirties, a white pullover draped stylishly across her shoulders, is fare collector, conductor, driver, and guide all at once. While they wait, passengers lean back, taking in the Promenade spectacle, snapping pictures, reading foreign newspapers. When enough of them have climbed aboard to suit Sylvie, she drifts back from car to car collecting the thirty-franc fare, periodically fishing in her money belt for change. Finally, the horn beeps and the train lurches forward. A tape supplies commentary in French and English.

Just outside the old town, the train scoots up boulevard Jean-Jaurès to Place Garibaldi, then begins to climb the Château Hill. "Don't bother to look for the castle," blares the tape, "there's nothing left." On the way up, they pass an artificial waterfall. At the top, they reach a plateau where several other little trains, their passengers momentarily disgorged, are parked. "Fifteen minutes," Sylvie calls out.

While Sylvie sits talking with a friend, her passengers disperse across the hilltop enclave. They buy ice cream. They wander among souvenir stands stocked with refrigerator magnets and shell-encrusted jewelry, baseball caps with Nice inscribed in phosphorescent pink.

From Terrasse Frédéric Nietzsche, they gaze over the red clay roofs and church steeples of the old town. The official altitude is ninety-two meters, about three hundred feet. High enough to command a stunning view. Low enough to hear the faint crackling of the waves as they spill over the rocks and pebbles along the beach.

The *train touristique* is, of course, the silliest thing you've ever seen. This golf-cart-scaled faux-locomotive, hauling a conspicuous cargo of ogling tourists at five or six miles an hour through four-hundred-year-old streets, is guaranteed to make you feel ridiculous. But it's fun. And indispensable if you want to see the *vieille ville* any way but on foot. Because it's skinny enough to slip, like a silent apparition, through *ruelles*, back alleys, crammed with pedestrians and the tables and chairs of sidewalk cafés.

Sometimes, a waiter sees Sylvie coming and slides a chair out of the way. Or Sylvie herself will stop to move a postcard rack jutting a few inches into her path. Today, though, she faces a more formidable obstacle. There, at the head of rue Benoît-Bunico as it crosses rue Rossetti, stands a white Volvo. Parked squarely in the middle of the street. Sitting there. Empty.

Sylvie honks.

Nothing happens.

She honks again—at first tentatively, then more insistently.

Her passengers settle back; they're not going anywhere. One, a Dutchman, gets out to snap pictures of the improbable scene.

Sylvie puts in a call on her portable radio. But no one comes to move the car.

There's no way to get around it, no way to move back.

The clock ticks. Sylvie waits. Her brood of passengers wait.

Still nothing.

And then a second *train touristique*, unaware of the roadblock, pulls in behind Sylvie's on rue Benoît-Bunico. Now it's both of them sitting there, *two* trainloads of tourists. Now it's a whole line of little white cars snaking all the way back from rue Rossetti.

In time, a man will appear at a window several stories up, he and Sylvie will shout, a seemingly unruffled young woman will scurry over to the Volvo, slide inside, and peel off down the street. But just now, on this summer day in high season, it's gridlock in old Nice.

∞

This is the year the French win soccer's World Cup, and Nice, like any other self-respecting French town, talks of nothing else. As the crucial match nears, televisions in cafés and *tabacs* blare into the street. On the night France finally triumphs, Nice goes mad. Horns beep and bellow. Children, aping their heroes, kick balls up and down the street. Young men climb atop the hoods of cars, waving flags. On the Promenade, traffic inches along, cars sound raspy Klaxons. Every face, it seems, is painted with the *bleu, blanc, et rouge* of the French tricolor. The air is thick with smoke from exploding fireworks.

As hours pass and the din heightens, you can pick out the tourists from the natives. Because they merely beam with pleasure rather than scream themselves hoarse. Tonight, on the streets of Nice, it is *interdit*, prohibited, not to smile. But whereas the smiles of the Niçois explode, those of the tourists seem thinner, more contained. Even now, at the madness's height, you can spot them by their gait—that strut, that shuffle, of people with all the time in the world, curious, watchful, taking it all in, but at a little distance.

Late that evening, a couple step out onto the balcony of their room in a Promenade des Anglais hotel, its façade much as it was during the Belle Époque, lit up in the night. From their perch, composed, they gaze down over the civic insanity. Then they turn to each other, smile, lightly kiss, and turn back inside.

∞

Outside Nice, on the Grande Corniche, in La Turbie, where Augustus erected his towering monument to Rome's victories, the tourists are coming—when the cruise ships make port, says the guide on duty, sometimes seven or eight hundred of them a day. So many that the parking's getting out of hand. So many that she thinks maybe they should restore the narrow-gauge railroad that ran up the mountain from Monaco until 1932, when an accident shut it down. Recently, a new walkway has been completed, the stream of tourists among and through the ancient stones and columns smoothed by steel pipe, cable, and judicious cuts right through the masonry. They put it in, says the guide, because tourists demanded it.

In Menton, just this side of the border, voices heard on the beach include many Italian ones. An old cemetery up a steep stone stairway, beyond a pair of churches, tells how once the British elite and others came here to die. Now, though, Menton swarms with life, every inch of beach covered by people, umbrellas, towels, mats, rafts, and toys. It's a family place, celebrating domestic pleasures. An old man, in a checked bathing suit that drops down from beneath a great expanse of belly, stands in the shallows, motionless, as if meditating on the rustle of water against his calves. A grandfather holds a child's hand. A heavily lipsticked woman, with dyed red hair and thick, callused hands, sits with her feet in the water, reading. Looking up, she can see, high in the cliffs above her, the line of cars and trucks snaking toward Italy.

In Monte Carlo, on a Saturday night, guards in livery stand in front of the casino, while tourists gawk at the procession of luxury cars—a Ferrari, an Aston-Martin, a Rolls. Their drivers pull right up and leave them; no parking hassles for them. The cars, of course, are part of the show: tourists line the low iron fence out front in order to glimpse celebrities and ogle their cars. An Indian positions his wife, in full sari, beside a yellow Lamborghini, frames the picture, and snaps it. Others immediately take their places. Hey, you don't see cars like *this* back home, says an Israeli woman posing beside a Ferrari. But in front of a car not even your own? Why? She looks at you as if you're crazy, or stupid. "Because," she replies evenly, "it is beautiful."

On the other side of the Var, outside Vence, visitors troop through the tiny Chapelle du Rosaire to see Matisse's stained-glass panels, all glowing greens, yellows, and blues. It's hard here not to pay homage—if not to God, then to Matisse's genius. But compared with many tourist sites, the chapel's hours are few; it's a working religious institution. Over the years, tourists would knock at the door expecting to be

admitted anyway and, turned away, fairly *beg* to be made an exception. So now the sign out front, along with posting the hours, adds: *"Merci de ne pas insister,"* Thank you for not insisting.

In Saint-Paul-de-Vence, a town near Vence best known for the writers and artists who gathered around its famous auberge, the Colombe d'Or, an American family, tired and grumpy, compare notes. They feel cheated. Why? The crowds, for one. And the ten-story underground parking garage. And the shops that together feel like an American shopping mall. But their teenaged son sees more darkly yet into their Riviera vacation. They've been all over, his parents priding themselves on the varied slices of it to which he's been introduced—hotels from seedy to luxurious; museums, beaches, and historic sites; perched villages, idyllic *calanques*, big cities—all so different. Nah, says the boy, not different at all, but just the same. The towns, built on hilltops or the sides of cliffs: piles of old houses crowded together. All with too much history and too few people living in them. All with darling little shops that sell crafts, dolls, miniatures, pottery, and other stuff that regular people don't need. All with old fountains, and cobbled back alleys, and scraggly cats.

∞

As the great August peak approaches, local newspapers track the story like a force of nature, the way American weather forecasters trail a hurricane as it gathers strength in the Atlantic before roaring up the East Coast.

In late July, the paper reports a particularly good May and early June, traditionally a "black hole" for Nice tourism. But this time it's been buttressed by a Microsoft conference that's brought thousands of visitors to Nice and by itself filled half the city's prime hotel space; ordinary tourists without reservations were left trooping from hotel to hotel begging for a room.

With the onset of August, tension mounts. " 'Black Saturday' in the Rhône Valley," says the front page of *Nice-Matin* on August 2; a telephoto shot captures cars, with bicycles and luggage lashed to their roofs, bumper to bumper. Paris vacationers faced "up to 650 kilometers of traffic jams before reaching the long-sought shore."

In the Alpes-Maritimes generally, another article reports, occupancy rates are up 7 or 8 percentage points from last summer. "The bulge of vacationers is expected beginning Tuesday."

Still another article, this one relegated to page ten, tells of thirty-five hundred trains placed in service for the weekend; two million travelers set to board them; young people stationed at seventy train stations, identifiable by their red cardigans, available to help them.

Then the rains come. After months of none at all, rain in August! "The rain spurs a new August rush," says *Nice-Matin*, this time to dry shops, museums, and backcountry towns. *"Plages désertes!"* says an article inside—beaches deserted! "The stones of the Prom' normally covered with bath towels in this season, yesterday showed themselves gray and bare."

The rain is soon gone, of course. And then, one day—it's August 10—the great wave crests. A single color photo in the middle of the page, nine inches square, spills over with the splendid azure arc of the bay and, beside it, the Nice beach aswarm with bodies. At the top, a single word, *"Complet!,"* full.

> They have arrived. In waves. En masse. Especially these past three days. The August arrivals are here, taking over everywhere, crowding every beach in the region, leaving La Côte's hotels *complet* from Menton to Théoule.

∞

In 1816, archeologist Aubin-Louis Millin climbed up to the old terrace, built atop the row of shops bordering the Cours Saleya, and from that vantage point looked out to sea. He saw fishing boats drawn up onto the shore, ships bound for Genoa and Marseilles, the mountains of Corsica barely visible in the distance. "Nothing so encourages meditation as the spectacle one enjoys on this terrace," he wrote.

One remains here for hours and still cannot get enough of it. However unchanging it might seem, it awakens in us thoughts of profound interest. The idea of our distance across the waters from other countries; the diversity of customs and mores of the people living in them; the thought of the dangers the sea poses to those who brave it; the immense commerce it promotes; the riches it has swallowed up; the products it bestows upon us. All these enthrall the imagination.

Today, up the Château Hill from where Millin looked out to sea, and almost visible from it, visitors stop beside a stone wall to look down upon the harbor, over to Mont Boron, and out to sea. A mosaic set in the ground nearby, portraying Ulysses' travels, bears the inscription: "Happy is he who, like Ulysses, has had a fine voyage." Cacti and shrubbery, like infantry scaling a ramparts, climb the hill's slope almost to the very top. Below lies a modest basin, with rows of small boats and yachts, and a long breakwater jutting into the sea. A three-masted sailing vessel is tied up at one dock. Tourists line up to board it; you can almost make out their faces from here. A big, yellow-hulled ferry bound for Corsica, its lines cast off, pulls away in a flurry of foam, its engines stirring the water, the sea left milky white behind it.

An American couple in their thirties watch these prosaic events unfold. He wears gray shorts and a university T-shirt; she a simple mauve skirt. Mostly, they watch in silence. But occasionally they comment about the boats; or wonder how long the ferry takes to reach Corsica; or compare it with one they took once to Sicily's Reggio di Calabria; she gives it her best full-throated accent, as if merely to utter the name brings back remembered pleasures.

They don't have the spot to themselves. A dozen other visitors are up here with them. Someone snaps a picture. A video camera whirrs. But there's no milling about among them; like the American couple, they stand beside the wall, stock still, as if intending never to go. The air is bright and sharp, the sun tempered by a bracing sea breeze, the port's muffled activity distant yet cozily close. A few steps away stands one of those bulky public binoculars that for five or ten francs affords a few minutes of a closer view. But no one uses it.

So, no, they don't leave just yet. For much longer than you'd think, for minutes on end, for a long, long time, they stay. Whatever it is they get from this view, this air, this time out of time, they want just a little more.

ABOUT THE ILLUSTRATIONS

SOURCES AND ACKNOWLEDGMENTS

To erect elaborate scholarly scaffolding around a book that honors leisure seems downright perverse. Still, I hope this book, primarily aimed at the general reader, may prove helpful to some who are professionally or otherwise interested in travel, tourism, leisure, the Riviera, or things French generally. So I offer here the high points of the research upon which this book rests.

I cite, first, the many personal accounts of visitors to Nice and its environs whom the reader has already met, like Tobias Smollett or Robert Allen.

A second broad category comprises those who, as scholars or journalists, have written *about* Nice or related subjects, and whose firsthand impressions of the place, if any, figure only secondarily.

Finally, although it is more customary to split off the debts one owes written sources, as in a bibliography, from those one owes friends, family, colleagues, informants, and others, as in an acknowledgments section, so neat a division doesn't fit here; accordingly, expressions of gratitude percolate all through this appendix.

VISITORS TO NICE

Individual accounts of visits to Nice and the Riviera—diaries, journals, memoirs, reminiscences—constitute this book's bedrock.

Some of them, certainly most of the unpublished ones, are rough and unrefined. Others have been worked over later by the travelers or their editors. Though many never actually appear in the book, all helped me understand Nice, the Riviera, and the travel experience through the ages. They are subdivided by the form in which they reached me—whether as archival record, published memoir, interview, or whatever.

Archival Accounts

Included here are journals, diaries, and letters, most of them never published. For access to them and for much other assistance, I am indebted to the patient, endlessly helpful professional staffs of the libraries and archives indicated.

Hagley Museum, Wilmington, Delaware: Louis A. Cazenove, Joanna Maria Du Pont, Natalie Driver (Wilson) Du Pont, Mary Pauline Foster.

Halifax, Nova Scotia, Public Archives (through Eileen M. Curran, Colby College): Richard Blair.

Harvard University, Cambridge, Massachusetts: Elizabeth Foster.

Huntington Library, Pasadena, California: Ellen Columba Anderson, Elizabeth Miller, John Westley Vandevort, Samuel Willard.

Maryland Historical Society, Baltimore: Jennie Reizenstein, Evan Philip Thomas.

Massachusetts Historical Society, Boston: George Bemis, George B. Emerson, William H. Gardiner, Margaret Morton Quincy Greene, Eliza L. Lothrop Homans, Arthur Howard Nichols, Ephraim Peabody, Sarah Putnam, Henrietta M. Schroeder, Louise Winsor.

New York Public Library, New York, New York: Laura Libbey.

Rutgers University Library, New Brunswick, New Jersey: Anne P. Heroy, Mary Burr Hulsizer, Anna Miller (Newkirk) Place, Robert Edgar Welsh, Anna B. Wilcox.

University of Virginia, Charlottesville, Virginia: Ethel L. Dickinson, Ella K. Fifes Haxall papers, Mr. and Mrs. John Thomas Toof.

Thanks to Antolin Garcia Carbonell of Miami, Florida, for letting me see extracts from the journal of his grandfather Antolin Garcia Alvarez.

Interviews

This book spans a time from the distant past to the present. For the recent past, I owe much of what I know to interviews and private correspondence with, or personal journals of, visitors to Nice whose travels I became aware of through a variety of means: John H. Connell, Richard Hecht, Jane Huddish, David D. Kane, Robert Lasson, Donald Launer, Bill and Louisa Newlin, Maya Pines, Mark Rickards, Sarah Schmidt, Victoria Secunda, Earle A. Taylor.

Thanks go as well to:

Richard Hauer Costa. See also "Somerset Maugham and the Driffield Position," in Mr. Costa's *An Appointment with Somerset Maugham*. College Station: Texas A & M University Press, 1995.

Roger Denkart, who alerted me to the Stanford University tour.

Kenneth Silver. For Mr. Silver's extensive published writings about artists on the Côte d'Azur, see "Scholars and Writers" below.

Several of those named above were kind enough to let me see various materials, from hotel stubs to college essays, that helped me to better understand their experiences. But I owe the following men and women a further debt of gratitude for permitting me access to their private journals: Helen Glazer, Abigail Green, Ming-Tai Huh, Anna Wolisin.

I wish to express special thanks to Robert Allen, who let me rummage through the correspondence and other rich personal records of his navy days. He and his warm, welcoming family extended me every kindness during my visit to Newton, Massachusetts, during a period before I myself moved to the Boston area.

Published Accounts

Accounts of visitors to Nice and the Riviera that have come to me through published books, journal articles, and anthologies appear here broken down by broad historical period.

A particularly useful resource was André Merquiol's *La Côte d'Azur dans la littérature française* (Paris: Jacques Dervyl, 1949), indicated below as "Merquiol."

Another was *Nice historique*, the journal of L'Academia Nissarda, now almost a century old. A special issue (no. 1–2, 1993) devoted to the Promenade des Anglais in the 1930s bears numerous accounts of visitors from that period, especially in Jean-Paul Potron's essay, pp. 37–61, "La Promenade des Anglais d'une guerre à l'autre," indicated here as "Potron/Promenade."

A number of visitors to Nice wrote books that, while taking on the outward form of history or guide, in fact read more like personal accounts, or otherwise bear a tone more flavorful or intimately knowledgeable than their titles might suggest. I've included these here rather than in the "Scholars and Writers" section.

An anthology containing numerous brief accounts of visits to Nice, which I discovered only after I'd finished writing, is *The South of France: An Anthology*, compiled by Laura Raison (New York: Beaufort Books, 1985).

Before 1815

Beatis, Antonio de. *The Travel Journal of Antonio de Beatis*. Edited by J. R. Hale. London: Hakluyt Society, 1979.

Beaumont, Albanis de. *Through the Maritime Alps from Italy to Lyons*. London: T. Bensley, 1795.

Bromley, William. *Remarks on the Grand Tour of France and Italy Performed by a Person of Quality, 1691.* N.p., 1705.

Brosses, Charles de. *Lettres familières sur l'Italie.* Paris: Firmin-Didiot, 1931.

Casanova, Jean-Jacques. In *Nice historique*, 1913, pp. 68–69.

Davis, J. B. *The Ancient and Modern History of Nice.* London: Tipper & Richards, 1807.

Dupaty, Charles. *Travels Through Italy.* Translated from the French by an English Gentleman. Dublin: Burnet, Byrne, and Moore, 1789.

Evelyn, John. *The Diary of John Evelyn.* Oxford: Clarendon Press, 1955.

Eyrard, Monsignor. *Voyage court, agréable et utile fait par Monsignor Eyrard (1787).* Edited by Wanda Rupolo. Rome: Istituto Nazionale di Archeologia e Storia dell'Arte, 1988.

Faraday, Michael. *Curiosity Perfectly Satisfyed: Faraday's Travels in Europe, 1813–1815.* Edited by Brian Bowers and Lenore Symons. London: Peter Peregrinus in association with The Science Museum, 1991.

Genlis, Comtesse de. In Merquiol, pp. 38–41.

Grégoire, Henri. *Rapport présenté à la Convention nationale.* Paris: Imprimerie Nationale, 1793. See also "L'Abbé Grégoire: Apôtre de la tolérance," *Sourgentin*, vol. 106 (March–April 1993), pp. 14–15.

Hospital, Michel de l'. In Merquiol, pp. 47–51.

Jefferson, Thomas. *The Papers of Thomas Jefferson.* Edited by Julian P. Boyd. Vol. 11. Princeton, N.J.: Princeton University Press, 1955. See also *Thomas Jefferson's Travels in Europe, 1784–1789*, edited by George Green Shackelford (Baltimore, Md.: Johns Hopkins University Press, 1995).

Lande, M. de la. *Voyage en Italie.* Yverdon: n.p., 1788.

Mortoft, Francis. *Francis Mortoft: His Book, Being His Travels Through France and Italy, 1658–1659.* London: Hakluyt Society, 1925.

Rigby, Edward. *Dr. Rigby's Letters.* Edited by Lady Eastlake. London: Longmans, Green, 1880.

Saussure, H. B. de. In A. Baréty, "Le Voyage de Nice Autrefois," *Nice historique*, 1913, pp. 117–34, 169–85.

Smith, James Edward. *A Sketch of a Tour on the Continent.* London: J. Davis, 1793.

Smollett, Tobias. *Travels Through France and Italy.* Edited by Frank Felsenstein. London: Oxford University Press, 1981.

Sulzer, Jean George. *Journal d'un voyage fait en 1775 et 1776.* Translated from the German. Rotterdam: L. Bennet, 1789. For a crucial foray into the University of California at Berkeley library that led to my obtaining this hard-to-find account, I wish to thank Laird Harrison of Oakland, California.

Thomas, Antoine-Leonard. In Merquiol, pp. 58–63.

Young, Arthur. *Travels in France and Italy.* London: J. M. Dent, 1915.

Remainder of the Nineteenth Century

Ackermann, Louise. In Merquiol, pp. 105–12.

Anonymous. In Les Amis du Musée Masséna, ed., *Les Anglais dans le comté de Nice et en Provence depuis le XVIIe siècle.* N.p., ca. 1934. This account appears on pp. 164–68 under the title "Journal de Voyage de Mrs. ***."

———. In Jacques Borge and Nicolas Viasnof, eds., *Archives de la Côte d'Azur.* Paris: Michèle Trinckvel, 1994. This account appears on pp. 103–13 under the title "Journal d'une dame de la haute société."

Auger, Hippolyte. In Merquiol, pp. 88–90.

Banville, Théodore de. *La Mer de Nice.* Paris: Poulet-Malassis et de Broise, 1861.

Bashkirtseff, Marie. *The Journal of Marie Bashkirtseff.* Translated by Mathilde Blind. London: Virago, 1986. See also "Marie Bashkirtseff et Nice," *Nice historique,* nos. 3–4, 1995. I defy anyone not to fall hopelessly in love with Mademoiselle Bashkirtseff.

Berlioz, Hector. *Memoirs of Hector Berlioz from 1803 to 1865.* Translated by Ernest Newman et al. New York: Dover, 1990.

Birchall, Emily. *Wedding Tour.* Edited by David Verey. New York: St. Martin's Press, 1985.

Blessington, Countess of. Marguerite (Power) Farmer Gardiner. *The Idler in Italy.* London: Henry Colburn, 1839.

Brewster, Margaret Maria. *Letters from Cannes and Nice.* Edinburgh: Thomas Constable, 1857.

Carter, N. H. *Letters from Europe.* New York: G. & C. & H. Carvill, 1829.

Charles-Félix, King of Sardinia. In P. Dieudé-Defly, "Séjour à Nice, en novembre 1826, de LL. MM. le Roi et la Reine de Sardaigne," *Nice historique,* July–August 1938.

Chateaubriand, François-René de. In Merquiol, pp. 92–99.

Cobden, Richard. *The European Diaries of Richard Cobden, 1846–1849.* Edited by Miles Taylor. Aldershot, England: Scolar Press, 1994.

Dickens, Charles. *Pictures from Italy.* Originally published in 1846. New York: Books, Inc., edition.

Dumas, Alexandre. In Merquiol, pp. 133–37.

Épinois, Anna, Henri, and Aurélie de l'. *De Nice à Gênes: Impressions de voyage.* Edited by Charles Astro et al. Nice: Action Culturelle Municipale, 1993.

Farr, William. *A Medical Guide to Nice.* London: John Churchill, 1841.

Fitzpatrick, Percy. *A Guide to Nice.* Nice: Nice Typographic Society, 1858.

Flaubert, Gustave. *Notes de voyages.* Paris: Louis Conard, 1910.

Fleming, Gertrude. In Eva-Marie Kroller, ed., *Canadian Travellers in Europe, 1851–1900* (Vancouver: University of British Columbia Press, 1987).

Hall, Adelaide. *Two Women Abroad.* Chicago: Monarch, 1897.

Herzen, Alexander. *Alexander Herzen: Letters from France and Italy, 1847–1851.* Edited by Judith E. Zimmerman. Pittsburgh, Pa.: University of Pittsburgh Press, 1995. See also Franco Venturi, *Studies in Free Russia,* p. 285 below.

Lee, Edwin. *Continental Travel, with an Appendix on the Influence of Climate amd the Remedial Advantages of Travelling.* London: W. J. Adams, 1848. See also Lee's *Nice and Its Climate* (London: Hope, 1854).

Meyerbeer, Giacomo. In Guillaume Borea, "Les Séjours de Meyerbeer à Nice," *Nice historique,* January–February 1938.

Millin, Aubin Louis. *Voyage en Savoie, en Piemont, à Nice, et à Gênes.* Paris: C. Wassermann, 1816.

Nash, James. *The Royal Guide to Nice.* Nice: Bensa, 1896.

Nietzsche, Frédéric. In *Sourgentin,* no. 68, September–October 1985. My thanks to Raoul Nathiez, editor of *Sourgentin,* for his trouble in dispatching to me from Nice several articles appearing in his excellent regional journal.

Paccard, Chevalier. In G. Borea. "Notes d'un hivernant avant l'annexion," *Nice historique,* 1939, pp. 81–91.

Rattazzi, Marie. *Nice la Belle.* Paris: Degorce-Cadot, 1868.

Segretain, Alexandre. In "Nice en 1860: Souvenirs du Général Al. Segretain," *Revue de Paris,* August 1960.

Silliman, Benjamin. *A Visit to Europe in 1851.* New York: A. S. Barnes, 1856.

Starke, Mariana. *Letters from Italy Between the Years 1792 and 1798.* London: R. Phillips, 1800.

Stendhal. *Voyages en France.* Paris: Gallimard, 1992.

Topliff, Samuel. *Letters from Abroad in the Years 1828 and 1829.* Boston: Boston Athenaeum, 1906.

Tothill, Mary D. *Pen & Pencil Notes on the Riviera and in North Italy.* London: Simpkin Marshall, 1880.

Victoria, Queen. In David Duff, *Victoria Travels: Journeys of Queen Victoria* (New York: Taplinger, 1971).

Twentieth Century

Adams, Eustace L. *The Family Sees France.* New York: Brewer and Warren, 1931.

Amory, Martha Babcock. *Wedding Journal of Charles & Martha Babcock Amory.* Boston: privately published, 1922.

Blasco Ibanez, Vicente. In Potron/Promenade, pp. 43–45.

Bransby, Leslie. *A Fortnight on the French Riviera.* London: Percival Marshall, 1951.

Cohn, Nik. "Riviera Gumshoe." In *Travelers' Tales France,* edited by James O'Reilly et al. (San Francisco: Travelers' Tales, 1995), pp. 325–35.

Ebert, Roger. *Two Weeks in the Midday Sun: A Cannes Notebook.* Kansas City, Mo.: Andrews & McMeel, 1987.

Flament, Albert. In Potron/Promenade, pp. 49–50.

Ford, Ford Madox. *Provence.* Hopewell, N.J.: Ecco Press, 1972.

George, Donald W. "Three Women of Nice." In *Travelers' Tales France*, edited by James O'Reilly et al. (San Francisco: Travelers' Tales, 1995), pp. 79–82.

Gibbons, Herbert Adams. *Riviera Towns.* New York: Robert M. McBride, 1931.

Gostling, Frances M. *The Lure of the Riviera.* New York: Robert M. McBride, 1927.

Graves, Charles. *The Big Gamble: The Story of Monte Carlo.* London: Hutchinson, 1951.

———. *The Riviera Revisited.* London: Evans Brothers, 1948.

Hall, Warren. *Azure Coast.* N.p., 1952.

Hallam Murray, A. H. *Sketches on the Old Road Through France to Florence.* London: John Murray, 1904.

Lartigue, Jacques-Henri. In *Recherches régionales Alpes-Maritimes et contrées limitrophes*, no. 3, 1993, p. 166.

Loveland, John Douglas Errington. *The Romance of Nice.* New York: Frederick A. Stokes, 1912.

Mais, S. P. B. *The Riviera: New Look & Old.* London: Christopher Johnson, 1949.

Morand, Paul. In Potron/Promenade, p. 17.

Murdoch, Nina. *Seventh Heaven.* Sydney, Australia: Angus & Robertson, 1930.

Newby, Eric. *On the Shores of the Mediterranean.* London: Lonely Planet, 1998.

Peattie, Donald Culross. *Immortal Village.* Chicago: University of Chicago Press, 1945. See also L. R. and D. C. Peattie, *The Happy Kingdom* (London: Blackie & Son, 1935).

Samoźwaniec, Magdalena. In Potron/Promenade, pp. 46–47.

Sutton, Horace. *Footlose in France.* New York: Rinehart, 1948.

SCHOLARS AND WRITERS

High Season in Nice is a work of popular history which, while dependent on visitors' firsthand accounts, also owes much to legions of scholars and other writers. I make no attempt to cite here all sources consulted—no articles from *Nice-Matin*, *Petit Niçois*, or *l'Éclaireur*, no popular magazines, brochures, or travel guidebooks. I do wish to record, however, some of the key books and articles on which I relied, and to which those interested might turn. These are broken down by periods in Nice's history (roughly following the text), or by broad topical categories.

Travel and Tourism in Nice and the Riviera

Blume, Mary. *Côte d'Azur: Inventing the French Riviera*. New York: Thames and Hudson, 1992.

Centre d'Études du Tourisme, Université d'Aix-Marseille. *Le Caractère saisonnier du phénomène touristique: Ses Conséquences économiques*. Aix-en-Provence: La Pensée Universitaire, 1963.

Decaux, Alain. *Les Heures brillantes de la Côte d'Azur*. Paris: Librairie Académique Perrin, 1964.

Devun, Jean. "L'Évolution de Nice de 1860 à 1960." *Recherches régionales Alpes-Maritimes et contrées limitrophes*, no. 1, 1971, pp. 1–29.

Gade, Daniel W. "The French Riviera as Elitist Space." *Journal of Cultural Geography*, Fall–Winter 1982, pp. 19–28.

Gonnet, Paul. "Un Moteur original de croissance régionale: Les Migrations d'agrément sur la Côte d'Azur (1860–1975)." *Bulletin de la Société d'Histoire Moderne*, vol. 15, no. 21 (1977), pp. 2–15.

Graves, Charles. *Royal Riviera*. London: Heinemann, 1957.

Haug, C. James. *Leisure and Urbanism in Nineteenth-Century Nice*. Lawrence: Regents Press of Kansas, 1982.

Michaud, Guy, and Jean-Pierre Jardel, eds. *Tourisme et Développement: Côte d'Azur–Riviera dei Fiori*. Paris: Presses d'Europe, 1979.

Musée de l'Automobiliste. *Les Routes en Provence-Alpes-Côte d'Azur au fil des siècles*. Paris: Maeght, 1993.

Nash, Dennison. "The Rise and Fall of an Aristocratic Tourist Culture—Nice: 1763–1936." *Annals of Tourism Research*, January–March 1979, pp. 61–75.

Pietri, Antoine. "Nice: Capitale touristique." *Actes du 83e Congrès National des Sociétés Savantes* (Aix-Marseille, 1958), bulletin (section de géographie), vol. 71, pp. 209–43.

Potron, Jean-Paul. *L'Image de Nice au travers des guides de voyage, 1800–1900*. Nice: D.E.A. Université de Nice, 1991. Heartfelt thanks to Monsieur Potron for his help in tracking down materials at the Bibliothèque du Chevalier Victor de Cessole, Nice.

Rudney, Robert. "The Development of Tourism on the Côte d'Azur: An Historical Perspective." In Donald E. Hawkins et al. *Tourism Planning and Development Issues*. Washington, D.C.: George Washington University, 1980.

———. "From Luxury to Popular Tourism: The Transformation of the Resort City of Nice." Ph.D. dissertation, University of Michigan, 1979. Mr. Rudney was unfailingly generous in letting me borrow materials that he used in writ-

ing his superb doctoral thesis, which concentrated on Nice between the
world wars.

Soane, John V. N. *Fashionable Resort Regions: Their Evolution and Transformation, with Particular Reference to Bournemouth, Nice, Los Angeles and Wiesbaden.* Wallingford, England: CAB International, 1993.

Souza, Robert de. *Nice: Capitale d'hiver.* Paris: Berger-Levrault, 1913.

General Histories of Nice and the Riviera

Barelli, Hervé. *Vieux Nice: Guide historique et architectural.* Nice: Serre, 1997.

Bordes, Maurice. *Histoire de Nice et du pays niçois.* Toulouse: Édouard Privat, 1976.

Castela, Paul. *De Nikaia à Acropolis: La Mutation de Nice.* Nice: Ciais, 1988.

Compan, André. *Le Comté de Nice.* Paris: Séghers, 1980.

Hildesheimer, Françoise. *La Vie à Nice au XVIIe siècle.* Paris: Publisud, 1987.

Latouche, Robert. *Histoire de Nice.* 3 vols. Nice: Ville de Nice, 1965.

Lenthéric, Charles. *The Riviera: Ancient and Modern.* Translated by Charles West. Chicago: Ares Publishers, 1976.

Livet, Roger. *Atlas et géographie de Provence, Côte d'Azur et Corse.* Paris: Flammarion et Éditions Famot, 1978.

Paccino, Charles. *L'Avenue.* Nice: Serre, 1983.

Raybaut, Paul. *Les Sources régionales du pays de Nice.* Paris: Fayard, 1979.

Greeks and Romans on the Riviera

Cimiez-Cemenelum, a Gallo-Roman Site and other brochures published by Musée Archéologique de Nice-Cimiez.

Hall, W. H. [Bullock]. *The Romans on the Riviera and the Rhône.* Chicago: Ares Publishers, 1974.

Mouchot, Danièle. *Le Musée d'Archéologie.* Nice: Action Culturelle Municipale, 1989.

The Grand Tour

Black, Jeremy. *The British Abroad: The Grand Tour in the Eighteenth Century.* New York: St. Martin's Press, 1997.

Hibbert, Christopher. *The Grand Tour.* New York: G. P. Putnam's Sons, 1969.

Mead, William Edward. *The Grand Tour in the Eighteenth Century.* Boston: Houghton Mifflin, 1914.

Nugent, Thomas. *The Grand Tour.* London: n.p., 1756.

Towner, John. "The Grand Tour: A Key Phase in the History of Tourism." *Annals of Tourism Research,* 1985, pp. 297–333.

The British on the Riviera

Les Anglais dans le comté de Nice et en Provence depuis le XVIIIe siècle. Edited by Les Amis du Musée Masséna. N.p., ca. 1934.

Howarth, Patrick. *When the Riviera Was Ours.* London: Routledge, 1977.

Isnard, Roger. "Les Anglais à Nice." *Nice historique,* October–December 1985, pp. 103–19.

Lough, John. *France Observed in the Seventeenth Century by British Travelers.* Stockfield, England: Oriel Press, 1985.

Maxwell, Constantia. *The English Traveller in France, 1698–1815.* London: Routledge, 1932.

Pemble, John. *The Mediterranean Passion: Victorians and Edwardians in the South.* London: Oxford University Press, 1987.

Stoye, John. *English Travellers Abroad, 1604–1667.* New Haven, Conn.: Yale University Press, 1989.

Smollett

Joliat, Eugène. *Smollett et la France.* Paris: Librairie Ancienne Honore Champion, 1935.

Prowse, W. J. "Smollett at Nice." *Macmillan's Magazine,* 1901, pp. 527–33.

Seccombe, Thomas. "Smelfungus Goes South." *Cornhill Magazine,* 1901, pp. 192–210.

From the Eve of the French Revolution to the Coming of the Railroad

Bodard, Pierre. "La Fuite des émigrés." *Sourgentin,* no. 85, January–February 1989, pp. 10–13.

Combet, J. "La Vie économique à Nice sous le Consulat et l'Empire." *Nice historique,* March–April 1924, pp. 59–64.

Costamagna, Henri. "Nice au XVIIIe siècle: Présentation historique et géographique." In *Aspects de Nice du XVIIIe au XXe siècles,* Annales de la Faculté des Lettres et Sciences Humaines de Nice, no. 19, 1973.

Durante, Louis. *Histoire de Nice.* Vol. 3. Turin: Favale, 1823.

Dyer, Colin. "Hivernants et habitants sur la Riviera Française: Nice et Cannes jusqu'à l'arrivée du chemin de fer." *Recherches régionales Alpes-Maritimes et contrées limitrophes,* no. 143, 1998, pp. 18–32.

Feliciangeli, Daniel. "La Développement de Nice au cours de la seconde moitié du XVIIIe siècle: Les Anglais à Nice." In *Aspects de Nice du XVIIIe au XXe siècles,* Annales de la Faculté des Lettres et Sciences Humaines de Nice, no. 19, 1973.

Nice's Riviera Neighbors

Banaudo, Jose, et al. *Sillons: Les Cartes postales anciennes racontent les Alpes du Sud.* 2nd edition. Nice: Serre, 1993.

Bennet, J. Henry. *Winter in the South of Europe.* London: John Churchill & Sons, 1865.

Bourrier, Michel, and Colette Bourrier-Reynaud. "Le Choléra niçois de 1835." *DH: Bulletin d'information,* vol. 54 (1989), pp. 27–33.

Boyer, Marc. "Hyères, station d'hivernants au XIXe siècle." *Provence historique,* 1962, pp. 139–65.

Brown, Alexander M. *Wintering at Menton on the Riviera.* London: J. and A. Churchill, 1872.

Cane, André. "Beaulieu, 1880–1914." In *Riviera,* edited by Brigitte Ouvry-Vial, *Autrement revue,* Paris, 1987.

Ebert, Roger. *Two Weeks in the Midday Sun: A Cannes Notebook.* Kansas City, Mo.: Andrews & McMeel, 1987.

Giorsetti, Louis, and Alain Tiberti. "Menton, création du tourisme." In *Loisir, environement et qualité de la vie sur la Côte d'Azur,* Annales de la Faculté des Lettres et Sciences Humaines de Nice, no. 24, 1976.

Graves, Charles. *The Big Gamble: The Story of Monte Carlo.* London: Hutchinson, 1951.

Greut, Anne-Marie. "Saint-Paul-de-Vence et la Colle-sur-Loup." In *Loisir, environement et qualité de la vie sur la Côte d'Azur,* Annales de la Faculté des Lettres et Sciences Humaines de Nice, no. 24, 1976.

Russians on the Riviera

Ellis, Le Roy. *Les Russes sur la Cote d'Azur: La Colonie russe dans les Alpes-Maritimes des origines à 1939.* Nice: Serre, 1988.

Guerra, Alain. *Itinéraire russe à Nice.* Issy-les-Moulineaux: Albatros, 1995.

Mosse, W. E. "The Russians at Villafranca." *Slavonic Review,* vol. 75 (June 1952), pp. 425–40.

Rouillier, Alain. "L'Aventure russe à Nice et sur la Côte d'Azur." *Sourgentin,* no. 123 (October 1996), p. 5. Introduction to issue devoted to Russians on the Riviera.

Venturi, Franco. "Russians, French, and Italians in Nice, Genoa, and Turin After the Revolution of 1848." In his *Studies in Free Russia,* translated by Fausta Segre Walsby and Margaret O'Dell. (Chicago: University of Chicago Press, 1982).

Belle Époque

Borge, Jacques, and Nicolas Viasnof. *Archives de la Côte d'Azur.* Paris: Michèle Trinckvel, 1994.

Gade, Daniel. " 'Tropicalisation' de la végétation ornementale de la Côte d'Azur." *Méditerranée*, no. 4, 1987, pp. 19–25.

Harris, J. C. *Décadence de Nice comme station d'hiver*. Pamphlet. Nice: n.p., 1884.

Haug, C. James. "Administrative Power in Nineteenth-Century France: The Case of Nice." *Historian*, vol. 50, no. 3 (1988), pp. 348–68.

———. "The Population Dynamics of a Tourist City: Nice, 1872–1911." *Proceedings of the Third Annual Meeting of the Western Society for French History*, 1976, pp. 421–33.

Lèques, Paulette. "Tourisme hivernal et vie mondaine à Nice de 1860 à 1881: Cercles et salons." *Aspects de Nice du XVIIIe au XXe siècles*, Annales de la Faculté des Lettres et Sciences Humaines de Nice, no. 19, 1973.

Liégeard, Stephen. *La Côte d'Azur*. Nice: Serre, 1988. First published 1887.

Mallet, Nicole. "Mutations de l'espace urbain à Nice sur le plan architectural de 1860 à 1878." Master's thesis, Université de Nice, U.E.R. Lettres et des Sciences Humaines, 1971.

Moreau, Guy Junien. *Le Casino de la Jetée-Promenade*. Nice: Gilletta, 1993.

Siffre, A., et al. "Les Capitaux et la région niçoise de 1880–1914." *Revue d'histoire économique et sociale*, vol. 53, nos. 2–3 (1975), pp. 360–85.

Steve, Michel. *L'Architecture Belle Époque à Nice*. Nice: Demaistre, 1995.

Hotels

Gautier, Marcel. *L'Industrie hôtelière*. Paris: Presses Universitaires de France, 1962.

Isnard, Roger. "L'Hôtellerie à Nice." *Sourgentin*, no. 50, ca. 1980, pp. 20–25.

Mori, Hiroshi. *Petits Hôtels in Côte d'Azur*. In Japanese and English. *Shotenkenchiku*, extra no., 1991.

Mortier, Marie-France. "Archives d'entreprise: L'Hôtel Beau-Rivage de Nice (1882–1969)." *Provence historique*, vol. 40, no. 160 (April–June 1990), pp. 217–32.

Potron, Jean-Paul. "Rêves de garnis et propos de palaces." *Recherches régionales Alpes-Maritimes et contrées limitrophes*, no. 3, July–September 1993, and other articles in this issue devoted to the Côte d'Azur hotel industry.

World War I

Schor, Ralph. "La Fonction d'accueil de Nice et la guerre de 1914–1918." In *Aspects de Nice du XVIIIe au XXe siècles*, Annales de la Faculté des Lettres et Sciences Humaines de Nice, no. 19, 1973, pp. 103–35.

———. *Nice et Les Alpes-Maritimes de 1914 à 1945*. 2nd edition. Nice: Centre Régional de Documentation Pédagogique de Nice, 1980.

———. *Nice pendant la guerre de 1914–1918*. Aix-en-Provence: La Penseé Universitaire, 1964.

Artists on the Côte d'Azur

La Côte d'Azur et la Modernité: 1918–1958. Exhibition catalogue. Paris: Réunion des Musées Nationaux, 1997.

Cowart, Jack, and Dominique Fourcade. *Henri Matisse: The Early Years in Nice, 1916–1930.* Washington, D.C.: National Gallery of Art, 1986.

Deflandre, Françoise. *Picasso à Antibes: Antipolis, 1946.* Paris: Réunion des Musées Nationaux, 1998.

Duclos-Arkilovitch, Jonathan. *Jazzin' Riviera.* Nice: ROM Editions, 1997.

Flam, Jack. *Matisse: A Retrospective.* New York: Wings Books, 1988.

Freed, Barbara F., with Alan Halpern. *Artists and Their Museums on the Riviera.* New York: Abrams, 1998.

Girard, Xavier. *Matisse in Nice: 1917–1954.* London: Thames and Hudson, 1996.

Herbert, James D. *Fauve Painting: The Making of Cultural Politics.* New Haven, Conn.: Yale University Press, 1992.

————. "Matisse and Derain on the Mediterranean Shore." In Judi Freeman, ed., *The Fauve Landscape* (New York: Abbeville Press, 1990).

Silver, Kenneth E. "An Invented Paradise." *Art in America,* March 1998, pp. 77–87.

————. *Making Paradise: Art, Modernity, and the Myth of the French Riviera.* Cambridge, Mass.: MIT Press, 2001.

Between the Wars

Fitzgerald, F. Scott. *Tender Is the Night.* New York: Scribner, 1933.

Fussell, Paul. *Abroad: British Literary Traveling Between the Wars.* New York: Oxford University Press, 1980.

Maugham, W. Somerset. "The Three Fat Women of Antibes" and "The Facts of Life." In *The Complete Short Stories of W. Somerset Maugham,* vol. 2 (Garden City, N.Y.: Doubleday, 1953).

Olivesi, Dominique. "La Promenade à Rebours: Une Vision politique contrastée." *Nice historique,* nos. 1–2, 1993, pp. 76–81.

Potron, Jean-Paul. "La Promenade des Anglais d'une guerre à l'autre: Approches littéraires." *Nice historique,* nos. 1–2, 1993, pp. 36–61.

Predal, René. "À Propos de Nice: Le Point de vue documenté de Jean Vigo." *Nice historique,* nos. 1–2, 1993, pp. 62–69.

Vaill, Amanda. *Everybody Was So Young.* Boston: Houghton Mifflin, 1998.

Williams, Maynard Owen. "Carnival Days on the Riviera." *National Geographic,* October 1926, pp. 467–501.

Congés Payés

Bordier, Roger. *J'étais enfant en 1936.* Paris: Éditions du Sorbier, 1996.

Cacères, Benigno. *Allons au-devant de la vie.* Paris: François Maspéro, 1981.

Chavardes, Maurice. *Été 1936: La Victoire du Front populaire.* Paris: Calmann-Lévy, 1966.

Corbin, Alain. *L'Avènement des loisirs, 1850–1960.* Paris: Aubier, 1995.

Le Cri des travailleurs, regional Communist Party newspaper.

Cross, Gary. "Vacations for All: The Leisure Question in the Era of the Popular Front." *Journal of Contemporary History,* vol. 24 (1989), pp. 599–621.

Elhadad, Lydia, and Olivier Querouil. "L'Apparition des congés payés." *Temps libre,* vol. 1 (1980), pp. 83–89.

Goujon, Paul. "Quand 1936 devient '36." In *Cent Ans de tourisme en France.* Paris: Le Cherche Midi, 1989.

Jackson, Julian. *The Popular Front in France: Defending Democracy, 1934–38.* Cambridge: Cambridge University Press, 1990.

Noguères, Henri. *La Vie quotidienne en France au temps du Front populaire, 1935–1938.* Paris: Hachette, 1977.

World War II

Braun, Michel, et al. *La Guerre dans les Alpes-Maritimes, 1939–1945.* Breil-sur-Roya: Éditions du Cabri, 1994.

Diamant, Zanvel. "Jewish Refugees on the French Riviera." *Yivo Annual of Jewish Social Science,* vol. viii (1953), pp. 264–81.

Felstiner, Mary Lowenthal. *To Paint Her Life: Charlotte Saloman in the Nazi Era.* New York: HarperCollins, 1994.

Gordon, Bertram M. *"Ist Gott französisch?:* Germans, Tourism, and Occupied France, 1940–1944." *Modern & Contemporary France,* 1996, pp. 287–98.

Kelman, Claude. "L'Activité des organizations juives dans la zone italienne en 1943." *Le Monde juif,* vol. 49, no. 149 (1993), pp. 90–94.

Klarsfeld, Serge. *Les Transferts de Juifs de la région de Nice vers le camp de Drancy en vue de leur déportation, 31 Aout 1942–30 Juillet 1944.* Paris: Les Fils et Filles des Déportés Juifs de France, 1993.

Klotz, Roger. "Images de Nice dans la littérature contemporaine: Les Amands du Paradis de Raoul Mille." In *Recherches régionales Alpes-Maritimes et contrées limitrophes,* no. 2, 1992, pp. 105–9.

Leslie, Peter. *The Liberation of the Riviera.* New York: Wyndham Books, 1980.

Marrus, Michael R., and Robert O. Paxton. *Vichy France and the Jews.* New York: Basic Books, 1981.

Panicacci, Jean-Louis. "Les Juifs et la question juive dans les Alpes-Maritimes de 1939 à 1945." *Recherches régionales Alpes-Maritimes et contrées limitrophes*, 1983, pp. 240–331.

———. *Les Lieux de mémoire de la Deuxième Guerre Mondiale dans les Alpes-Maritimes.* Nice: Serre, 1997.

———. *Nice pendant la Deuxième Guerre Mondiale: De l'occupation italienne à la fin de la guerre.* Nice: Faculté des Lettres de Nice, D.E.S. d'Histoire, 1970.

———. "Le Tourisme dans les Alpes-Maritimes." In A. Beltran et al., *La Vie des entreprises sous l'occupation: Une Enquête à l'échelle locale* (Paris: Belin, 1994).

Zuccotti, Susan. *The Holocaust, the French, and the Jews.* New York: Basic Books, 1993.

Since World War II

For the postwar period especially, my account profits from unpublished material found in Nice's Archives Municipales; in the Lycée Régional Hôtelier et de Tourisme de Nice; as well as from the Lycée's rich fund of news reports, trade-journal accounts, and other published material bearing on Nice tourism. The following represents a sample.

"Avant-Projet concernant l'organisme à créer pour la direction la surveillance et l'exécution de la propagande touristique française en U.S.A." 1948.

"La Clientèle touristique de la Côte d'Azur, 1952–1960," Comité Régional de Tourisme, 1961.

"Hôtels de la ville de Nice: Établissement d'un ordre de priorité de reconstitution des biens sinistres," 1947.

"Motels de la Côte d'Azur," 1953.

"Projets de thèmes publicitaires à exploiter au Japon," Délégation Régionale Riviera–Côte d'Azur, 1975.

"Rapport sur l'activité touristique à Nice au cours de la saison d'été 1947," and comments concerning it attached.

"Rapport sur la situation actuelle des hôtels de catégorie 'une étoile' à Nice," Syndicat des Hôteliers de Nice.

"Réunion des représentants à l'étranger des services officiels français du tourisme et des délégués régionaux," Nice. Commissariat General au Tourisme, April 18–23, 1966.

Wackermann, Gabriel. "Comportement touristique sur la Côte d'Azur: Actualité et perspective," L'Office Municipal de l'Action Culturelle et de la Communication de la Ville de Cannes, 1986.

Other material dealing primarily with the postwar era includes:

"Les Années d'après-guerre à Nice." *Sourgentin*, no. 131, special issue, May 1998.

"Côte d'Azur: Le Rêve californien." *Geo*, no. 74, special issue, April 1985.

Dodge, David. *The Rich Man's Guide to the Riviera*. Boston: Little, Brown, 1962.

Greene, Graham. *J'Accuse: The Dark Side of Nice*. London: Bodley Head, 1982.

Maurice, René Louis, and Ken Follett. *The Gentlemen of 16 July*. New York: Arbor House, 1982.

Médecin, Jacques. *Nice: Onze Ans de vie commune*. Paris: Presses de la Cité, 1977.

History of Travel and Tourism, Generally

Casson, Lionel. *Travel in the Ancient World*. Baltimore, Md.: Johns Hopkins University Press, 1994.

Corbin, Alain. *The Lure of the Sea: The Discovery of the Seaside*. Translated by Jocelyn Phelps. London: Penguin, 1995.

Feifer, Maxine. *Tourism in History: From Imperial Rome to the Present*. New York: Stein and Day, 1985.

Krotz, Larry. *Tourists: How Our Fastest-Growing Industry Is Changing the World*. Boston: Faber and Faber, 1996.

Lencek, Lena, and Gideon Bosker. *The Beach: The History of Paradise on Earth*. New York: Penguin, 1999.

Lofgren, Orvar. *On Holiday: A History of Vacationing*. Berkeley: University of California Press, 1999.

Stowe, William W. *Going Abroad: European Travel in Nineteenth Century American Culture*. Princeton, N.J.: Princeton University Press, 1994.

Sutton, Horace. *Travelers: The American Tourist from Stagecoach to Space Shuttle*. New York: Willliam Morrow, 1980.

Towner, John. *A Historical Geography of Recreation and Tourism in the Western World, 1540–1940*. New York: John Wiley & Sons, 1996.

Turner, Louis, and John Ash. *The Golden Hordes: International Tourism and the Pleasure Periphery*. New York: St. Martin's Press, 1976.

Withey, Lynne. *Grand Tours and Cook's Tours: A History of Leisure Travel, 1750 to 1915*. New York: William Morrow, 1999.

Travel and Tourism in France

Babeau, Albert. *Les Voyageurs en France depuis la Renaissance jusqu'à la Révolution*. Geneva: Slatkine Reprints, 1970. Originally published in Paris, 1885.

Boyer, Marc. *Le Tourisme*. Paris: Éditions du Seuil, 1972.

Burnet, Louis. *Villégiature et tourisme sur les côtes de France.* Paris: Hachette, 1963.

Cribier, Françoise. *La Grande Migration d'été des citadins en France.* Paris: Éditions du Centre National de la Recherche Scientifique, 1969.

Furlough, Ellen. "Making Mass Vacations: Tourism and Consumer Culture in France, 1930s to 1970s." *Comparative Studies in Society and History,* vol. 40, no. 2 (April 1998), pp. 247–86.

Levenstein, Harvey. *Seductive Journey: American Tourists in France from Jefferson to the Jazz Age.* Chicago: University of Chicago Press, 1998.

Other Travel and Tourism Scholarship

Herewith a small sample, not particularly about the Côte d'Azur, of the burgeoning literature on tourism as a subject of cultural, anthropological, economic, and environmental study.

Butler, R. W. "The Concept of a Tourist Area Cycle of Evolution: Implications for Management of Resources." *Canadian Geographer,* vol. 24, no. 1 (1980), pp. 5–12.

Buzard, James. *The Beaten Track: European Tourism, Literature, and the Ways to Culture, 1800–1918.* Oxford: Clarendon Press, 1993.

Dann, Graham. "Writing Out the Tourist in Space and Time." *Annals of Tourism Research,* vol. 26, no. 1 (1998), pp. 159–87.

Fussell, Paul. "Travel, Tourism and 'International Understanding.'" In his *Thank God for the Atom Bomb and Other Essays* (New York: Summit Books, 1988).

Herbert, D. T. "Artistic and Literary Places in France as Tourist Attractions." *Tourism Management,* vol. 17, no. 2 (1996), pp. 77–85.

Hunter, Colin, and Howard Green. *Tourism and the Environment: A Sustainable Relationship?* New York: Routledge, 1995.

Leed, Eric J. *The Mind of the Traveler: From Gilgamesh to Global Tourism.* New York: Basic Books, 1991.

Smith, Valene L., ed. *Hosts and Guests: The Anthropology of Tourism.* Philadelphia: University of Pennsylvania Press, 1977.

Williams, Allan M., and Gareth Shaw. *Tourism and Economic Development: Western European Experiences.* London: Belhaven Press, 1988.

Williams, Stephen. *Tourism Geography.* London: Routledge, 1998.

Illustrated Books

The visual pleasures of the Côte d'Azur have inspired many photographic and illustrative treatments. The ones listed here helped bring back memories of Nice on many a wintry New England day.

Châteauneuf, Charles Martini de. *Affiches d'Azur*. Nice: Gilletta, 1992.

Christ, Yvan. *Les Métamorphoses de la Côte d'Azur*. Paris: Balland, 1971.

Lartigue, Jacques-Henri. *Lartigue's Riviera*. Paris: Flammarion, 1997.

Ollivier, Gabriel, and Georges Trubert. *The French Riviera*. Paris: Éditions Sun, 1959.

Pollini, Eva. *All Nice and Surroundings*. Florence: Bonechi, 1983.

Quinn, Edward. *A Côte d'Azur Album*. Edited by Martin Heller. Zurich: Zurich Museum of Design, 1994.

Robichon, Jacques. *Côte d'Azur*. Paris: Éditions Sun, 1976.

Miscellaneous

Fuller, Margaret. *These Sad but Glorious Days*. New Haven, Conn.: Yale University Press, 1991.

Hardin, Garrett. "The Tragedy of the Commons." *Science*, vol. 162 (December 13, 1968), pp. 1243–48.

Siegfried, André. *Aspects du XXe siècle*. Paris: Hachette, 1955.

Twain, Mark. *The Innocents Abroad*. N.p., 1869.

FURTHER ACKNOWLEDGMENTS

Among the many besides its visitors with whom I talked while in Nice and environs, I wish specifically to thank Monsieur and Madame Buvron, Hôtel Trianon; Georges Cavaglione; Jacqueline Roth Chagnaud, Fondation Sophia Antipolis; Michèle Chevis, Lycée Régional Hôtelier et de Tourisme de Nice; Dominique Demangel, Archives Municipales; Sylvie Grosgogeat, Nice Office du Tourisme et des Congrès; Judit Kiraly; Teijo Koljonen, Finnmatkat; Anne Lechaczynski, Verrerie de Biot; Jacqueline Ollier; Pierre-Hugues Polacci; Ursula Paolozzi; Aurore Renaut; Bill and Mara Robinson; Janet Ruiz, American Consular Agency; Jacqueline Serrano; John Willms, American Legion, Côte d'Azur chapter.

Thanks to Martin and Elena, to Sylvie of Train Touristique, and the many shop proprietors, hotel receptionists, guides, and others who helped me better understand the Riviera tourism industry. One of them was a spice vendor just outside Èze who lamented that she'd grown weary of customers who couldn't be bothered with a simple *bonjour* or *merci*. To you, mademoiselle, from me and all the other tourists: *Merci mille fois*.

Thanks also to Isabelle Lambert, Patricia Rossi, Martin Evans, Susan Graven, and others affiliated with Stanford University who graciously included me in their visit to Monte Carlo and Nice; to the staffs of Bibliothèque Anglo-Américaine, Bibliothèque Municipale, Archives Municipales, Bibliothèque du

Chevalier Victor de Cessole; and to the proprietor of Libraire Magellan, rue d'Italie, whose aisles I clogged for too many afternoons.

No words can adequately express my thanks, appreciation, and respect for Suzanne Costantini, chief librarian at Lycée Régional Hôtelier et de Tourisme de Nice. Instantly grasping what I was up to, she brought to my project enormous imagination and profound understanding of the resources of her library, and proved a deep well of information on all matters touristic in the region.

In the United States, I am particularly indebted to the following: Ronald Becker, Rutgers University Special Collections; Kristin Cooper, Virginia Renner, and Mary L. Robertson, Huntington Library; Gregg Drinkwater, University of California at Berkeley; Barbara Freed, Carnegie Mellon University; Sandra B. Freitag, American Historical Association; Daniel W. Gade, University of Vermont; Bertram Gordon, Mills College; James Housefield; Tina Hummel, Washington, D.C.–based historical researcher, for her help at the earliest stages of my research; Jane Keller, Baltimore; Arthur Magida, Baltimore; Nandini N. Nadkarni, Southeast Missouri State University; Mark Page, San Francisco; Frank Santilli, Bel Air, Maryland; Frances Sellers, Baltimore; Peggy Shaffer; Geoff Tweedale, Manchester, England; Carol Vaeth, University of Baltimore; Robin D. Wear and Margaret Hrabe, University of Virginia Special Collections; Jim Weeks; Pam Wight.

Among librarians and archivists, in addition to those cited above, I wish to thank those at the French Library and Cultural Center, Boston; the Eisenhower and Peabody Libraries of Johns Hopkins University; Library of Congress; University of Maryland, College Park; Massachusetts Institute of Technology; Towson University.

At the University of Baltimore and, since the summer of 1999, at MIT's Program in Writing and Humanistic Studies, my colleagues have invariably proved friendly and supportive. I thank them.

I thank also Marie-Camille Havard, my patient French teacher in Baltimore, who improved some of my embarrassingly bad French correspondence, read through the manuscript, and kindly helped me at several other points in the research and writing.

I have checked a number of the more difficult translations with native speakers of French, including Marie-Camille Havard and, in the French section of MIT's School of Humanities, Arts, and Social Sciences, with Agnes Trichard-Arany, Sabine Levet, and Odile Cazenave, to all of whom I am grateful. But any errors or misreadings in these translations are necessarily my own.

At Viking Penguin, I wish to thank Barbara Grossman, this book's first champion; Wendy Wolf, who, taking over midway through, took it on as her own and gave it the benefit of her editorial intelligence; Beena Kamlani, Bruce Gif-fords, and the many others at Viking who helped bring this book into being (as well as their counterparts at Little, Brown in England).

I would like once more to thank Vicky Bijur. This is the fourth book, over fifteen years, for which she's stood beside me: who could ask for an agent more sensible, loyal, or diligent?

And who knows how much a book owes its author's family? My wife, Judy, knows. My son, David, knows. I wish the debt were smaller.

INDEX